KU-295-728

5406000022862

MANAGING SACRED SITES

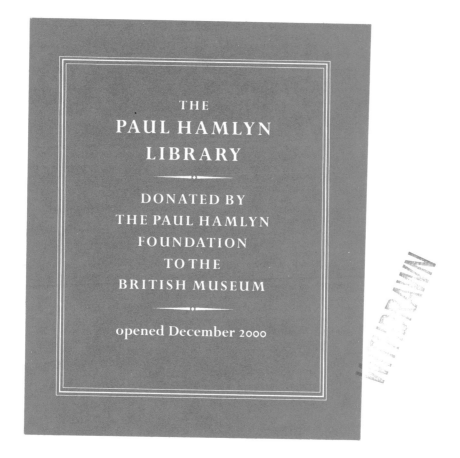

THE

PAUL HAMLYN
LIBRARY

DONATED BY
THE PAUL HAMLYN
FOUNDATION
TO THE
BRITISH MUSEUM

opened December 2000

Also available from Continuum:
Aronsson: *The Development of Sustainable Tourism*
Bray and Raitz: *Flight to the Sun: The Story of the Holiday Revolution*
Godfrey and Clarke: *The Tourism Development Handbook*
Leask and Yeoman (eds): *Heritage Visitor Attractions*
Lennon and Foley: *Dark Tourism: The Attraction of Death and Disaster*
Tribe *et al.*: *Environmental Management for Rural Tourism and Recreation*

Managing Sacred Sites

Service Provision and Visitor Experience

Myra Shackley

Professor of Culture Resource Management
Nottingham Business School
Nottingham Trent University

THOMSON

Australia • Canada • Mexico • Singapore • Spain • United Kingdom • United States

338.4791 SHA

THE BRITISH MUSEUM

THE PAUL HAMLYN LIBRARY

THOMSON

Managing Sacred Sites

Copyright © 2001 Myra Shackley

The Thomson logo is a registered trademark used herein under licence.

For more information, contact Thomson Learning, High Holborn House, 50-51 Bedford Row, London WC1R 4LR or visit us on the World Wide Web at:
http://www.thomsonlearning.co.uk

All rights reserved by Thomson Learning 2004. The text of this publication, or any part thereof, may not be reproduced or transmitted in any form or by any means, electronic or mechanical, including photocopying, recording, storage in an information retrieval system, or otherwise, without prior permission of the publisher.

While the publisher has taken all reasonable care in the preparation of this book the publisher makes no representation, express or implied, with regard to the accuracy of the information contained in this book and cannot accept any legal responsibility or liability for any errors or omissions from the book or the consequences thereof.

Products and services that are referred to in this book may be either trademarks and/or registered trademarks of their respective owners. The publisher and author/s make no claim to these trademarks.

British Library Cataloguing-in-Publication Data
A catalogue record for this book is available from the British Library

ISBN 1-84480-107-1

First edition published 2001 by Continuum
Reprinted 2003 by Thomson Learning

Printed in the UK by TJI Digital, Padstow, Cornwall

'Come no closer! Remove the sandals from your feet, for the place on which you are standing is holy ground.'

(Exodus 3:5)

Contents

List of Figures

LIST OF FIGURES

List of Tables

Acknowledgements

The writer is greatly indebted to the many friends and colleagues who contributed references, suggestions and ideas for this book, and to Nottingham Trent University for supporting much of the relevant fieldwork. Special thanks are due to David Airey, Jean Chadha, Lionel Davies, Bob Gibson, Tove Oliver and Karen Smith. Specific illustrations were provided by Nick Harding/Audrey Stocks (Fig. 6.1), and Robben Island Museum, South Africa (Fig. 9.1). Unless otherwise stated all other photographs are from the writer's own collection.

Preface

This book examines the concept of sacred sites as visitor attractions, looking at the nature of their 'product', the way in which that product is 'sold' to visitors (whether or not any money is actually involved), the nature of the visitor experience and the links between the sacred site and associated service providers, including accommodation, merchandising, catering, etc. Any examination of the operations management at sacred sites will immediately distinguish such sites from other visitor attractions: the way the site is managed, for example, which will almost certainly be as a not-for-profit operation where providing services for visitors is not regarded as the core business. The managers of sacred sites will seldom recognize themselves as such, but might prefer to identify themselves primarily as facilitators of worship, custodians of a site or building. If a sacred site becomes a tourist attraction its visitors are unlikely to be drawn exclusively (or sometimes at all) from the religious tradition to which the site belongs. Such visitors may be unaware of its customs and rules of behaviour.

The site manager is almost always starved of resources with his (operating sacred sites is an almost exclusively male prerogative) operations grossly under-capitalized. Moreover, he will probably see dealing with planning or financial issues or other aspects of operational management as something that he neither wishes to get deeply involved with nor has the ability to cope with at the required level. The managers of sacred sites are usually religious leaders, to whom concepts such as product development and strategic planning may be quite foreign. And perhaps, in spiritual terms, this is a good thing. Yet when sites become visitor attractions, which may necessitate coping with thousands, and sometimes millions, of visitors each year, operations management is no longer a luxury, but becomes essential. Management methods vary and site managers have to perform a delicate balancing act. On the one hand they need to preserve the site, which may be ancient, fragile and weighed down by traditions that means that the installation of visitor facilities becomes unfeasibly expensive, if not downright impossible. Yet to conserve the site requires money (and sufficient cash will never be forthcoming from worshippers), and money comes, directly or indirectly, from visitors. But visitors will be unhappy about paying for an experience which they did not enjoy or which was marred by inadequate facilities: lack of information, for example, a poorly guided tour, or overcrowding. Visiting a sacred site is, or should be, an emotive experience and site managers are also charged with the task of preserving that elusive spiritual quality referred to as 'spirit of place'. At the same time they must facilitate the religious use of the site (if, indeed, the site is active) and cater for the frequently-conflicting demands of worshippers and visitors. Site managers may have to cope with heavy but uneven visitor flows, or with special festivals and events that may attract crowds running into the millions. Their staff will generally be drawn from some form of religious establishment and not always supplemented by professional managers, especially in the Developing World. In the Developed World matters are simplified by easy access to professional advice, funding sources, the relevant committees and professional associations; but in the Developing World managing a sacred site is frequently accomplished by merely letting things happen, hoping that the deity will provide. Which he usually does. Sacred sites often rely heavily on volunteers to assist with day-to-day operations, with all the problems that provides. Sacred sites attract the emotionally vulnerable; they are not (primarily) commercial operations yet are functioning in a commercial world where customers have become more discerning and more critical, can choose between competing destinations and have easier access to information.

The range of sacred sites in the world is enormous, and the problem of classifying them could be tackled in any number of ways. They could be divided, for example, by religious tradition, by the level of site utilization, by the balance between the worshipping community and the number of tourist visitors. They could be categorized by management type (sacred or secular, public or private sector) or by size (which can vary from a small shrine to tens of square miles of cultural landscape). They could be divided roughly on the basis of the number of visitors which each receives, on the premise that the difficulty of managing a sacred site is in direct proportion to the number of people who visit it, or by the length of time the visitors stay. A typology of visitors could also be constructed, perhaps on the basis of the distance they have travelled, which could be a pilgrimage of several hundred miles or a journey just round the corner from their homes. The context of a sacred site could be a means of classification, for example whether it was urban, rural, linear, nodal, or how it was linked to other attractions. It might form part of a pilgrimage or cultural route or have been included in a marketing promotion which encouraged visitors to sample a number of linked attractions in the course of one tour or visit. An even simpler division of sacred sites would split off those sites actively used for worship from those which, while still visited by tourists, are in religious terms only of historical or archaeological interest. But few sites are really fossil – even major sites such as Stonehenge still attract a worshipping community of Druids despite the fact that the tradition which they represent died out centuries ago and 99 per cent of visitors would not consider the site as sacred, but classify it as an historical monument.

This book has taken rather an operations management approach, not dividing by context or tradition but trying to get an overview of the problems and issues faced by sacred sites which have become visitor attractions. But this is not a 'how to manage your site' manual, but a series of reflections on the nature of sacred sites and their visitors, and the interface between them. Specific examples are included by means of short case studies woven into the fabric of each chapter, which serve to focus the attention of the reader on a specific problem or issue, and on how it is being approached. The nature of the 'product' being offered by sacred sites is considered, and the difficulties experienced in promoting or developing a 'product' which is not being 'sold' to the customer in any straightforward commercial sense. This relates directly to the quality of the experience received by visitors, and how this can be maintained in sites with very large visitor numbers and minimal financial resources. Examples are included to illustrate ways in which this problem has been solved at sites from many different religious traditions across the world. Because of the challenges faced in coping with large visitor numbers, sometimes on an episodic or sporadic basis, one entire chapter is devoted to the management of visitor flows. This can take place at a range of scales from macro (pilgrimages, or the hosting of sacred and secular festivals and events with large visitor catchment areas) to the micro scale (how visitors can be moved through the site with minimal disruption to worshippers while at the same time ensuring a high quality of experience). Later chapters examine the concept of cultural landscapes surrounding sacred sites, including problems with managing natural resources in sacred groves, springs and mountains, leading into a discussion of the effect of sociopolitical change on visitation to sacred sites – always a topical issue. Towards the end of the book there has been included a chapter on so-called 'secular' sites, by which is meant non-ecclestiastical sites which may be seen as holy by their visitors, and which are often of immense significance to particular social, racial or ethnic groups. This category would include the slave forts of West Africa, Holocaust sites in Europe and sites which have become the foci of secular pilgrimage, such as

Robben Island in South Africa. The book ends with some reflections on the role that sacred sites play in contemporary society, and how those roles are changing.

The motivations of visitors to the thousands of sacred sites that form part of our global heritage are complex and multidimensional. Some are seeking a life-changing experience, others merely somewhere to while away a wet afternoon. Some wish to worship, others to marvel or just to explore. The managers of sacred sites have to cater for all these needs while avoiding the temptation to reduce the site to the level of a secular attraction. Visiting a sacred site should be an essentially spiritual experience, uncontaminated (as far as possible) by technical and commercial realities. Sacred sites should offer the attendee a window on infinity. As Albert Einstein once famously said 'The fairest thing that we can experience is the mysterious'. It is the task of sacred sites to manage the mysterious and reach for the sublime, while coping with the prosaic. Whatever the shape of the postmodern world, increasing numbers of people are going to be looking at sacred sites for some means of defining a more acceptable reality.

CHAPTER 1

Sacred Sites – An Introduction

Part of the diversification of the late twentieth century quest for religious experience includes not only 'traditional' sites sacred to the great monotheistic religions (Christianity, Judaism and Islam) but also contemporary pilgrimage and 'New Age' sites. Some indication of current levels of interest in visiting sacred sites can be seen in the vastly increased numbers of people going on pilgrimage. As a result, Spain has now reopened the medieval pilgrim hostels on the route to Santiago de Compostela, one of Europe's most important pilgrimage destinations, and it is estimated that 3.5 million pilgrims per year make a visit (Bywater, 1994). But this is only a fraction of the 12 million ordinary tourists who visit the cathedral of Notre-Dame in Paris each year, making it the most popular tourism attraction in Europe. Managing such huge volumes of visitors to these sacred sites presents immense challenges, not least in balancing the need to conserve the fabric of the site with the provision of a special experience for the visitor. Sacred sites perform many functions for their visitors. For the worshipper, or adherent of a particular religious tradition, they may be places which witness to a message or value system, as well as being a place of encounter with the numinous and an interesting artefact. For the tourist they may be (or contain) great works of art, they may be visited for their architecture, their setting, their atmosphere or simply as part of a great day out. The literature about sacred sites includes atlases of holy places (Wilson, 1997), pilgrimage and travel guides (e.g. Brockman, 1997; CCB, 1992) and academic works grounded mainly in the literature of tourism management (Carmichael *et al.*, 1994, Vuconic, 1996), theology (Brown and Loades, 1995; Holm and Bowker, 1994) or cultural geography (Park, 1994).

It is possible to distinguish several major categories of sacred site, although categories overlap and many sites could fit quite reasonably into any of several categories. Table 1.1 suggests a classification, and adds some examples, most of which are discussed elsewhere in this book.

Table 1.1 Classification of sacred sites

Category	Type	Examples
1	Single nodal feature	Canterbury Cathedral, Emerald Buddha (Bangkok), Hagia Sophia (Istanbul)
2	Archaeological sites	Machu Picchu (Peru), Chichén Itzá (Mexico)
3	Burial sites	Catacombs (Rome), Pyramids (Giza)
4	Detached temples/shrines	Borobudur, Ankgor Wat, Amritsar
5	Whole towns	Rome, Jerusalem, Assisi, Varanasi, Bethlehem
6	Shrine/temple complexes	Lalibela (Ethiopia), Potala (Tibet), St Katherine's Monastery (Egypt)
7	'Earth energy' sites	Nazca Lines (Peru), Glastonbury
8	Sacred mountains	Uluru, Everest, Tai Shan, Athos, Mt Fuji
9	Sacred islands	Rapa Nui, Lindisfarne, Iona, Mont-St-Michel
10	Pilgrimage foci	Mecca, Medina, Mt Kailash, Compostela
11	Secular pilgrimage	Robben Island (RSA), Goree (Senegal), Holocaust sites

Category 1 sites are more or less isolated nodes of activity, though seldom standing entirely alone, generally being surrounded by supplementary buildings such as minor churches, temples and shrines as well as various types of visitor facility. When such sites proliferate over a discrete area they may constitute a cultural landscape. Although these supplementary attractions may also be visited, the major attraction is the primary motivation and focal point of a tourist's visit. Many are linked to ancient pilgrimage trails or by more modern tourist routes to other elements of a visitor attraction network. Canterbury Cathedral, for example, is not only a stand-alone attraction but also part of an ancient pilgrim route from London, 55 miles away. It attracts worshippers, pilgrims and tourists, much as it has done for the last 1600 years.

Category 2 (archaeological sites) consists of sites which may once have been sacred but which today are seldom, if ever, utilized for their original religious function but survive merely as archaeological sites. They have become visitor attractions where the visitor is likely to be a tourist rather than a pilgrim, making a trip for historico-cultural rather than religious reasons. Such archaeological sites may also be attached to trails, routes or other related sites. Machu Picchu in Peru,

Figure 1.1 'New Age' worshippers at the sacred sun stone, Machu Picchu

for example, may be reached by tourists directly by rail but is also the culmination of the ancient Inca Trail, once a ceremonial road and now a trekking route. It is walked by adventure tourists rather than pilgrims, but a minority of visitors to the site are people with a religious motivation since Machu Picchu is also considered one of the 'earth energy' sites of Category 7, venerated by those interested in 'New Age' spirituality. Machu Picchu was (arguably) an Inca sacred site but is undoubtedly visited by most tourists merely as a cultural tourism attraction. However, the motivations of individual visitors differ and although the bulk of visitors arrive on a short organized day-trip from Cuzco many others come for spiritual reasons (Fig. 1.1) and may stay longer. There is much 'New Age' interest in the area and some tour operators offer participation in reconstructed Inca rituals and ceremonies held in unusual settings and 'power places'. A typical advertisement reads 'in this excursion we will learn about the ancient rituals of the Incas and participate in a pilgrimage to several of their places of worship, in a search to purify and energize our souls and bodies. The pilgrimage will start in Cuzco and will take us to Machu Picchu and other historic sites' (http:/// www.kontikitours.com/spiritual.html). Customers for such a tour consider that the site's status as a 'power place' is related to its location within three high peaks of exceptional power, forming an energy triangle. Category 2 sites also include archaeological urban complexes of a primarily sacred nature, of which a good example is the Toltec/Maya ceremonial site of Chichén Itzá in Mexico. Many folk healers and other descendants of the Maya still come to pray to the old gods for rain and other needs, and food offerings are left on makeshift altars. But such visitors are only few in number; by far the majority of people coming to visit the site are international tourists wishing to see the famous pyramids, ball courts and sacred well (*cenote*) of the site. The Acropolis in Athens might be a better example for this category, visited for its historical significance and architectural glories but not considered actively sacred (despite its temples) since the religious beliefs to which it was central no longer exist (Davies, 1994).

Category 3 includes diverse burial sites including those still being used (such as the Père Lachaise and Highgate cemeteries in Paris and London), which also act as visitor attractions for those wishing to visit the graves of the rich and famous. It also includes long-abandoned burial sites such as the Catacombs of Rome, and those sites which, although their original function was for burial, are visited today for quite different reasons. A good example here would be the Pyramids of Giza, because they were once tombs. The caves of Ajanta in India, a major Hindu centre for pilgrimage, might also be included in Category 3 although their primary function was never burial. Many of the shrines and temples in Category 4 also function as the end point of pilgrimages, or as centres which stage specific events and festivals, such as the Temple of the Tooth in Sri Lanka. However, some (including the Buddhist temples of Borobudor and Ankor Wat in southeast Asia) have become relict archaeological sites literally isolated from the contemporary world as islands in a sea of jungle. Moreover, both Angkor and Borobodur are sociopolitically isolated from the dominant contemporary religion of the country in which they are located. Category 4 sites also includes Christian shrines such as those commemorating appearances of the Blessed Virgin Mary (like Fatima in Portugal or Medjugorje in Boznia/Herzgovina). The 'whole town' Category (5) is more difficult to define but it is intended to include coherent urban areas which contain a number of discrete shrines, churches, temples or other sacred sites within them. Of course they also contain a large number of secular buildings, as well as all the infrastructure of modern life and its tourism industry. They may be linear (as in the shrines along the banks of the Ganges at Varanasi), or consist of groups of settlements belonging to one tradition dispersed over a cultural landscape (the *Pays Dogon*, Mali). These may be currently in use by the same worshipping tradition which built them (Assisi), be mainly restricted to one faith (Rome) or include sites sacred to many faiths (Jerusalem).

The shrine/temple complexes mentioned as Category 6 are essentially a Developing World phenomenon. Perhaps the best examples are the rock-cut church complex at Lalibela in Ethiopia (also a site which acts as a focus for pilgrimage and festivals within the Coptic church). Another example can be found in the Potala palace in Tibet with its complex of shrines, temples, offices – for many the epitome of Tibet, and a national symbol. The Buddhist shrine complex at Nara, Japan, could also be included here although most of its visitors do not come for religious reasons, as can the isolated monastic complex of St Katherine in the Sinai desert (Egypt). The 'earth energy' classification of Category 7 is far more difficult, but would include sites not belonging to any recognized religion and often grouped under the heading of 'New Age'. They are frequently located at sites with historical or archaeological significance (as at Nazca in Peru or Glastonbury in the UK) but have been taken over by a more contemporary ideology and may function as attractions for 'New Age' pilgrims. The activities of such groups may clash with others who consider themselves as the original 'owners' of the site, exemplified by the conflict between 'New Age' travellers and Druids at Stonehenge in the UK (Bender, 1999), and between 'New Age' tourists and young Native Americans at Bighorn Medicine Wheel in Wyoming, USA (Price, 1994).

Mountains are sacred in many traditions; sometimes just the mountain itself (as at Mt Kilauea, Hawaii), sometimes because of the complex of religious buildings which has grown up around it (such as Mt Athos in Greece or the Tai Shan range in China). This sanctity can sometimes include the whole of a sacred cultural landscape around the mountain itself, as in the Everest region of Nepal, the area around Uluru (Ayers Rock) in Australia or the hinterland of Mt Sinai. Islands are also a special case, Category 9, because of their geographical isolation. This frequently has the function of enhancing their perceived sanctity because of the difficulty of reaching them, and also because they are perceived as somehow set apart from the rest of the world. Many are also foci for pilgrimage (such as the Celtic Christianity sites of Iona and Lindisfarne in the UK). Delos, the Greek island formerly sacred to Apollo, is merely an archaeological site of little religious relevance today. Rapa Nui (Easter Island) is significant since virtually the whole island may be considered an outdoor museum, punctuated by the giant statues (*moai*) bearing witness to a religious tradition that is no longer practised. The pilgrimage foci of Category 10 are the centres (usually urban) which act as end points of pilgrimages, typified by Mecca/Medina for Muslims and Compostela for

Christians. In the Buddhist/Hindu tradition Mt Kailash in Tibet would fall into this category, but is also a sacred landscape. Shrines such as Lourdes which have developed into huge religious tourism attractions could also belong here, as could other pilgrimage foci which may be locations used for special events and festivals rather than ongoing pilgrimage. Examples include the Kumbh Mela sites on the Ganges in India, Turin (when the Shroud is being exhibited), or Oberammergau when the Passion Play is being performed. The final category, 11, consists of sites which function as secular pilgrimage centres, and it has been included since its component places are frequently regarded by their visitors as sacred. The sacredness here does not derive from their association with any particular religious tradition, but rather because they represent a particular belief, moral or value system. Classic examples are the Holocaust sites of Germany and Poland, especially Dachau and Auschwitz-Birkenau which are the most heavily visited. One could also include sites significant as markers in the human quest for freedom (Robben Island in South Africa) and Ellis Island in New York, as well as the former slave forts of Senegal and Ghana, of immense emotional significance to thousands of African-American pilgrims each year. Category 11 also includes the Hiroshima Peace Memorial in Japan, the Anne Frank House in Amsterdam, and Masada in Israel, which are all of symbolic significance to particular ethnic or religious groups.

Sacred places not necessarily ancient – many of the modern Marian sites important to Roman Catholics are relatively recent, as are the sites sacred to Mormons exemplified by the nineteenth-century rise of Salt Lake City in Utah, USA, as the sacred focus of a new religion. Visiting places which contain sacred relics has always been a popular activity. In Europe such relics were often the treasured possession of a church and marked in some physical way the continuity of the faithful with those who had given their lives for faith in Christ. Relics were often reckoned to have special powers which could, for example, heal people. In the twelfth century in Europe relics played a major role in religious life, not only bits from bodies of martyrs but 'Our Lord's shoe, his swaddling clothes, blood and water from his side, bread from the feeding of the five thousand and the Last Supper . . . The rods of Moses and Aaron, relics of St John the Baptist' (Bethell, 1972: 67). It was desirable to be buried near the relics of saint or martyr to gain their protection, but space was obviously limited in a church. Many churches expanded in size to bury the dead within their walls, but as time went on churchyards and cemeteries immediately outside the church building took on the nature of sacred places for the burial of the dead. One of the most interesting examples of attitudes towards death and sacred places is currently found in British crematoria. Crematoria have become popular only since the 1960s, but now c. 70 per cent of people dying in the UK are cremated. Crematoria are not run by churches but largely by local authorities within the public sector, but funeral services are usually conducted by ministers of religion. Increased numbers of people think that crematoria are sacred places because of their association with the dead, and the rites performed for them (Davies, 1994). The foci of religious attention can also change in other ways, as in Tibet where the sacred focus of Tibetan Buddhism has shifted from Lhasa, now under the political control of China, to the person of the Dalai Lama himself and his court at Dharamsala in India which has become a place of pilgrimage.

SACRED SITES AS VISITOR ATTRACTIONS

Within academic studies of the tourism system (Cooper *et al.*, 1998), sacred sites are classified as visitor attractions, localities which act as the motivation for a tourist journey and constitute one of the three most important elements of the tourism system – the others being accommodation and transport (Inskeep, 1991). There are numerous definitions of what constitutes a visitor attraction, such as Middleton (1994) 'A designated permanent resource which is controlled and managed for the enjoyment, entertainment, and education of the visiting public'. However, this implies that tourism is the core business of the attraction, which is not necessarily true for sacred sites. But few sacred sites attract only worshippers, and at most sites those who come to worship, pray or meditate are in a minority. The majority of visitors are often tourists who see the site as a visitor attraction which just happens to be a sacred site, rather than the other way round. So what is the real core business of such a site? It is, undoubtedly, to provide a focus and facility for those who wish to worship, pray or meditate, but it may need to welcome large numbers of those who do not wish to do any of these things in order to earn its keep. However, unlike other visitor attractions within the leisure industry, sacred sites seldom offer a product in which entertainment figures strongly, although many include a strong educational element. Gunn (1988) divides visitor attractions into short-stay touring attractions and longer-stay focused attractions. Inskeep (1991) considers that attractions are either natural, cultural or artificially created, and Lew (1987), who reviewed some attraction typologies, noted that they tended either to be an ideographic listing of attractions, or to be taken from an organizational perspective utilizing factors such as capacity, spatial and temporal scale, or to be derived from a cognitive perspective incorporating the tourist's perceptions and experience of attractions.

The 1980s marked a watershed in the evolution of the visitor attraction with dramatic changes in consumer leisure time, income, technology and tastes. Traditional attractions such as castles and museums became supplemented by technology, and the very idea of visitor attractions developed as a subject for a philosophical debate which surrounded the heritage industry (Hewison, 1987). Some commentators of the period saw heritage as nostalgia, distorting history for the benefit of tourism, but this is less significant in religious tourism though prominent in the development of managed attractions. Thus the traveller to York can visit the great Minster church in a way which is merely continuing 1500 years of tradition, but a visit to the Jorvik Viking centre which incorporates a 'ride' and other paraphernalia of the heritage industry is getting quite a different experience in which issues of authenticity will inevitably surface. Who is the customer for the 'product' which is produced by a sacred site, and what is the nature of that product? Few would dispute that the tourist paying an admissions charge to a site such as the Acropolis is in the position of being a customer of the heritage tourism industry, but the issue of customers at sites which form integral parts of active religious traditions is rather more contentious. Visitors to sacred sites have a far wider range of motivations than, for example, visitors to a theme park. Walsh-Heron and Stevens (1990) considered that in order to qualify as such, a visitor attraction must set out to attract visitors and day visitors from resident or tourist populations, and to be managed accordingly. It must also provide an appropriate level of facilities and services to meet and cater to the demands, needs and interests of its visitors. Visitor attractions need not necessarily charge for entry but they must still be managed for the benefit of their visitors. The authors also suggested that the provision of a 'fun and pleasurable experience and an enjoyable way for customers to spend their leisure time' is significant, but this is contentious. Few would dispute the ability of sites such as Auschwitz to attract large numbers of visitors, and the experience offered may be educational and emotive but it is certainly not entertaining. However, some sacred sites may offer entertainment as well, perhaps included in festivals or special events from concerts to dramatic performances.

Broadly speaking, visitor attractions can be either

- components of the natural environment
- man-made buildings, structures and sites designed for a purpose other than attracting visitors (such as religious worship), but which now attract substantial numbers of visitors who use them as leisure amenities
- man-made buildings, structures and sites designed to attract visitors including those purpose-built to accommodate all their needs, such as theme parks
- special events.

Sacred sites can be found within any of these these categories – even the purpose-built visitor centres at sacred sites such as the Marian shrine at Knock, Ireland, would qualify (Swarbrooke, 1995). 'Visitors' can include local residents, foreign tourists, those taking a day-trip and those staying in the area. Attractions can be permanent (such as elements of built heritage) or temporary (a particular festival or event). In the case of natural and man-made sites not designed for tourism, the main management issues centre around coping with problems caused by visitors, environmental impacts such as pollution and erosion and the effect of tourism on the original purpose of the site or building (such as a cathedral, mosque or temple). It can be quite difficult to pigeonhole some sacred places. For example, cathedrals are seldom seen as purpose-built tourism attractions yet it could be argued that they were pegs in the earliest tourist activity, namely pilgrimage. They were always designed as places to welcome tourists and visitors but not for the volume of non-worshipping visitors they are receiving at present. Sacred sites as visitor attractions are seldom managed with the sole aim of either increasing visitation or turning large profits. Revenue generation may be important but it is generally considered secondary to the core business of the attraction, which is some form of worship. There are exceptions to this rule, for example the Borobudur temple already referred to, which was once a major Buddhist pilgrimage site but is now the principal peg of Indonesia's tourism industry. It is a Buddhist site of historical interest in an increasingly militant Islamic country, which is managed entirely as a tourist attraction to encourage increased visitor numbers and spend.

Sacred sites can attract very large volumes of visitors and also grow significantly as a result of increased pilgrim and tourist traffic. Lourdes began as a pilgrimage site in 1858 and has since experienced a steady increase in its population from 4000 to 18,000 residents, by contrast with other neighbouring Pyreneen cities whose populations are declining. Other shrine destinations such as Loreto and Fatima (Portugal) have grown from villages to cities as a result of the pilgrim trade. Mecca, in Saudi Arabia, which depends exclusively on the pilgrim trade now has a resident population of over 500,000 people, and Varanasi in India over 600,000 as a result of the immigration of workers and service personnel as well as in-migration of pilgrims who decide to settle there (a common phenomenon). Rinschede (1992) looked at the growth of the townscape in Lourdes where the core, nearest the shrine, includes as usual a gathering place and merges into the religious centre. This is then surrounded by other establishments including monasteries, hospitals, souvenir shops, travel agencies, parking and transport. For such a small town Fatima had 52 religious communities totalling 500 people, as well as 37 hotels. Lourdes had 370 hotels but Mecca only four, because pilgrims making a *hajj* stay in temporarily-erected tent cities or camp in the open air. In-migration of settlers attracted by the perceived sacredness of a place can significantly distort the socioeconomic dynamic. In all major pilgrimage destinations a plethora of souvenir businesses develop near the centre and major hotels, whether in Bethlehem or Bombay. These are supplemented by religious hawkers, vendors and other travelling salesmen at peak times.

The catchment area of sacred sites is very varied, and related to the different motivations of visitors. Many sites, for example, attract local people on a daily basis, but national and international visitors only for special festivals or events or at particular times of year. Changing travel patterns are also a factor. A remote temple site in Asia that once only attracted local visitors may now find itself suddenly accessible to international visitors as a result of improvement in air or road transport. The increased numbers of pilgrims making the *hajj* to Mecca, for example, is not unrelated to easier, cheaper and faster air access as well as to considerable investment by the Saudi Arabian authorities in improved visitor facilities.

OWNERSHIP AND MANAGEMENT

Sacred sites are seldom under private ownership, and this is both good and bad. Most are managed by voluntary organizations, including charities, religious sects and religious organizations whose main priority is often site conservation and the encouragement of worship, with secondary objectives including education, mission, and perhaps the offering of hospitality. Some sacred sites are included within the public sector, and are under government or local authority control. Again, the priorities of their site managers are likely to include conservation and education, but other factors such as public access, the function of the site as catalyst for tourist development and the need to generate income may also be apparent. In the UK the Association of Leading Visitor Attractions (ALVA) was formed in 1989 to represent Visitor Attractions that welcome more than one million visitors per year. Its membership includes various cathedrals and it has become both a major forum for the exchange of management information, and a powerful pressure group. The management of any individual site may be complicated for historical reasons and may consist of a single dominant individual, a clerical heirachy or management by committee. This is true both at the level of the individual site where various different organizations have an interest, and indeed at the level of an entire city, such as Jerusalem. The presence of a sacred site often results in the growth of an entire tourist destination in much the same way that a grain of sand acts in an oyster to foster the development of a pearl. Sometimes, the sacred site is the entire destination, as at Easter Island, or Anthony Island. The provision of facilities such as accommodation, catering, merchandising, transport and parking expands and develops the significance of sacred sites. This may require the public-sector provision of infrastructure working in conjunction with voluntary sector management of the site and private-sector development of specific facilities. Sacred sites do not form part of chains, and cannot be franchised. No two have the same sets of issues and problems, and no two are alike.

Attractions inevitably have a considerable economic impact on the surrounding area. This may not be reflected in the funding of the sacred site itself, and it is common to find an underfunded site desperately in need of cash for conservation surrounded by a sea of profit-making private enterprises. Sacred visitor attractions provide relatively few paid jobs, and those that do exist are paid poorly, with the majority of employment created in the field of ancillary services. Much of the expenditure of individual visitors contributes little towards site maintenance, especially if there is no compulsory entrance fee, with visitor spend being directed towards catering, crafts, souvenirs and accommodation, mainly provided by the private sector. Such expenditure does have a multiplier effect within the local and regional economy, but in purely financial terms a sacred site is usually a liability, rather than an asset, to its management.

VISITOR MOTIVATION

What benefits do visitors expect and receive from sacred sites? The most obvious include an opportunity for worship, or the acquisition of spiritual merit merely through having made the visit. Less obvious benefits include status, nostalgia and education. Visitors expect to receive a range of services (although expectations will vary with site location and level of development) which might include the provision of adequate management, information, accessibility and visitor facilities, but rarely include value for money. The primary motivator for a visit, and the primary expected benefit, centres around the issue of visitor experience, how the site conveys its spiritual message, its 'spirit of place'. Historically, the motivations of visitors to sacred sites may have changed greatly over the years. To take a small example, local festivals such as well-dressing in Derbyshire, UK, which involved the decoration of village wells with elaborate floral displays, used to be a religious activity which guaranteed the well-being of the village community. Now such events have become visitor attractions. The changing nature of tourism to any sacred site in the Developed World is also related to easier access, increased disposable income, more leisure time (paid holidays), increased personal mobility (car ownership) better information (fax, websites, the media), and better marketing of special events (Hall and Weiler, 1992). Sacred sites need to be accessible for visitors, most of whom arrive by road, although many ancient sites were originally visited on foot or horseback. In the Developed World the need to transport far greater numbers of people to a site than had originally been envisaged can create difficulties. It can also produce entirely new developments in transport, such as the new airport which has opened at Knock in Ireland, purely to cater for the pilgrimage trade.

At times it is difficult to see where the sacredness of some sites resides. Glastonbury, in the UK, is a case in point. Glastonbury village is rather surreal, on the surface just another Mendip town but on closer inspection full of shops selling meditation candles, Indian headdresses and a Hemp Shop 'which seems to cover every conceivable aspect of marijuana, apart from marijuana' (Thorncroft, 1997: 31). Glastonbury has always attracted the mystic fringe, thanks to its Tor, an ancient mound rising a sheer 500 feet from the surrounding marshlands. The twelfth-century Abbots of Glastonbury became some of the most prosperous in the land by their fortuitous discovery of the bodies of, reputedly, King Arthur and his Queen Guinevere in the Abbey grounds. They also encouraged the myth that Joseph of Arimathea had not only visited Glastonbury but planted his staff in the ground, creating a flowering thorn of which three specimens can be seen in the town today. Contemporary Glastonbury performs many functions and aims to attract the lucrative 'New Age' pilgrim trade with such emotive legends. But it also attracts the casual tourist, shoppers, visitors to the beautifully-maintained monastic ruins and the peaceful atmosphere of the Tor, supposedly an 'earth energy' place. Christian visitors often visit the site as part of a trip which includes the cathedral at Wells and some longer-stay visitors might be taking a holiday which includes not only these sites but also other sacred sites such as Stonehenge and Bath.

Visits to sacred sites can be motivated by secular, rather than religious, stimuli. This has certainly been the case for the seventeenth- and eighteenth-century Jesuit missions built in the land of the Guaranis in Argentina/Brazil, located in the heart of tropical rainforest and designated as World Heritage sites in the mid 1980s. Localities that can be visited include the ruins of São Miguel das Missões in Brazil, together with San Ignacio Mini, Santa Ana, Nuestra Señora de Loreto and Santa María la Mayor in Argentina. They are the remnants of a remarkable experiment in community living on the borders of Argentina, Brazil and Paraguay where the Jesuits started to found farming villages in which the different Guarani tribes could feel cultural and ethnic unity. Each was self-governing under the supervision of a priest, working closely with traditional chiefs (caciques). Their produce supported the community, with a surplus given to the sick or to the church or paid in taxes to Spain. The experiment came to a sudden end in the second half of the eighteenth-century, partly as result of new frontier treaties between Spain and Portugal but mainly because of expulsion of Jesuits from Spanish and Portuguese dominions. The political and religious autonomy of the missions had been seen as a threat to

Spanish imperial power. After the communities dispersed, the missions fell into ruin. The sites entered public consciousness again as a result of the release of the film 'The Mission', starring actors Robert de Niro and Jeremy Irons. Previously, few had heard of the sites which are now, in common with neighbouring Iguaçu Falls, experiencing a rapid growth in visitors who do not come because the sites are sacred, but because they are famous. The Missions are visited as cultural tourism attractions, not as sacred sites.

PERCEPTIONS OF SACRED SPACE

It is an ancient Chinese tradition, but shared by many cultures, to see one's own land as the centre of the world, and thus intrinsically sacred. Specific locations within that land can derive their sacredness from some natural quality or by human association. Mountains and rivers are natural sacred places which may be reflected in man-made structures. For example, the Himalayan mountains in Hinduism are mythologically represented in some Hindu deities and also reflected in the architecture of Hindu temples whose pinnacles are viewed as mountain peaks. In Japan, the actual land is considered sacred by the Japanese people in a way that produces deep-seated nationalist feelings especially evident during times of war. There are many parallels here with the notion of Israel as the Promised Land, given by God, a long-standing biblical tradition which underpins contemporary Middle Eastern politics.

A sacred site both exists within sacred space and contains sacred space within it. Sacred space has been defined by Jackson and Henrie (1983: 94) as 'that portion of the earth's surface which is recognized by individuals or groups as worthy of devotion, loyalty or esteem'. It is usually sharply distinguished from the profane world around it. Wright (1966) invented the word 'geopiety' to refer to the recognition of certain areas as sacred, meaning devotion and loyalty towards a perceived sacred space. The perception of sanctity is central to this idea since sacred space exists only for those who know its characteristics and the reason for its delineation. This is at the root of many problems associated with the management of sacred sites. Although such sites are recognized as sacred by their worshippers, who behave accordingly, tourists may not perceive the site as sacred and behave in an inappropriate manner, creating tension. Although the majority of sacred places are associated with perceived supernatural events (mystico-religious sites), others, as we have already seen, evoke feelings of sanctity or esteem which may be non-religious. The Cenotaph War Memorial in London was recently desecrated by a protester: this caused universal outrage, since the memorial had acquired sanctity by its association with the dead, perceived as having given their lives in the cause of freedom. Similarly, the ancestral home of a family may be perceived as sacred by that family, without religious significance. Many people also have sacred spaces within their homes which may be overtly religious (such as a statue of a saint, a crucifix or a house altar) or more secular (such as framed photographs of a dead relative or friend). Others may designate an area as 'sacred' in the sense that it is not to be disturbed and must be treated with respect, and this can be anything from a desk to the corner of someone's study.

The reason that a space is designated as sacred may be difficult to work out and may reach beyond recorded history into a individual's psyche or a community's mind. Homelands become sacred space which have been assigned sanctity as a result of events occurring there. Although sacred sites vary in size and shape they share the characteristic of being relatively permanent and inspiring respect and devotion. Religious sacred places and homelands occur in most cultures as ways of structuring space. Most people feel an emotional tie to a portion of space designated as 'home' where they were reared as a child, and which evokes feelings of non-religious sanctity. But people need not have lived in their own sacred 'homeland'. Israel is recognized by Jews as their homeland with second- or third-generation immigrants often referring to their grandparents' original country as 'homeland' even when they have never visited it. A historical site may also become sacred because of an event associated with it that need not be (but can be) religious. Perceived esteem or sanctity discriminates such sites from the profane world. An individual's view of sacred space is stratified with different levels of perceived sanctity. It usually consists of a local area with many sacred places, a regional level with fewer and an international level with fewer still. Levels of sacredness also increase in relation to the nearness of the tradition, as well as with geographical proximity. As an example the Garden of Gethsemane is sacred to all Christians, whereas a local family church or cemetery creates reverence and nostalgia mainly among those who live nearby or have relatives buried there. Christian beliefs endow churches and cemeteries with the attributes of places where communications with another world occur. Homelands are viewed through filters of patriotism and nostalgia so that the area of space considered as sacred therefore varies from the infinite to a finite point. Christians, after all, see the entire cosmos as sacred since it was created by God. Sacred sites may also have great impact on landscape; indeed, they may result in the construction of entire cities. Religious views tend to be relatively permanent and spaces associated with mystico-religious sites are also permanent, whereas homelands associated with religion are variable in terms of permanence.

CASE STUDY: MORMON PERCEPTIONS OF SACRED SPACE

Jackson and Henrie (1983) presented an interesting example of the way in which sacred space is defined in Mormon culture. Mormons are a Christian sect who believe that their founder Joseph Smith talked with God. The authors aimed to test out the idea that sacred sites can be divided into three categories (mystico-religious space, homelands and historical sites) utilizing a sample survey asking Mormons to rank their attitude to different types of Mormon sacred sites with regard to perceived relative levels of sanctity. Mormons temples are sacred because faithful Mormons believe that it is necessary to visit them to perform rituals essential for their salvation. The temples (the most significant of which is at Salt Lake City) are not open to non-Mormons and, indeed, only to those Mormons judged worthy by their bishop. Like all temples they are viewed by believers as sites where communication occurs between earth and heaven. There are fifteen Mormon temples in the USA, whose construction signifies permanence and gives to the Mormons in the surrounding area a piece of space consecrated to religion. Other Mormon sacred sites include the Sacred Grove near Palmyra, New York, where Mormons believe that Joseph Smith spoke with God. Mormons also revere the sites of the Holy Land (such as Bethlehem). Mormon homelands may be their ancestral family home, present residence or even a state, and the whole of Utah was used as a possible homeland in the project since it was from here that the Mormon faith diffused outwards from 1900 onwards. It is regarded as the Mormon homeland to which converts were encouraged to migrate. Other homeland sites include Jackson County, Missouri, which Jospeh Smith had said in 1832 was Zion. Although Mormons were driven out of Jackson County in 1839 their church doctrine teaches that they will return and build a millennial city and temple there. Major historical sites included the Lincoln Memorial in Washington (all Mormons were US citizens), Joseph Smith's birthplace and other sites such as Nauvoo, Illinois, a city developed by the Mormons where a temple was constructed. A sample size of 500 questionnaires was returned and results clearly showed that the Salt Lake Temple was regarded as the most sacred place for Mormons, ranking higher than the future city of Zion where Mormons believe that the resurrected Christ will live. The Salt Lake temple had symbolic connotations in relation to the struggles of the early Mormon pioneers in Utah; leaders met there and it is believed that they received direct revelations from God. Other mystico-religious sites were regarded as less sacred as they were not directly related to early church members, and this category included sites in the Holy Land, such as Bethlehem. Mormon chapels, places of regular meeting, were not regarded as highly sacred. Among the homelands the state of Utah was sometimes rated as sacred, more by those who had visited it than by those who had not. The survey also suggested that historical sites associated with religious history were regarded as more sacred than secular sites (such as the Lincoln Memorial), as might have been expected.

The case suggests that for this community, as with most others, sites associated with mystico-religious phenomena were regarded as the most sacred. Historical sites varied in perceived sacredness depending on whether they were associated with secular or religious history. It is interesting that sites *not* directly associated with church leadership were thought of as less sacred than those that were, even a major biblical site such as Bethlehem. And places where regular secular activities happen (Mormon chapels are multi-functional and include classrooms, a cultural hall and sometimes a gym) were rated as less sacred than those sites purely devoted to prayer and worship. The more use a place received the less it was regarded as sacred. One wonders, then, whether there is connected with this phenomenon the 'aura' of sacredness surrounding sites which are seldom used for worship but where worship has previously been very significant. Certainly, an act of worship carried out in a supermarket or airport waiting room is less likely to put the worshipper in touch with the transcendent than a service carried out in temple, mosque or cathedral. The desire to be at least fleetingly in encounter with the numinous is probably the main reason for the rise in interest in visiting English parish churches and cathedrals at a time when Christian worshipping communities are dropping in numbers. If church leaders wish to convey the presence of the almighty and encourage a spiritual atmosphere, then worship in secular space will clearly not suffice. Another point of interest from the case is that the cultural landscape of Utah was rated more sacred by those who had been there than by those who had not. But the ratings dropped again if the respondent had visited Utah often, suggesting that perception of a place as sacred is reinforced after one visit but lessens with familiarity. This phenomenon is familiar to all those who have ever worked within sacred space who may horrify visitors by their casual attitude to a sacred building with whose workings they are over-familiar. Staff working within a temple or cathedral have a view of its sacredness very different from that of visitors; awe diminishes if you have to clean the brasses. Expanding this point, one might therefore expect a Muslim always to view Mecca as sacred but especially so if he has once made the *hajj*, though less so if the pilgrimage has been made frequently. Unfortunately, no survey data exists to confirm this. Family homes were not regarded as very sacred in this case study, doubtless a reflection upon the nature of American society with its high degrees of geographical and social mobility. This supports Eliade's (1981) contention that when a territory is permanently settled by a group it is regarded as sacred ground. In the case of Utah the perception of the state as sacred space, a cultural and religious landscape, affects the economy, population migration and church doctrine. Utah receives considerable in-migration despite rapid growth in membership of the Mormon church elsewhere and despite pleas from Mormon leaders to stop the process.

RELIGIOUS TOURISM

The beginnings of religious tourism, and thus the idea of pilgrimage to special, sacred places, goes back a very long way indeed. In fact, one could make a strong case for such behaviour starting with early humans paying sequential visits to paint cave walls at sites such as Lascaux, France. Sacred sites become numerous with the rise of urban societies, although many had been essential components of pre-classical civilizations such as that of Egypt where pilgrims were attracted to festivals at temple sites at Abydos, Thebes, Luxor and Karnak. Today, such sites attract visitors not because they are seen as sacred religious sites but because they are significant cultural tourism attractions. The same is true for the temple complexes which characterize the pre-classicial civilizations of Central and South America, and this is a function of increased cultural distance. Greek festivals had a strong religious character with supraregional centres such as Athens, Ephesus, Delphi and Olympia where athletic competitions also had a religious emphasis but this contributes little to the experience of today's visitors. It is undeniable that the medieval period in Europe saw a great rise in tourism based on religion, arguably the first manifestation of mass tourism. It also saw a growth in services geared to the needs of religious travellers, such as hostels and guide books to facilitate visits to shrines. Huge distances were travelled and well-established routes developed (Chapter Nine). Feifer (1986) discusses the history of medieval tourism when most travellers were either merchants or pilgrims. Far more recently, right at the beginning of package travel, religious excursions played an important role in the history of Thomas Cook as a tour operator (Rinschede, 1992).

Religious tourism may be short-term (a visit to a site or pilgrimage centre to participate in an event, conference or meeting) or longer-term (such as a journey along a pilgrimage route). It is dominantly a group activity where social interaction within a group of believers is a vital component of the experience. Such a group can be composed of people from the same church, temple or mosque or of family groups or parties of friends. Hard data about the volume and value of the pilgrimage business is difficult to come by. Morinis (1984) in a wide-ranging study of pilgrims to three sites in West Bengal, India noted that only 11 per cent were travelling alone, 65 per cent came with family members, 12 per cent with friends and 12% with organized tours. Rinschede (1992) notes that 30 per cent of pilgrims to Lourdes came in groups, making them highly visible, requiring special facilities and (because they were registered) easier to record – unlike the usual situation in Asia. Pilgrimage sites in western countries are predominantly accessed by road (Rinschede, *op. cit.*); at Lourdes the figure is 62 per cent arriving by car, at Fatima it is 90 per cent and some sites in the USA and Canada reach 100 per cent. At Lourdes 69 per cent of pilgrims are female – partly since the site is a Marian shrine, but this gender imbalance is common at all Catholic pilgrim sites. Conversely, 65 per cent of pilgrims to Mecca are male, which is related to the position of women in the Islamic world and religion.

The role of the travel industry in any cultural tourism product is relatively small, and particularly so in relation to the management of sacred site tourism, with the exception of the organization of pilgrimages. Management of any cultural tourism product is complicated since it occurs in an open system which includes many facets which are just a way of life, or non-tourism functions. Cultural tourism, for example, may include church services, street life, views of a castle and visits to a museum, but the tour operator sells these elements as part of a whole cultural tourism experience, together with commercial products such as accommodation, transportation and food. Management of an open system is much more difficult than that of a closed attraction such as a theme park, as all its elements may be subject to different management systems and all may be unpredictable.

Visitors to sacred sites may be divided into two basic groups: those whose primary purpose is to gain a religious experience (including pilgrims) and the potentially far larger group of those whose major motivation is visiting an element of the world's religious heritage. Patterns of systematic religious tourism and pilgrimage are constantly altering in response to factors such as political change, site accessibility, particular promotions and events in religious calendars. The most significant of these was the rise in such travel during the year 2000, when between 20 million and 50 million visitors were expected just in Rome. Purposive religious tourism (as opposed to the opportunistic visiting of a sacred site in the course of any leisure or business trip) is especially significant for the coach industry, and also in rail and air charter travel. Visiting sacred sites (particularly when there is a large concentration of such sites within an urban centre) is also a major motivation within the European-short-break market, since a very high proportion of all visits to major religious centres lasts only for a single day or a two-night stopover. Domestic religious travel (often involving small, highly-specialized direct sell operators) is a growth market. Religious tourism also has merchandising implications – annual sales of religious souvenirs in Italy are estimated at US$255m (Bywater, 1994) and 200 shops in Lourdes depend on sales of religious objects. The tourism industries of countries such as Israel and the Vatican city are entirely dependent on sacred sites. In Israel, for example, 95 per cent of all visitors go to Jerusalem and more than 60 per cent to Nazareth and Bethlehem. Such tourism is relatively recession-resistant, but it is highly vulnerable to political uncertainties (Boniface, 1995).

Sacred sites can be classified in a number of ways, with most classifications being effectively based on site type and location, rather than on the religious tradition represented. It is also possible to categorize visitor motivations, which tend to polarize between the 'worshipper' on the one hand and the 'tourist' on the other. However, there are substantial degrees of overlap. Visiting sacred sites is an activity that is nested within a framework of cultural and religious tourism, with sacred sites producing some interesting management challenges in a way not experienced by secular visitor attractions. The managers of sacred sites may see their primary function as being conservation and preservation of both site and religious tradition, as opposed to provision of facilities for visitors. Sacred sites are arguably the oldest type of visitor attraction within the tourism system but few were designed to cope with the volume and flow of today's visitation patterns and the expectations of today's visitors, issues which will be dealt with in the next two chapters.

CHAPTER 2

Visitor Experience

The nature of the experience offered by a sacred site to its visitors is highly complex, particularly since it is largely intangible and may include elements such as nostalgia, a closeness to God, 'atmosphere' and the spiritual merit of a visit, on which it is impossible to put a monetary value. But such sites are also in the business of providing a service (sometimes literally as well as metaphorically). The visitor experience is composed of a number of elements, which may include:

- The journey to reach the site
- The characteristics and atmosphere of the site
- The influence of staff and site management
- Availability of visitor services
- Occurrence of special events, festivals, etc.

The journey to reach the site may be a very significant component of the experience, particularly for religious tourists and pilgrims who may have built up a high level of spiritual anticipation, sometimes for many years. The length and frequency of the actual physical journey to the site may vary, from an annual visit to a local shrine for a festival to a cross-country pilgrimage that can involve travelling hundreds of miles. The pre-visit stage of anticipation and planning is also affected by travelling companions (visiting sacred sites is a very social business, few travel alone), who reinforce group bonds and make the experience even more special for members of the party. Whatever their motivation, every visitor arrives at the site with a set of expectations which will have been generated by previous visits, conversations with previous visitors, photographs, television programmes or any combination of these influences, or merely exist simply in the imagination of the individual. Sometimes a mismatch between imagination and reality can have serious psychological effects such as 'Jerusalem Syndrome', a well-documented medical condition where sufferers (of many different faiths) are simply unable to cope with the spiritual pressure of their visit to such a significant location whose emotional power can literally be overwhelming. 'Jerusalem Syndrome' has become a recognized, if transient, complaint. Some sufferers disintegrate physically, spiritually or psychologically. Others suffer the delusion that they are characters from the Bible (Jesus is the favourite but many also identify with Moses, King David, Elijah, John the Baptist and the Virgin Mary). Affected persons might take up the clothes and mannerisms of the persons they are convinced that they are. Another aspect of the condition is that sufferers occasionally take violent action – in 1969 an Australian tourist tried to burn down the al-Aqsa mosque in preparation for the Second Coming of Christ that he thought was imminent. Several hundred cases of people with Jerusalem Syndrome enter local hospitals each year, and the authorities worried about extra severe outbreaks during the celebration of the new millennium in 2000.

Once the visitor has arrived at the site of his or her choice the nature of the experience is also affected by the availability of suitable visitor services, which may include interpretation, transport, parking, accommodation, catering, signage, guiding and merchandising, as well as by the attitude of site staff and managers. Indeed, staff (using the term flexibly) may themselves be an intrinsic component of the experience since those who tend the site in a religious capacity whether priests, mullahs, monks or lamas are generally perceived by the visitor as part of the total experience being consumed. The level of importance attached to interaction with staff will vary depending on the motivation of the visitor. For a Roman Catholic visiting Rome, for example, a chance sighting of a Cardinal will be highly significant and exciting, but for a non-religious tourist the Cardinal's spectacular clothing and elevated clerical status merely contributes to an exotic photo-opportunity devoid of religious value. Similarly, Buddhists visiting remote shrines in the Himalayas will place a high spiritual value on an encounter with a saffron-robed lama, whereas for the cultural tourist the lama is merely a part of the experience.

Cultural change and cultural distance condition many aspects of visitor experience at sacred sites. Fifty years ago, for example, most Christian visitors to churches or cathedrals in Europe would themselves have been churchgoers, and the nuances of dress and office visible within the premises were familiar in a way that they are not to contemporary visitors. Dress, vestments, lights, incense, smells, colour and ceremonial add greatly to the quality of visitor experience at sacred sites, whether at High Mass in a cathedral or a temple ceremony in Tibet. There is legitimate religious cause for concern when the requirements of non-worshipping visitors affect the production of this kind of ceremonial in an attempt to make it more 'relevant' or understandable.

Visitors to a sacred site are also themselves components of the experience that it offers. Worshippers at a service are a part of that service, and watchers of sacred dance reciprocally contribute to the nature of their experience. Since each visitor comes with his or her own set of prejudices, values, attitudes and expectations the nature of the experience is different for everyone. Obvious generalizations can be made, for example the differences in experience between a member of the same worshipping tradition and those of a worshipper of a different tradition. Clear differences will also exist between the ways in which the experience is perceived by those of different gender, age or race. But the experience cannot be standardized, no two sacred sites are ever alike, and it is difficult to enforce any kind of quality management system to enhance experience consistency. The experience cannot be stored and it is perishable, although the visitor can take away a tangible memory in the form of photographs or souvenirs. This makes it very difficult to balance supply and demand – hence the difficulties of managing capacity constraints in sacred sites. Intangibility, combined with complex visitor motivations that might include spiritual fulfilment, mean that visits to sacred sites have a high propensity for spiritual uplift but can be catastrophic for the life of an individual if they go wrong. A pilgrimage to Jerusalem may be anticipated for years: having a poor experience is more than just a holiday disaster and may have serious implications for the person's spiritual health or belief system. A visitor experience cannot be returned like a faulty piece of goods, and may have involved extensive travel and investment of time, money and emotion. Visiting sacred sites is a fragile process, for many reasons.

BUILDING THE EXPERIENCE

In tourism terms the experience of visiting a sacred site starts long before the actual visit, and includes the following stages:

Stage 1 Anticipation: This may be accompanied by research or information-gathering, or by religious preparation such as fasting.

Stage 2 The Journey: The journey to the site may be accompanied by carrying out special rites, or wearing of special clothing. Unlike other heritage attractions the visitor's objective may not necessarily be to reach the site as quickly as possible; indeed, the journey may form an integral part of the visit.

Stage 3 The Visit: The rest of the visitor experience is based on the time spent at the site, but will be affected by preconceptions accumulated on, and before, the journey.

Stage 4 The Return: The return journey is used to mull over the principal features of the experience. These may be intangible (spiritual benefit, comfort, experience of transcendence) or physical, such as healing, and may also include the accumulation of tangible artefacts such as souvenirs or relics.

Some sacred sites have very high levels of repeat business if the perceived quality of experience is high (as in people who continually revisit a much-loved shrine), but the same visitor will be discouraged from coming again if the nature of the experience changes. The commonest ways in which this happens are when major building work has been started which alters the perceived 'spirit of place', or when the site is viewed as overcrowded. Other familiar complaints include intrusive guides and (especially) the introduction of admission charges.

Many complex models of travel behaviour have been constructed (e.g. Gnoth, 1997) which attempt to assess the factors influencing decision-making behaviour, as well as those affecting the quality of the experience. After making the decision to visit a site (thus metaphorically or literally purchasing its product), the visitor continually evaluates his or her decision until the visit is undertaken (which may be some considerable time after the purchase). Much of the literature of consumer satisfaction measures satisfaction either against expectation or against actual experience. Satisfaction is defined as a holistic emotional response to a situation or event that matches or exceeds expectations (Gnoth, 1994; Ryan, 1995). Knowing what customers expect is undoubtedly the most critical step in delivery quality service. Unfortunately, the consumer suffers from an incomplete data set at the time that expectations are formed, and in some cases this is deliberately engineered by the tourism industry to present an edited image of a particular site. Visitors to the Pyramids in Egypt, for example, are often surprised to find that they are in a suburb of Cairo, since marketing brochures show a level desert plateau with the monuments outlined against the sky. However, such selectivity can rebound since visitors' expectations are unlikely to be met, and they may be disappointed. The nature of the visitor experience at a sacred site is also potentially emotional in a way that a visit to a castle or theme park is not. The emotional attachment of the visitor to the site develops primarily through knowledge acquisition and actual social interaction with other different groups. This shapes the visitor's expectations and subsequently affects his or her behaviour. Levels of satisfaction or dissatisfaction depend on whether those expectations have been met at all stages during the progress of the visit. The nature of a visitor experience to a sacred site will also be affected by the visitor's emotional attachment to the site, and by the social experience of others in the group with him or her. Easily the most significant factor in forming the nature of the on-site experience is the way in which the sacred site presents and maintains its 'spirit of place'.

MAINTAINING A 'SPIRIT OF PLACE'

Reverence for sacred places has existed since the world's earliest settled farming communities, and possibly before. Today, there is a great deal of interest in issues to do with sacred sites, both in their meaning and in their management. In earlier times, visiting a sacred site meant an encounter with the holy, and a visitor experience that might include a call to move beyond the self. The vast majority of today's cultural tourists do not have such motivations, but part of the challenge of managing visitors at sacred sites lies in difficulties associated with an interface between the sacred and the profane. The introduction of qualitative elements such as 'a sense of the numinous' or a 'spirit of place' makes the visitor experience difficult to classify. The writer noted with interest the way in which remarks made by visitors to the opening of the Tate Modern art gallery in London's Bankside during May 2000 closely mirrored those of visitors to cathedrals. Tate Modern visitors commented that they were impressed by the vastness of the space (the gallery is a converted power station), a space which made them feel insignificant yet also excited and involved. Comments included approval of the way in which light had been used in the design of the facility, at the level of provision of visitor facilities (especially catering) and the fact that entry was free. Visitors also commented favourably on the way in which the space was free of the hushed whispering common in galleries and cathedrals and museums, and that they were encouraged to talk, interact and run about. The Tate Modern and its exhibits were contrasted favourably with the crass superficiality of the Millennium Dome (which was seen as a competing visitor attraction but has since closed). Such comments indicate that the architects of Tate Modern had succeeded in creating a powerful 'spirit of place', an atmosphere which both welcomed and intrigued visitors yet provided them with the opportunity to experience something out of the range of their normal lives. It is extremely difficult to do this at a 'secular' site, easier if the site is seen by its visitors as sacred and thus already possessed of an appropriate and distinctive atmosphere.

CASE STUDY: MAINTAINING A SPIRIT OF PLACE AT NINSTINTS, BRITISH COLUMBIA

The lower the number of visitors the easier it is to manage visitor impact and maintain a 'spirit of place', retaining that elusive spiritual quality which attracts visitors to sacred sites in the first place and provides them with an uplifting experience. The atmosphere of shrines and temples where worshippers have congregated for millennia may be very distinctive, but it is also possible to encounter open-air sites which produce a powerful spiritual impact on their visitors. One good example may be found at the abandoned Haida village of Ninstints on Anthony Island, the southernmost of the Queen Charlotte Islands off the coast of British Columbia, in Canada (Shackley, 1998f).

Ninstints was once a large and flourishing village of the coastal Haida Native American people, but all that is left now are the collapsed remains of log houses and an extraordinary collection of intricately-carved but heavily-weathered totem poles. It is these poles that have resulted in World Heritage designation being given to the site, which is regarded as sacred by many Native American people. Today, the visitor to Ninstints can see more than two dozen of the great totem poles which were formerly dotted throughout the village, in a quietly magical setting of great solemnity recalling the stone monoliths (*moai*) of Easter Island (Fig. 2.1). The village is located in an enchanted forest of many-coloured moss, giant tree ferns and seemingly endless varieties of trees. The cedar poles are bleached by the weather, rotting and tilting towards each other, and mixed up with the remains of seventeen log houses. Glimpses of the carved faces and figures of beavers, bears, dogfish and thunderbirds stare out from the moss-covered remains. Ninstints feels like a sacred place, and is often referred to as a 'natural cathedral', full of Haida ancestral forests spirits surviving in a green world of unchanging silence. So powerful is this impression that otherwise staid historians and archaeologists have been known to refer to Ninstints as one of Canada's holiest places (e.g. MacDonald, 1983: 1).

Contemporary Haida people view Ninstints as their most sacred site, to be conserved at all costs. During the 1990s they successfully lobbied for helicopter flights and floatplane landings to be banned so that all visitors must come by water, by either inflatable boat or sea kayak. Weather conditions ensure that the site is accessible only between July and September, and it receives fewer than 1000 visitors per year. There are no

Figure 2.1 Haida totem poles at Ninstints (Anthony Island), British Columbia, Canada

visitor facilities: no catering, marketing or signage and no interpretation except that provided personally by the Watchmen, a small group of Haida who are descendants of the original inhabitants of the island. Visitors land on the beach at high tide, register with the Watchmen and then walk around the abandoned village of Ninstints. Watchmen (whose activities are funded by Parks Canada) sometimes offer to take visitors to the other six Haida sites on the island, including two burial caves. They may welcome visitors into their longhouse for a chat and a cup of tea. Watchmen keep a visitor utilization record and have the powers to limit visitors to twenty at a time, and to evict or exclude the unwelcome. Watchmen are all volunteers, trained by means of classes that take place over the winter and involve not only record-keeping and visitor skills but also traditional crafts such as drum-making and spruce root weaving. Watchmen are intended not just to guard the site but also to act as culture brokers and interpreters, a programme which is both successful with visitors and highly regarded by the Haida themselves.

There are no visible tourism impacts at Ninstints and today's visitor will see the site looking much as it did at the time it was abandoned in the late nineteenth-century, as a result of a smallpox epidemic (Shackley, 1998f). Today, Ninstints is the focus of contemporary Haida nationalism, a memorial to days of greatness and a living symbol of the former power and wealth of the Haida people. The Haida welcome visitors to their ancient sites, since this provides an opportunity for education, but also raises their own consciousness and awareness of the extent of what has been lost. The visitor to Ninstints has the benefit of the almost tangible presence of Haida ancestors, an experience perhaps unique, certainly unsettling but (one hopes) sustainable.

What makes the visitor experience at Ninstints so powerful? It is easy to unpack the constituent factors, which are dominated by the isolation of the site, its beauty, and the need to reach it by sea. As has already been noted, the nature of the visitor experience is formed by expectation and journey as well as the actual visit itself. Here, the visitor needs to exercise considerable ingenuity (and great expense) to get him- or herself to a remote island with very restricted access. Few do so unless motivated by an interest in Haida culture. The experience involves not only difficulty but also an element of danger, and it can be physically taxing. It is always undertaken as part of a like-minded group, and must be planned carefully well in advance. If the visitor is in fact a member of the Haida nation then the trip contains substantial elements of pilgrimage; if not, then the visitor is still likely to have an informed interest in Haida culture. The site is famous (at least in Canada) for its beauty and remoteness, and the visual image of the abandoned totem poles in their forest setting are quite well known. Visitors come expecting to be impressed, and they are not disappointed. Ninstints is arguably the most remote tourist attraction in Canada. The isolation of the site, its perfect quietness and the necessity for arriving by sea, as its original inhabitants did, usually make a profound impression on the visitor. Only one group of visitors may arrive per day, permitting a tranquil and satisfactory experience, without crowding. The presence of the Watchmen not only controls visitor access and behaviour but also enhances the nature of the experience. They are the classic example of site managers and staff who are themselves a vital element of the visitor experience. The Watchmen have constructed traditional log cabins and maintain a watch rota, as well as a visitors' book that acts as a record of all who have come to the sites. This is interesting, since poor record-keeping is a particular feature of sacred sites, even those in the most developed countries. Watchmen are well trained and highly motivated, and have plenty of time. They enjoy explaining the religious and technological aspects of Haida culture, using oral histories. Clearly, the Haida perception of the site as sacred is transmitted by them to visitors, but the site itself has a peculiar atmosphere. Visitors often treat it as an open-air cathedral and, indeed, its spirit of place is reinforced by its remoteness and its beauty. Here, an atmosphere of reverence is created not by the presence of numerous other worshippers, or by the feeling that the site has been a focus for worship for many years, but by an absence of the modern world which enables the visitor to feel the site as it once was. Ninstints is an archaeological site where no rituals or ceremonies are now performed but for contemporary Haida it is a vital element in their history. For non-Haida visitors it provides a unique window on what the world of the Haida was like, by preserving the site as it was, unreconstructed, uninterpreted and untouched by any evidence of tourist activity.

AUTHENTICITY AND VISITOR EXPERIENCE

The visitor experience at Ninstints is authentic in the sense that the site has not been reconstructed, and that interpretation is only provided by the descendants of its inhabitants. This authenticity is a quality which is greatly sought-after in the experience of visiting a sacred site, and may constitute a vital element in visitor expectations and thus in the quality of the eventual experience. However, the absence of authenticity does not mean that the quality of the experience is inevitably adversely affected. A visitor to the Sea of Galilee, for example, who is searching for a quiet lakeside experience where he or she can imagine the presence of Christ and his disciples is in for a rude awakening. The lakeside town of Tiberias where the majority of visitor facilities are located is seedy, messy and unromantic. A McDonalds fast-food restaurant overlooks the waters of the Lake (a companion to the McDrive-In a short distance uphill towards the village of Cana'a), and hungry cats scavenge for the remnants of St Peter's fish thrown to them by diners at the lakeside cafés. Yet despite this lack of calm and authenticity the Sea of Galilee does provide a powerful experience, but more by association and mental image than by reality. Eating a simple meal of bread, wine and grilled fish in the artificial surroundings of Tiberias still has a curiously sacramental quality. St Peter's fish (*moust*) is a basically uninteresting bony lake fish, yet to eat it freshly-caught from the Sea of Galilee is special, a simple meal sanctified by the place. Today, far from being remote and storm-tossed, the Sea of Galilee is frequented by large tourist cruise ships, ferries and small power boats. In quiet corners small traditional-style fishing boats can still be seen with their occupants looking embarrassed at casting their nets overboard, as if caught out in some chronologically or sociologically unacceptable activity. The searcher for enlightenment is unlikely to find it here, even in the splendidly-named Galactic Internet Café, next to McDonalds and within site of Caperneum.

Many visitors to Israel come expecting greater authenticity than this, hoping for a spirit of place untouched since Biblical times. Many are disappointed, since the sacred atmosphere that they expected has long since been submerged in a wave of constructed chapels, mosques, temples, courtyards and homes. In some cases the precise location of the original sacred event associated with a particular site either has been largely obscured or is highly debatable. For example, visitors to the Church of the Holy Sepulchre in Jerusalem are asked to believe that points within the present building mark the precise site of Christ's burial, crucifixion and the last four major events in the Stations of the Cross. It is just the same in Bethlehem, where visitors are shown the precise position of the manger in the stable in the Church of the Nativity. Wars have been fought over such locations, and even if the churches do cover the authentic spot where the event occurred its true site is now submerged under walls, pictures, lamps and silverware. The churches are full of noisy pilgrims, and even noisier tour guides. The emotional appeal of the Christian sites of Jerusalem to their visitors is still very great. Millions of tourists and pilgrims tramp the present Via Dolorosa each year even though the existing route is only one of several that Christ might have taken. However, this seems curiously unimportant and indeed merely of historical interest since it is the symbolism of the journey that is significant. Today, walking the route is more of an obstacle course than a sacred experience. And yet the power of the places is manifested in the combined belief and joy of visitors, a sort of collective wish fulfilment. No amount of street vendors and souvenir stands selling plastic Crowns of Thorns can destroy the perceived authenticity that is in the mind of the believer.

The case study of Ninstints, discussed above, noted that one of the most distinctive features of its atmosphere was the total silence, which allowed the visitor to contemplate the site without contemporary realities getting in the way. Yet it is a curiously western idea that sacred sites have to be quiet to be holy. Most have always been loud and noisy. New visitor attractions at ancient sacred sites can acquire also their own aura of sanctity. At the point where the river Jordan leaves Galilee, for example, upriver from where Jesus was actually baptized, a local *kibbutz* has developed a most successful baptismal site where baptismal services are held in a series of tiered fishpond-like arrangements let into the River Jordan. Gowns, certificates, gift shop and bazaar are provided and baptismal services held every day between the hours of 8 a.m. and 7 p.m. The site is extremely popular, especially with overseas visitors who come to be 'born again' and find the experience powerful and disconcerting. The fact that the immediate facility is both new and artificial seems to be less significant than its location on the undeniably authentic River Jordan.

In the world of sacred site tourism it is occasionally difficult to distinguish between the real and the staged. Take, for example, the example of several American sites associated with the Shaker movement which are an increasingly fashionable element of the American cultural tourism industry, largely because of high levels of interest in Shaker furniture and craftsmanship. Shaker sites date from the initial foundation of the Shaker movement in 1747 as the United Society of Believers, which comprised a series of Christian semi-monastic communities scattered throughout the northeastern corner of the United States. Shakers practised equality of sexes and races, common ownership of goods, celibacy and pacifism within their villages. Of the original communities only one, Sabbathday Lake, remains an active Shaker community today, although there are many others which have been transformed into museums and interpretative centres. At Sabbathday Lake the community follows a monastic rule, farming 18,000 acres of land and supplementing their income with craft production. The website (http://www.shaker.lib.me.us/about.html) details the philosophy, theology and history of the community . Sabbathday Lake includes a museum (open seasonally) within its perimeter which utilizes six of the existing eighteen original Shaker structures. It was originally started by community members with an educational aim. Part of the attraction for visitors is the possibility of meeting 'real' Shakers, actual members of the community, as opposed to interpreters. The site offers a structured tour programme six days a week during designated community 'work' time, and also welcomes visitors to share in an active experience of work and worship with the community. However, it asks that privacy is respected (meaning that visitors refrain from entering enclosed off-limits areas, a common problem for religious communities). Specific attractions, apart from the people (who exert exactly the same fascination for visitors as do the Haida Watchmen at Ninstints), include the huge collection of Shaker artefacts which contains famous examples of furniture and wooden objects. However, it is interesting to speculate in what way the visitor experience at this religious site differs from the experiences offered by other Shaker centres such as the museums and visitor centre of Hancock Shaker Village (http://www.hancockshakervillage.org/). Visitors have similar opportunities to get information about Shaker beliefs, and to see Shaker artefacts. However, at

Sabbathday Lake the site is still active in the sense that it is still a working and praying Shaker community (Gleeson, 1994). The other sites provide an equally educational experience but without that element of authenticity. The need, clearly felt at Sabbathday Lake, to delineate areas where visitors were welcome and also areas where they were off-limits is using a standard method of site zoning, discussed below and widely applied. The fact that visitors frequently transgress those limits at religious sites is not unrelated to the quest for authenticity since they are aware that a sacred site is like an iceberg with most of the action out of sight of the viewer.

There is always a desire to get behind the scenes, to penetrate beyond the stage and view the workings behind it (MacCannell, 1973). Many sacred sites involve a certain level of recreated heritage although some authors (e.g. Uzell, 1989) argue that this is impossible as visitor perception of the past will always be influenced by their present-day attitudes and values. Certain aspects of cultural heritage can be recreated, within limits, as at Colonial Williamsburg. The same is true of certain sacred sites where it is only the presence of tourists, often greatly outnumbering worshippers, which has resulted in the preservation of either the site or some rite, sacrament, festival or event that takes place within it. Sometimes the site has remained sacred even when, like Hagia Sophia in Istanbul, it has survived extraordinary changes since its original construction. At Hagia Sophia these include multiple reuse, earthquakes and stripping of altars, but the sheer immensity and size of the building, and the length of time over which it has been visited as a holy place, conveys a sense of sanctity.

Visitors need to feel that they have come into a holy place, even if (by most architectural standards) it is a design disaster, as is the Church of the Holy Sepulchre. Atmosphere is not dependent on taste, but it may be related to behaviour and it is sometimes necessary to enforce specific regulations. For example, tour groups visiting the Church of the Annunciation in Nazareth must be silent, a good thing as the sound of loud voices raised in comment or commentary breaks the spell, contextualizing the visitor too firmly into the present day (as well as being frequently seen as disrespectful). Yet Christian churches were not always places of silence, but it has always been customary to be reverent when entering them. This brings us to a discussion of behaviour norms in sacred sites, and their impact on the nature of the visitor experience.

DRESS AND BEHAVIOUR

There are frequently certain expectations of dress and behaviour imposed on the visitor to a sacred site. Some may be enforced for reasons of safety or conservation, such as the shoe-covers and face masks provided for visitors to the tomb of Nefertari in the Valley of the Kings, to minimize visitor impact on the tomb fabric and paintings. Some regulations may be related to particular religious traditions or trends; others may just be the result of historical precedents. Few are shared by all visitors to the site, and thus provide many opportunities for discord between different groups. Expected behaviour at sacred sites clearly differs widely between sites from different cultural and religious traditions and in different geographical areas (Simpson, 1993). The issue of noise has already been mentioned, and the need to control the volume of a noise in sacred sites may be acute. This is felt most intensely in the large cathedrals of western Europe which have now become major visitor attractions and where there is a tradition of associating silence with reverence. A visitor accustomed to such cultural norms who then makes a trip to a Buddhist monastery in the Himalayas is likely to be struck by the apparent informality of activities; monks will be wandering in and out during ceremonies, sometimes chatting to friends or drinking tea. Only during periods of meditation is silence thought to be necessary. In North America and western Europe there is a culturally-conditioned dislike of crowds; people are uncomfortable being jostled by a large crowd which they see as an intrusion on their private space, as well as a potential security threat. This is not necessarily the case elsewhere, and the critical threshold beyond which people feel that a site is overcrowded is culturally influenced. In Asia, shrines and temples are often crowded to bursting point and at major festivals it may be impossible to move for the sheer press of people watching a procession. Westerners often feel intimidated by this, worried by the intimacy of being physically in contact with such a large number of people, and also worried by feeling that they might have their pockets picked or be assaulted in the mass of people. Easterners, more used to crowds, may feel more comfortable in such a situation and the very presence of a large crowd of people may add to their enjoyment, creating a feeling of solidarity within the worshipping tradition, enhancing the religious experience. Many Asian festivals are thronged with tightly-packed people drawing as much enjoyment from the fact that they are associating with so many like-minded individuals as they are from the festival itself. Unfortunately, there is very little primary data available to give feedback on perceptions of overcrowding at sacred sites.

Because of the change in cultural norms in the west many contemporary church and cathedral visitors do not come from backgrounds containing any religious experience, making them unaware of previously-accepted behaviour norms such as keeping their voices down and behaving reverently in the presence of God. This provides an interesting dilemma for site managers. Christian cathedrals, for example, traditionally impose a basic dress code that bans the wearing of revealing tops, beachwear, and shorts (at least for women). Many visitors are unaware of such unwritten rules and feel that, if they are not believers, they should not be subject to the same rules. One English cathedral was recently faced with a problem since its old-fashioned stewards objected to male visitors wearing hats (traditionally frowned upon). Unfortunately the cathedral was particularly popular with American tourists, many of whom habitually wore baseball caps that they were reluctant to remove. Two possibilities existed – condone the wearing of caps and welcome the visitor, or insist that the caps be removed, making the wearer feel uncomfortable and unwelcome and denying him the chance of entering into the presence of God. In the end, the stewards took the former course.

Visitors to Muslim sites must also accept a dress code: at some sites (such as the Ummayad mosque in Damascus) females must wear a black *abbaya*, completely covering their head and clothes. This conforms to local norms but is unpopular with many western visitors who object to compulsorily being issued with such a garment that may be less than clean. Minor behaviour modifications, such as the wearing of a headscarf or removal of shoes, are generally seen as more acceptable. Married women wishing to approach the Wailing Wall in Jerusalem must wear a headscarf, and it is only since 1945 that female visitors to Christian churches were not expected to do the same. Visitors to temples in Japan must remove their shoes and leave them outside, sometimes a source of stress since some westerners are convinced that the shoes will be stolen and are often unhappy about being shoeless

Figure 2.2 Visitor regulations at St Katherine's Monastery

in a public place – again, a cultural norm. In Japan, additional anxiety is often created by the fact that the slip-on sandals sometimes provided to replace the missing shoes are often too small for large western feet. A visitor to St Katherine's Monastery on Mt Sinai must be 'modestly dressed' (Fig. 2.2), which excludes shorts on either men or women. Visitors will not be admitted unless they conform, but the monastery keeps a supply of cotton cover-up robes for the importunate. Despite the fact that the dress code is clearly stated on a notice-board outside the main entrance many visitors try to sneak in, often complaining loudly that such a code is unreasonable and cannot possibly apply to them. Why? The complainers are not usually religious people (who, as a group, are generally happy to accede to any regulations which promotes an atmosphere of reverence) but tourists.

The prohibition of shorts is a world-wide phenomenon and few sacred sites allow unlimited amounts of flesh to be displayed. Visitors to temples in Bali must wear a sarong (although this is widely ignored) to cover shorts, and a temple sash to show respect. Ignoring dress codes is universally taken as insulting, and can sometimes cause embarrassment to visitor and visited alike. The writer has previously noted (Shackley, 1995) an incidence of a visitor to some Buddhist temples in Nepal who deliberately ignored the recommended dress code and entered the temples wearing shorts. He was deeply embarrassed to be followed round the site by a gang of small boys stroking his brown hairy legs, which they found fascinating having never previously encountered an adult whose legs were uncovered. At many sacred sites there is a general policy of 'no shirt, no shoes, no service' – the exception being the Episcopalian church in Key West, Florida, a very informal town, which has a notice outside (prominently displayed), reading 'No need to wear formal clothes – Jesus didn't'. Jain temples prohibit the wearing of leather, and also ask that women do not visit while menstruating. The former request is usually complied with but the latter gives problems. It is unlikely that western women forming part of a non-Jain visitor group would elect not to enter the temple while menstruating since this could be seen as unacceptable gender differentiation. There is still a certain taboo about discussing menstruation in western society. A female member of a mixed tourist group is unlikely to wish to discuss her menstrual cycle with complete strangers. It seems likely that the prohibition is widely ignored, although clearly this is impossible to check.

Dress is one way of expressing reverence. It also demonstrates familiarity with the cultural and religious norms of the site or building and avoids embarrassment. Reverence can also be expressed in posture. Within a Christian sacred site, for example, pilgrims may be distinguished from tourists by the adoption of a reverent posture, often with hands folded as in prayer. A quiet demeanour is often used to convey reverence, together with the use of ritual gestures such as genuflexion. The use of ritual objects such as a rosary in the Christian tradition, Muslim prayer beads or a Buddhist *mala*, also distinguish worshipper from tourist. Other gestures include the physical turning of prayer wheels, lighting of candles or joss sticks, and the use of specific postures such as kneeling, praying with hands outstretched or prostration. Visitors accustomed to utilizing certain objects, gestures or postures as part of their prayer may find it irritating if others do not share their customs, and especially difficult if non-worshippers take inappropriate photographs of rituals they do not understand, merely as additional local colour. There is a very widespread view that uncontrolled photography is inappropriate in a sacred place. This can manifest itself as a total or partial ban, especially on equipment-intensive video photography or flash photography that can damage fragile textiles and paintings. Photographing worshippers is often seen as an invasion of privacy. Many sites forbid photography altogether, or limit it to persons who have paid for a permit, which provides an extra opportunity to generate revenue. There has recently been considerable adverse publicity about the offence given to local people by tourists trying to photograph the 'burning *ghats*' alongside the river Ganges in Varanasi, where deceased Hindus are cremated. This is seen as not only insensitive but also downright sacrilegious. However, the proper treatment of sacred places is a matter of respect, not always enforceable by management and sometimes complicated by an extensive cultural distance between the function and purpose of the site and the background of its visitors. There are some examples of site managers taking a strong line when visitors behave in an unacceptable fashion. The main attractions for visitors to Bhutan, a small Himalayan country 200 miles east of Sikkim, are the fortress-monasteries or *dzong*, which even Bhutanese are not supposed to enter unless wearing their traditional dress and carrying a ceremonial scarf. Bhutan maintains strict controls over tourism and in 1988 suddenly closed its temples and *dzongs* to foreigners because of complaints that poor visitor behaviour was affecting their sanctity. The sites were eventually reopened as a result of pressure from the tourism industry and assurances that international visitors would receive better briefing about the correct mode of behaviour. It is undeniable that the adoption of a collective code in behaviour, dress and activities by visitors to sacred sites can enforce a sense of solidarity among worshippers. Unfortunately, it can also accentuate divisions between worshippers and tourists. The management of behaviour is very difficult to enforce, and largely accomplished by consensus. But the behaviour of fellow visitors materially affects the nature of the individual visitor experience as it modifies the 'spirit of place' of the site.

CHAPTER 3

Managing Visitor Impacts

Visitor impacts on sacred sites can be broadly grouped into two major categories: those that affect the physical resource itself, and those that in some way diminish the quality of the experience of visitors (both tourists and worshippers) without any physical effects on the fabric of the site. Clearly this is an oversimplification, and there are many subcategories of impact that could be added. The constant need to balance the requirements of visitors with those of worshippers also has a psychological impact on site managers. Some of the impact of visitors is economic, although at sacred sites positive economic benefits from visitors are more likely to be received by external privately owned enterprises than by the site itself. Crime, as a social impact of tourism, is not absent from sacred sites, with theft and vandalism being its most common manifestations. However, there are recorded instances of rape, grievous bodily harm and even murder. Crime is particularly common at major festivals and events where large numbers of people are gathered together in circumstances that are difficult to police. In terms of sacred sites with a substantial built heritage component (by far the majority), the principal categories of physical impacts related to visitor activity are summarized in Table 3.1. Of course, not all sacred sites do include built heritage. At natural sacred sites, such as groves, mountains, lakes and springs the types of visitor impact may include disturbance to wildlife, damage to vegetation and soils, changes in species composition, removal of wildlife, pollution by refuse or litter, hydrological and geomorphological effects and habitat loss.

Table 3.1 Physical impacts of visitor activity

Agent of Change	Physical Impact	Impact on Visitor Experience	Example
Theft of artefacts	Loss of resource	Diminished quality of experience	Removing tiles from Taj Mahal
Vandalism/graffiti	Damage to Resource	Diminished quality of experience	Carving of initials on Nativity Grotto
Accidental damage	Wear and tear	Diminished quality of experience	Fabric erosion in cathedrals
Pollution (fouling)	Damage to resource	Diminished quality of experience	Urine at Giza Plateau
Pollution (noise)	May undermine fabric	Diminished quality of experience	Church of Holy Sepulchre
Pollution (litter)	Reduced attractiveness	Diminished quality of experience	Mt Everest area
Microclimatic Change	Fabric damage	Diminished quality of experience	Egyptian tombs
Crowding	Leads to physical damage	Diminished quality of experience	

DELIBERATE PHYSICAL IMPACTS – THEFT AND VANDALISM

The management of the physical impacts of visitor activity usually has some financial implications. Vandalism and graffiti may incur considerable expense in both prevention and remedial action. Managers frequently take the view that prevention is better than cure, to be accomplished by visitor education and the provision of adequate information from guides and notices. Visitors to sacred sites often seem to require some actual physical contact with a sacred object or element of the site fabric: merely to be in its presence or within the site is not enough. This is often manifested either in touching the object (such as a statue of a saint or Buddha), or kissing the object, which not only erodes the artefact but is a deeply unhygienic practice which can spread disease. In the Basilica of St Peter in the Vatican the thirteenth-century bronze statue of St Peter made by Arnolfo de Cambio has had the toes of its right foot worn away by the lips and fingers of pilgrims. This erosion has been accomplished since 1857 when the reigning Pope, Pius IX, unwisely granted a 50-day Papal Indulgence to anyone kissing the foot of the statue after making his or her confession. Few sites are vandal-proof and their sacred status does not deter souvenir hunters. Even the remaining olive trees in the Garden of Gethsemane in Jerusalem have had to be fenced off to avoid damage, protecting them from over-enthusiastic people who would like a cutting. Cuttings from the trees are actually legally available at pruning time, by payment of a small inducement to the gardeners. A similar system is worked at the monastery of St Katherine in the Sinai Desert, which shelters a flourishing descendant of the Burning Bush (a specimen of *Rubus sanctus*). Today, monks sell cuttings from the Burning Bush (or its modern descendant) to visitors, an activity which has not only stopped the illegal taking of cuttings but also generates revenue for the monastery.

Many ancient buildings have had to employ Perspex™ screening to cover the walls in stairways, passageways and vulnerable areas, not just to prevent erosion from the continual friction caused by the clothing of visitors but also to deter visitors from taking souvenir samples of the fabric and scratching graffiti. Where this is not done (as in some of the tombs in the Valley of the Kings, Egypt) the erosion of the wall paintings is very obvious. Unfortunately, defacing walls with graffiti is a common practice and can be seen even in the holiest of sites such as the Church of the Holy Sepulchre, Jerusalem, in which graffiti have been scratched into the glass screening in the area known as St Helena's cave, where the remains of Christ's cross were supposedly discovered. However, one man's graffito is another man's historical inscription. In the Church of the Nativity in Bethlehem part of the walls are Perspex-covered to prevent graffiti but in other areas interesting ancient inscriptions and graffiti have been outlined in black to increase their visibility. In St Peter's, Rome, Michelangelo's wonderful white marble statue called the *Pietà*, which shows the Virgin Mary cradling the crucified Christ in her arms, is surely one of the most famous sculptures in the world. It was made when the artist was only 24, and is located in its own chapel to the right of the main entrance. However, now it is possible to view the sculpture only from some distance away through a glass screen, installed after an attack by a religious fanatic armed with a hammer in 1972. Visitors are discouraged by officious stewards from lingering by the screen, presumably to deter any attempts to make a closer inspection.

The removal of a piece of a site may seem to us as vandalism but for the believer it can appear as the acquisition of a sacred relic. A relic, whether a fragment of wall tile or a remnant of the body of a saint, is literally priceless; it is a way of coming into direct contact with a higher reality which can usually only be approached in prayer, meditation, worship or sacrament. A relic somehow makes a hole in the wall that separates the human from the divine, the visible from the invisible, the mundane from the transcendent. Relic-taking also goes on at modern sites, with modern relics including pieces of building fabric removed from Nelson Mandela's cell in Robben Island. Another example can be seen at the Milk Grotto in Bethlehem, which supposedly marks the spot where Mary, Joseph and Jesus are supposed to have rested during their flight to Egypt. The legend says that Mary was nursing the baby Jesus at the time and let fall a drop of her milk, turning the rock of the cave from red to chalky white. Ever since then the site has been visited by Christians and Muslims who share the belief that possessing a piece of the rock increases a nursing mother's milk and fertility. Unfortunately, this causes pilgrims to chip off pieces to take home, although the practice has now been forbidden. Nor are open-air sites and cultural landscapes immune from such vandalism. Mt Haleakala on the Hawaiian island of Maui is sacred in Polynesian legend. Today, the famous volcano crater is a National Park and tourist attraction, but rangers grew concerned at the increasing numbers of visitors who would remove a stone from the site as a souvenir. A novel means of prevention was adopted whereby the rumour was circulated that the removal of stones incurred the curse of the God Maui, to whom the site is sacred. Very little stone removal takes place today, and there have been cases where the National Park authorities have received stone samples posted back to them from all over the world by guilty parties. Exactly the same problem of souvenir-taking was experienced at Uluru (Ayers Rock) in Australia, a site sacred to Aboriginal people. Other locations have used substitution as a management method, rather than superstitition, with commercial replacement of the original by a packaged product. Throughout Israel, for example, the pilgrim can buy a small pack of genuine Holy Land soil, Jordan water, spikenard ointment (supposedly used by Mary Magdalene and containing frankincense) and holy oil.

Theft, clearly, is not only a tangible impact of visitor activity but diminishes the site resources. It is an unfortunate fact that just as the sacredness of a site is no barrier to vandalism it is also no barrier to theft. Indeed, sacred sites by their very nature are high-risk areas with long opening hours, minimal security and over-reliance on the fact that God will take care of his own. There is a very fine line between theft and souvenir-taking. Airey and Shackley (1998) studied the Islamic monuments of Bukhara and Samarkand in central Asia. Neither site has serious over-visitation problems but both sites are plagued by a type of vandalism where domestic visitors and Muslim pilgrims occasionally remove tiles or pieces of plaster as souvenirs of the holy places they have visited within those cities. Exactly the same phenomenon has been observed at the Taj Mahal where small pieces of inlay are frequently removed, although here it is less likely to be for religious purposes than for resale to international tourists as souvenirs.

CASE STUDY: EROSION AND VISITOR IMPACT
AT LALIBELA IN ETHIOPIA

Carlisle (1998) studied the famous complex of ancient rock-cut churches at Lalibela in Ethiopia, a significant pilgrimage destination for Coptic Christians and still actively in use for worship today. She concluded that four types of physical erosion of the fabric were apparent, namely cracks in the rock, granular disintegration, scaling and erosion. The degradation process involves a variety of contributing factors including the heterogeneity of the rock, people walking on and around the church area, the effect of rainwater, the encroachment of residential land-use and the formation of nitrates in the rock. The church's contents are also suffering degradation and there are few means of providing safe and secure storage for ancient artefacts. There is frequent handling of hand-crosses, ancient manuscripts, prayer sticks, drums, umbrellas, robes and carpets by priests and tourists, children and local people, which over the years has caused excessive wear and tear. Natural causes such as the humidity of the buildings, the hydrology of the churches, the passing of time, dust and the action of wind, insects and sunlight also have an effect on the deterioration of articles within the church. Flash photography is also contributing to colour deterioration of façades, paintings and costumes. Problems are made worse by the lack of restrictions over the areas where local people, pilgrims and tourists can walk in the church site. They are even allowed to walk on the surrounding walls of the monolithic churches and on top of the connecting tunnels. The heavy walking boots of international visitors contribute to the erosion of the rock, as well as to everyday wear and tear through constant treading. Safety of individuals is not taken into consideration and there are many steep, rocky and slippery steps to negotiate. Another problem that has arisen recently is that of sanitation in the village compounds situated within the close vicinity of the church site. Deterioration of the church walls is resulting from urine seeping into the ground from nearby households, causing nitrates to dissolve the rock. Finnida (a Finnish NGO working in the area on town planning and local community development) is keen to rectify this problem and there is also discussion of resettlement of families living within the church area. It is a sensitive issue as there are no determined boundaries of the church site (Carlisle, 1998). To implement conservation management, working within Lalibela's environmental and human carrying capacity, would require a number of changes to the running of the church sites. First, fragile areas would have to be closed, either temporarily or permanently, while archaeological research takes place. Secondly, visitor access needs to be controlled and, thirdly, some way must be found of preventing the theft and selling of priceless artefacts. As is common in Developing World sacred sites (and many in the Developed World as well), no detailed inventory of all movable heritage within the site exists. Problems are exacerbated by the fact that Ethiopia is now deriving substantial foreign exchange earnings from incoming international cultural tourism, increasing the numbers of visitors reaching the sites. However, in terms of numbers, international visitors are far outweighed by domestic visitors to Lalibela at the times of major Coptic festivals. At present the churches lack the funding for necessary conservation, although it is possible that their status as a World Heritage site may provide financial assistance in the future.

A similiar issue was identified by the writer in the Tibetan kingdom of Mustang (also called Lo). Lo was among the latest of the Buddhist kingdoms of Nepal to open its borders to visitors, who have only been allowed to travel there since 1992 (Shackley, 1993 and 1995). Its *gompas* (temple-monasteries) contain an as yet uncatalogued collection of artwork including statues, *thankas* (ritual paintings on silk) and wall paintings. Some of the latter are in very poor repair and one unfortunate by-product

Figure 3.1 Buddhist monastery at Lo Manthang, Nepal, now open to visitors

of tourism in Lo has been a spate of serious art thefts (Shackley, 1995). Among the first projects to be funded by the revenue obtained from tourism to some of the major monasteries was the installation of security screening at important *gompas*. Tourism to these sacred sites in Lo also provides an interesting example of the positive economic benefits that can accrue to the site from good visitor management. The monastic authorities in Lo instituted a standard visitor fee for *gompas* of 100 Nepalese rupees, paid directly to themselves rather than to tour operators or government agencies. It goes towards financing both the monastery schools and restoration projects, and is thus felt by most visitors to be money well spent. Visitors to sacred sites are notoriously reluctant to contribute funds just for the general good of the site, but are usually willing to pay a fee or make a donation for a specific project. The lamas of Lo are happy to welcome visitors, and not just because they are sources of revenue. Buddhism is traditionally a tolerant religion and the monks welcome the opportunity to meet westerners and, where possible, to share a little Buddhist philosophy. Indeed, when it was realized in Lo that visitors to *gompas* might be stealing artwork the High Lama actively opposed any regulation of visitor activities on the grounds that this was against Buddhist principles of tolerance and free will but he eventually compromised on the issue of security screening.

CASE STUDY: THEFT, SOUVENIRS AND CULTURAL CHANGE – AN EXAMPLE FROM THE *PAYS DOGON* (MALI)

The Dogon people live in the imposing Bandiagara Escarpment 75km east of Mopti in Mali, a region known as the *Pays Dogon*. Their villages consist of a maze of sandy-coloured stone houses with flat roofs that merge imperceptibly into the stone of the Escarpment, punctuated by the cone-shaped thatched roofs of the square-towered granaries and divided by small winding lanes. The entire Escarpment is a World Heritage Site, classified as a cultural landscape. All aspects of Dogon life have cosmological significance and reflect Dogon animist religious beliefs. Partly because of their geographical isolation, and partly due to their fierce independence, the Dogon have retained old beliefs and practices longer than many African people and most remain animists, although some have now converted to Islam. Each village, as well as each individual family house, is laid out in the shape of the human body. The village centre contains a *togu*, or men's shelter, supported by woodcarvings representing Dogon ancestors, now sometimes deliberately defaced to prevent theft or sale. All Dogon art and ritual has strong associations with death and the spirit world, with houses, statues, stools, locks and other artefacts carrying symbolic meaning in their design.

Western anthropologists' interest in Dogon culture began after the pioneering work of the French ethnographer Marcel Griaule who studied Dogon society from 1930 to 1950 (Shackley, 1997). Dogon art, particularly their statues and woodcarvings, is famous and much sought-after by collectors who offer huge prices, especially for grave goods and statuettes robbed by the Dogon from the burial caves of the Tellem people who were the previous inhabitants of the vertical Bandiagara cliffs. Dogon obtain the Tellem artefacts by tomb-robbing from the Tellem mortuary caves in the vertical cliffs behind their villages. There is collusion between international art dealers and local people, and a network of art thefts and exports has developed. Tellem wooden headrests are the oldest wooden artefacts in sub-Saharan Africa and, together with Tellem finger bells, ceramic pots, statuettes and parts of old musical instruments, can command high prices since they are irreplaceable. Tourism is the major source of income to the *Pays Dogon*, which can reasonably claim to be Mali's major cultural tourism attraction, but much concern has been expressed about the close relationship between increasing international tourism and the decreasing visibility of authentic Dogon artefacts.

The whole of the Dogon escarpment is effectively a sacred site, which is currently becoming a popular cultural tourism attraction. Most of the problems connected with the pillage of Dogon antiquities are posed by the international art market which sells mainly to institutions and art connoisseurs, but ordinary tourism has become a major factor in the artwork leakage. Antiquities are, theoretically, objects produced in an unreclaimable past. For the visitor a piece of ethnic art collected in a journey evokes a cultural otherness, emphasizing the cultural and temporal distance between host and guest, as well as evoking the nature of the visitor experience. The cultural gap means that the object may be seen merely as a curiosity or a commodity rather than an essential building-brick of the social identity of the host society.

Since a tourism visit is essentially intangible, the purchase of a souvenir or artwork imparts tangibility to the process as well as enabling the visitor to feel that he has obtained possession of a small part of the cultural heritage of his hosts. The more distant that culture is from his own, the more necessary such a purchase becomes. Most visitors to Mali are from European backgrounds and know relatively little about the religious beliefs of the Dogon. They do not see the purchase of artwork as the purchase of a relic or an essential element of Dogon culture, but

Figure 3.2 Woodcarvings on sale in the *Pays Dogon*, Mali

merely as a souvenir. Copying sacred artwork is a universal practice and many traditional artisans (including Dogon carvers) who copy antiquities for sale to visitors, see this as an acceptable perpetuation of their ancient culture combined with the chance to make some money. Some Dogon villagers claim that very few genuine antiquities remain, with most already having gone to dealers; the remaining authentic sacred objects are available only at a very high price. Poverty, as a result of drought, has previously created opportunities for illicit traders to buy art from the Dogon at below market prices. The Dogon are being robbed of their cultural heritage, albeit with their active collaboration, and losing their collective memory. However, it is up to them to decide what elements of their traditional culture and spirituality are important, since cultural identity is not static.

DAMAGE AND DECAY

Theft, vandalism and graffiti are all types of physical impact that are deliberate, and to a certain degree predictable. With sufficient resources they can be prevented or controlled, and in any case they are carried out by a tiny minority of visitors. Other types of visitor impact are involuntary, and usually related to the presence of larger numbers of visitors than the building can comfortably support (Baron and Byrne, 1987). We have already seen (above) the impact of poorly-controlled visitation to the rock-cut churches of Lalibela, and the way in which visitor impact and natural disintegration is inextricably connected. An equally good example comes from Egyptian sites in the vicinity of Luxor, ancient Thebes. All of the Theban monuments are under constant threat from a lethal combination of rising water levels and saline intrusion, continual archeological activity and high levels of visitation. In the Valley of the Kings and Valley of the Queens that contain the most famous Egyptian tombs (including that of Tutankhamun), such threats are intensified by the physical features of the area. The local limestone is unstable and greatly affected by moisture and vibration and by natural hazards such as the earthquake in 1992 and recent heavy rains. The paths and walls built around the groups of tombs also contribute to the risk of flood damage as they create conduits for the torrents of water and, despite records of previous floods, no damage-limitation measures had previously been put in place (Rivers, 1998). Tombs are periodically closed to visitors for protection, study or restoration, including some of the most famous such as that of Seti I. The famous tomb of Tutankhamun, the only one discovered largely intact, still contains the body of the pharaoh lying within his sarcophagus. All the rest of his grave goods are now in Cairo Museum, together with the wonderful gold funeral mask and gold inner coffins. Despite the charge of an additional fee and its small size, the tomb attracts nearly 300,000 visitors per year. Conservationists are convinced that the volume of visitors is a major threat to the tombs in the Valley of the Kings, as the presence of large groups of people increases humidity and vibration levels and escalates the rate of deterioration. Clearly, the tombs were never designed to be entered on a regular basis. Attempts have now been made to control visitor flows and shut tombs for maintenance, with the result that up to 30 per cent of the tombs in the Valley of the Kings can be closed at any one time. The huge volume of visitors is thought to have been a contributory factor when a roof collapsed in the tomb of Seti I, fortunately closed at the time (Rivers, 1998). Results of a study on the recently restored tomb of Nefertari by the J. Paul Getty Conservation Institute showed that 125 people staying in the tomb for an hour would produce the equivalent of three gallons of water poured onto the walls. It was concern about visitor impacts on the tomb which led to the decision to impose a limit of 150 visitors per day, and various measures were tried by the Department of Antiquities to manage these restrictions. Entry is by special tickets which are currently issued on a first come, first served basis with the result that queues form at the ticket office more than two hours before opening. The daily visitor quota is being strictly maintained and the tomb's microclimate helped by its solar-powered air-conditioning. Groups of no more than a dozen visitors at a time are allowed inside, remaining for no more than ten minutes, with the compulsory wearing of protective face masks and shoe covers to protect the fragile and beautiful wall paintings.

Figure 3.3 Visitor shuttles in the Valley of the Kings, Thebes, Egypt

Many other sacred sites also are affected by a combination of natural deterioration and human activity, including the temples of the Acropolis in Athens whose very fabric is threatened by the extremely high levels of air pollution. On really bad days, private traffic is banned. Nor are such problems absent at open-air sites. The Nazca Desert is a high plateau located on the coast of Peru about 250m south of Lima. It is home to one of Peru's most famous visitor attractions, the Nazca Lines. The Nazca people were a complex agricultural society wiped out after the Spanish conquest, and principally remembered for their weaving, pottery and sacred ground art. The Nazca Lines are over 1500 years old and apparently drawn so that they could only be appreciated from the air. The figures are thought to be of religious significance, not designed to be seen by human eyes, and there are many opinions about how they were constructed. Within the thousands of lines, five types of figure seem to dominate. These include long straight lines, large geometric figures, drawings of plants and animals, rock piles, and figures decorating hillsides. The drawings of animals are perhaps the most famous and include representations of birds, spiders, fish, and monkeys. The lines vary from 15 cm to 15 m in width and can run for several km. Their patterns were created either by removing the dark surface stones from the desert and placing them in the desired shapes, or by scraping away the thin brown surface sediment by walking or sweeping to expose creamy pink soil underneath. The area has a dry, stable and arid climate so that the configuration of the light-coloured lines has remained unchanged for centuries. Since the 1950s Nazca has been the focus of much legitimate archaeological activity and a large amount of fringe 'New Age' activity as well, since it is considered to be a 'power place'. The orientation of the lines does indeed seem to have some astronomical interest, with the result that the area is now included in many fringe publications which claim extraterrestrial origin for the artwork. The cumulative result is that Nazca now attracts increasing numbers of tourists, particularly since the political situation in Peru has stabilized and permitted investment in visitor facilities. Site-management issues include the requirement for visitors to take a guided tour, prohibitions on the use of off-road vehicles and a ban on walking over the lines or removing stones. Balloon tours, recently started, are proving a successful way of controlling access, though expense prohibits all visitors from being able to take one.

Of course, not all the problems affecting sacred sites are the result of their visitors, although visitor pressure can accentuate pre-existing difficulties. Catastrophic natural damage to sacred sites can occur in a very short time. In December 1999 a terrible storm hit France causing structural damage estimated at US$60–70m, with many major historical sites severely affected. The stained-glass window in the upper chapel of Sainte-Chapelle in Paris was destroyed, and there was extensive damage to the upper terraces of Notre-Dame where spires had been snapped off by hurricane-force winds. This was particularly unfortunate as Notre-Dame had just completed a major decade-long restoration project. The basilica of St Denis had windows blown out, and the towers of the Gothic cathedral of Chartres were closed for a while due to a risk from falling stones.

Many sacred sites have great difficulty in raising funding for running repairs, and even greater problems in raising the huge sums of money required to cope with natural disasters such as earthquake, fire and flood. Unfortunately, the extreme antiquity of the fabric of many sites means that conservation problems are both acute and chronic. The problem of souvenir-taking from Bukhara's magnificent Islamic monuments has already been mentioned, but this pales into insignificance by comparison with conservation problems caused by alterations in surface drainage such as the filling-in of many of the city's ancient canals. Conservation work has involved replacement of damaged brickwork and the construction of new foundations, but difficulties with saline groundwaters are compounded by the fact that the new bricks used in restoration are made from local clays, also heavily saline. The only bricks exempt from the problem seem to be those made to a traditional recipe involving eggs and camel milk, which cannot now be replicated. Examples of these famous bricks have survived intact in the Kalyan minaret and Ismail Samani mausoleum but modern attempts to duplicate the recipe have failed. The current Uzbek government is unable to match the money and conservation expertise to which the country had access when it was part of the former Soviet Union, although some of the earlier Soviet restoration projects are of dubious quality. Some money has been raised from overseas sources, including the Arab league and UNESCO.

Unfortunately, the inability of national governments to cope with the many structural problems of their sacred sites is widespread and many have needed to appeal for international help. A good example comes from the rock-cut churches of Cappadocia in Turkey. These Byzantine structures date from the seventh century (although some were probably inhabited earlier by Christian hermits). The churches are either hollowed out of rock cones or tunnelled into cliff faces, and many contain magnificent frescoes. The sites were gradually abandoned and neglected until the 1920s and 1930s when the writings of a French priest, Fr Guillaume de Jerphanion, drew them to the attention of both scholars and tourists. Peasant families had made homes in the caves, and the delicate tufas which had made church construction possible in the first place were eroding. Rain was soaking into decorated surfaces, fading colours and flaking paintwork. The area is also tectonically unstable and some sites have been destroyed by earthquakes. Today, many of the churches are being restored as the result of an international appeal by UNESCO and the region has become a major destination for both cultural tourism and pilgrimage.

PSYCHOLOGICAL IMPACT

Crowding not only can stimulate accidental damage to a building, but will certainly have a detrimental effect on the overall visitor experience (Berger and Norman, 1995). It can cause actual damage as people jostle to get the best view, take the best photograph or get close enough to touch a famous relic, statue or tomb. Large crowds also cause temperature and noise pollution – a large stone recently fell from the ceiling of the Ramses temple in Abu Simbel in Upper Egypt, probably as a result of the loosening of its setting by continual visitor noise. Helicopter noise and the vibrations of helicopter landings are also believed to be having such an adverse effect on Machu Picchu that they have now been banned. Not only were the helicopters affecting the fabric of the site, but they were also having a severe effect on the nature of visitor experience. Crowding can also affect the nature of the worshipping environment, which can be seen in the following case.

CASE STUDY: WESTMINSTER ABBEY

Westminster Abbey in London is a World Heritage site, an architectural masterpiece which summarizes 900 years of British history. It includes the tombs of kings and queens, and monuments to the great and famous. It has been the setting for every Coronation since 1066 and numerous other royal occasions, but is also a church dedicated to regular worship as well as to the celebration of great national events. It has an unusual status as a 'Royal Peculiar', different from the status of a parish church or cathedral, and comes under the jurisdiction of a Dean and Chapter responsible only to the reigning monarch. Westminster Abbey evolved from a Benedictine monastery, which offered hospitality to visitors, into a huge and complex operation which today offers visitor services of quite a different kind. Some are religious – including the provision of resources for worship, prayer, preaching, and teaching and the availability of a priest or religious sister for consultation or confession. Others are related to the need to manage its 3.5m visitors per year – an astonishing total of 16,000 visitors each busy day. Westminster Abbey is generally regarded as a very well managed sacred site. Research carried out by consultants for the ALVA (Association of Leading Visitor Attractions, of which the Abbey is a member) showed that 80 per cent of its visitors rated their visit as good or excellent, 89 per cent thought the marshals (stewards/guides) were helpful and 90 per cent would recommend a visit to their friends. These good opinions are the result of a programme entitled 'Recovering the Calm', introduced to the Abbey early in 1998 to help worshippers and visitors to co-exist in harmony.

As such an integral part of Britain's heritage the Abbey welcomes large numbers of international visitors. Because of its strategic location, it became a well-known meeting place where visitors forgot that they were in church, and worshippers were upset by visitors talking and milling about. This destroyed the spiritual atmosphere of the cathedral. 'Recovering the Calm' (http://www.westminster-abbey.org) employed the techniques of flow management and zoning to reduce crowding by moving visitors along a pre-determined route eastwards from the North Transept, including the historic cloisters, and leading to the Nave before exiting via the Great West Door. A new 'welcome' leaflet was produced, together with revised sound guides in several languages and the option of taking a tour with the Abbey's vergers. Guided tours are strictly limited to 26 visitors per guide, and an attempt made to space out the parties. But the experience is expensive – a £5 admission charge is levied in a bid to discourage the unmotivated. Charging for admission to sacred sites is always contentious but visitors to Westminster Abbey have always paid for access to particular areas such as the royal chapels, and other comparable sites such as St Paul's Cathedral and Canterbury cathedral were already charging. The money raised from entry charges is used largely for maintenance and restoration of the Abbey's fabric for which the Dean and Chapter are responsible with few grants available.

The new strategy has resulted in the Abbey becoming quieter and visitors still being satisfied with their experience. Tourists seem to value the calm and space of the Abbey that provides an opportunity for reflection and prayer. A two-minute prayer for the world and its needs is said on the hour, with visitors invited to participate – an idea which is now a common practice in many cathedrals. One result of the programme is that noise levels have been reduced by 50 per cent. Public worship continues to be the main emphasis day by day, and special provision has been made in St George's Chapel and St Faith's Chapel for those who wish to sit and pray. The programme seems to be working as both visitor and worshipper numbers are rising.

The use of zoning and other visitor-flow control methods will be discussed in the next chapter. The use of a price control as a crowd deterrent is interesting, since pricing is such an emotive issue on sacred sites. Many visitors feel that to charge for access to the presence of God is outrageous. Others are happy to pay to access sites of other religious traditions, but not if the site belongs to their own. Few quarrel with the basic concept of discouraging the uninterested who are just using the site as a convenience, but such pricing structures have to have flexibility for those who are local people, worshippers or those who do not wish to take a tour. The Westminster case is also interesting because once again a member of staff (in this case the priest or nun on duty) is not only an intrinsic component of the product being offered but also a visitor attraction in his or her own right. The Chapter House at Westminster Abbey appeared in the Heritage Monitor 2000 list of historic properties which had increased their visitation by more than 20 per cent (from 95,546 in 1998 to 115,233 in 1999). The Abbey itself attracted 1,268,215 visitors during 1999, placing it fourth in the league table of visits to English cathedrals after Canterbury, St Paul's Cathedral and York Minster.

Westminster Abbey was driven to adopt desperate crowd-control methods since it is one of a series of must-see visitor attractions in London. Many cities in England also have cathedrals which function as the crucial focus of their tourism industry (as at Durham or Lincoln); in other locations, such as York, the existence of a cathedral and associated historic sites has acted as catalyst for newer visitor attractions; and there are a few urban centres where the cathedral is the only thing to see in the town. At Chartres in France the cathedral dominates tourism to the small town of around 40,000 people, with town and cathedral inextricably linked in most people's minds. Chartre's Cathedral receives one million visitors each year, more than twenty times the town's population, and provides classic visitor-management problems. Cathedral visitors are often just making a brief stop-off in a chain of attractions which might include Paris, Versailles and the Loire Valley. Stays are short and rapid visitor-turnaround gives problems with parking. The process of gathering a group together creates noise and crowding, putting pressure on adjacent facilities and eroding historic structures. Like most cathedrals the site is welcoming increasing numbers of day visitors who are relatively uninformed about its historical and architectural qualities which they are being invited to observe. A visitor survey in 1991 (Glasson *et al.*, 1995) led to proposals for maintaining economic benefits, conserving the historic context and adding value to the visitor experience by the construction of a substantial 'gateway' visitor centre adjacent to the cathedral. This will supplement the visitor experience by providing essential information, as well as extending visitor dwelltime and spending levels through the offering of attractions and events. However, the scheme requires a combination of both local and national finance. Unlike Westminster Abbey, Chartres Cathedral is a state-owned monument marketed internationally as a jewel of French culture, with the mismatch between international image and local resourcing which is very common with major cultural tourism attractions.

VISITOR IMPACT ON CULTURAL INTANGIBLES

It is relatively easy to assess the impact of visitors on the physical fabric of a sacred site, and to devise ways of controlling it. However, the presence of visitors may also have an impact on intangible factors, not only on the nature of the visitor experience but also on the very nature of the attraction itself. One excellent example of this comes from anthropological studies of visitors and sacred dance, performances of which are popular tourist attractions in many Developing World countries. Such events are often colourful and seen as exotic or mysterious by the visitor, able to transport him or her temporarily into a wilder and more primitive world. Almost anyone can respond at some level to dance, but dance presented to tourists runs the danger of losing much of its original meaning (Shackley, 1997, 1996b). Sometimes, the performance is altered to take into account the expectations and wishes of the audience. The result is often 'ethnic' or 'tribal' dances which are staged for visitors in a form that is simpler and shorter than the original. Visitors are denied information about symbolic meaning, and asked to appreciate the performance at a purely visual level. They may be unwilling to sit through repetitious and complex dances, and tourist performances typically condense or amplify parts of the ritual at the expense of others. The majority of ritual dances were previously performed as part of festivals attracting local people, but many have now been transformed into commodities appropriate for consumption by tourists (Shackley, 1996c). The presence of visitors at sacred rituals affects performance, outcome and audience. Any alteration of ritual in order to please guests alters the cultural legacy of the hosts by modifying the transmission of a shared aesthetic and collective identity. Some interesting developments have been reported. Sweet (1989) reports on a Zuni Pueblo dance in south-western USA which has now been modified to include dancers burlesquing tourists. The Zuni, whose pueblos are a famous cultural tourism attraction, apparently distinguish four principle categories of tourists which they satirize in the dance: a 'New York' type, a 'Texan' type, a 'Save-the-Whale' type, and a 'Hippy'. Hippies, for example, appear as comic figures who attempt to join dances uninvited and ask endless questions about drug availability.

Masked dances and festivals occur throughout the world and are especially an element of cultural tourism. The use of masks in dance performances forms part of an archetypal continuum of dance, costume and magic which usually expresses beliefs and ideas about deities and demons. The material used for mask-making varies: in African dance, for example, most masks are of wood whereas in the Himalayas masks are typically constructed of plaster (Shackley, 1996b). The writer studied the masked dances of the Himalayas as tourist performances (Shackley, 1996c), noting that some of the masks are between 300 and 500 years old. If destroyed or damaged (by fire, theft or simple attrition) identical replacements are made, a process now facilitated by revenue from visitors who come to watch the dances. Charging visitors for admission to masked dances is therefore sometimes seen as a way of paying for essential replacement and repairs to costumes and masks, and thus of ensuring cultural continuity as well as a high standard of performance. Further cash can sometimes be earned by creating replicas of masks for sale to visitors, a practice that occurs wherever masked dances are held. However, not all masks are considered suitable for reproduction as some have religious significance which preclude their being made generally available.

Many writers have stressed the significance of cultural tourism in strengthening performing arts. McKean and Noronha (1992), for example, argue that tourism has led to the strengthening of the Balinese arts and crafts tradition. Balinese dances

Figure 3.4 Tourists watching specially-staged masked dances in the *Pays Dogon*, Mali

performed traditionally in temples may become forms of entertainment for visitors, but the opposite process also occurs. This blurs the distinction between the sacred and profane, a distinction which becomes increasingly difficult to make in scenarios where dancers continue to wear consecrated masks and obtain religious benefits although they are dancing specially for tourist audiences. Nor is the popularity of masked dances as tourist attractions confined to Asia. The chance of seeing masked dances has been mainly responsible for the growth of tourism to the Dogon people of Mali whose enormous repertoire of masks are classified according to the roles played in sacred performances. The Dogon are also well known for their masked sacred dance rituals which are held at various traditional intervals to accompany festivals such as the Sigui (every 60 years), the Dama (every few years) and annual harvest festivals (Fig. 3.4). New abbreviated versions of these festivals have been developed for tourism, for which the visitor pays both in cash and in kind, by providing beer for the troupe. Tourist dances are only loosely based on the originals with greater floor time given to the more elaborate masks and dramatic choreography with the true meaning of the dance often blurred, especially for the younger dancers. Today only a small number of Dogon, usually *hogons* (medicine men) have accurate and deep knowledge of the meaning of their art and rituals. Such dance performances have begun to act as major motivators for tourism with some travel companies timing visits to the *Pays Dogon* to coincide with the early June dance festivals held before the planting season. Dogon masks and costumes are thought to possess intrinsic energy, a concept tied up with ritual possession. This also occurs in the Himalayas where masked monks take on many of the attributes of the deities or demons that they are portraying, creating genuine fear among audience and performer alike.

Every sacred site consists of a physical (tangible) element and an intangible element. The physical element may simply be an item of landscape, a spring, sacred grove or sacred mountain, but – however simple – it will be of some spiritual or religious meaning to its visitors. Visitors come to encounter the spirit of the site and to understand its meaning, to be in some way changed by it. This is what has been termed as 'visitor experience'. But visitors also consume the site, psychologically for its spiritual benefit and physically by the impact of their presence. Although it is undeniable that the more concentrated the visitors (and the larger their numbers) the greater the physical impact of their presence will be, all visitors, even in small numbers, have some impact. Very few sacred sites were constructed to cope with the visitor numbers that they may now experience. In some cases (such as Egyptian tombs) they were not designed for visitors at all. In other cases, such as a major cathedral, they were designed to cope with large numbers of visitors over relatively short periods, not tens of thousands of visitors passing through the building each day, and every day. The physical impact produced by such high visitation levels is significant. All visitors to a sacred site will have some impact, whether they wish to or not. Some visitor impacts are deliberate (theft and vandalism), others are thoughtless (litter, pollution, noise), still others are accidental (abrasion of artwork or fabric in passing). In the past, most sacred sites have not applied visitor-management strategies but simply tried to let their visitors wander freely throughout existing structures. Restriction of access, by whatever means this is accomplished, always runs up against the universal feeling that equality of access to sacred sites ought to be a cultural norm. Only recently has it been realized that if visitors are not controlled the site cannot be managed and the resource, certainly in the long term, will become unsustainable. Already many Egyptian archaeologists are quoting a period of less than 100 years ahead by which time they think all tombs in the Theban necropoli will have to close because of a combination of natural and visitor pressure. It seems inevitable that visitors have to be managed for the benefit of sacred sites, as well as the other way around, and one set of techniques to do this (the management of visitor flows) is discussed in the next chapter.

CHAPTER 4

Controlling
Visitor Flows

As has already been discussed in the previous chapter, very few sacred sites take active steps to restrict overall visitor numbers, usually for religious reasons. However, even when not limiting numbers many sites actively manage their visitors by controlling visitor movements in some way, an exercise that is referred to as the management of visitor flow. At some sites with very small visitor numbers this is purely notional, and may take the form of simply directing visitors to areas of particular interest via signboards or stewards. But for sacred sites with very high levels of visitation, managing visitor flows can be a necessity to optimize multiple use of the site – well illustrated by the example of Westminster Abbey. Visitor flows can be managed in various ways. Sometimes, visitor access to a site is controlled by the type of transport required to reach it. The easiest access systems to control are, inevitably, to islands and the most difficult are at complex urban sites. At Ninstints, an island off the remote coastline of British Columbia, visitor flows are easily managed since all must arrive by sea in parties of no more than twenty visitors at a time. At Robben Island access is only available via scheduled ferry departures, so the most basic method of controlling visitor numbers is to limit the capacity of the individual boats, and the number of sailings. Exactly the same is true of ferry sailings to the pilgrimage island of Iona. Visitor access to Rapa Nui (Easter Island), a remote destination in the middle of the South Pacific, is subject to the airline monopoly of Lan Chile (Shackley, 1998e) and the number and distribution of visitors to the *moai* is intrinsically linked to airline operating schedules. However, this pattern is now being disrupted several times a year by cruise ships that disgorge several hundred visitors at a time during a very short period, creating great pressure on visitor facilities. Visitor access to the Celtic sites on Lindisfarne island in the UK is controlled by the tide, which permits access only at low tide (Fig. 4.1) when the

Figure 4.1 Causeway to Lindisfarne Island flooded at high tide – with a motorist who had ignored the warning notices

causeway road is exposed and the footway linking the island to the Northumbrian coast can be crossed.

Such methods limit physical access to a sacred site, but it is also possible to control social access by policies that include the implementation of booking and queuing systems, which may or may not be associated with various types of charges. Charging for access to sacred sites is a highly emotive issue and one that frequently causes disagreement on the grounds that access should be universal, a human right. It is argued on moral, religious or ethical grounds that sacred sites should not exhibit socially divisive means of limiting their visitors. However, in reality access to sacred sites is never equal. Any site is accessed selectively, either by self-selection on the grounds of consumer choice or by the employment of some other criterion. This might be the physical fitness of the visitor (if the site or pilgrimage destination is difficult to reach), his or her financial fitness (if a charging system is utilized), or even social or religious fitness (manifested as membership of the appropriate group). Visitor access to sacred sites is also related to motivation and, inevitably, to site management and site interpretation.

Access can be limited by poor or non-existent road transport, or even lack of suitable parking. Some sacred sites are accessed by exotic means. Since 1999, visitors to the ancient site of Jericho in the Jordan Valley of Israel can now reach the neighbouring Monastery of the Temptation, high on a mountainside above the village, by a new cable railway. The paired red and black cable cars take visitors up to the monastery and are a private-sector Palestinian investment project, accompanied by a plush new shopping mall at the Jericho terminus. The cable-cars stop for undeniably panoramic views of Jericho and the northern end of the Dead Sea, but the development is controversial. Many claim that the railway is a visual pollutant and destroys the 'spirit of place' of the area, although it undoubtedly maximizes visitor access to the Monastery (previously limited to those capable of making the hard climb). However, the reason for its construction was not to assist with visitor flow but to generate revenue in a West Bank area with little access to tourism development funding. There are precedents – down the valley visitors to Masada (a site of great significance to Jews) have the option of taking a cable railway if they are unwilling to risk the steep path, but on this Israeli territory aesthetic arguments seem to have been overlooked.

CASE STUDY: SEASONALITY AND VISITOR ACCESS TO IONA

The islands of Iona, off the west coast of Scotland, and Lindisfarne, off the Northumbrian coast, are the main centres associated with a revival of interest in Celtic Christianity in the British Isles. Iona is famous for its associations with St Columba, who used the island as a base for missionary and teaching work in the sixth century AD. Even before then Druids had recognized Iona as a place of special spiritual quality, and there are 35 megalithic standing stones on the island testifying to even earlier belief systems. Celtic Christianity blended with, and enhanced, Druidism in the shared belief that the divine is inherent in all things – the Druid symbol of a circle became incorporated into the Christian cross resulting in the 'Celtic Cross' which is a popular motif today. St Columba's monastery was subject to regular Viking raids including a famous massacre of its 68 monks in AD 806. Iona now houses an ecumenical semi-monastic community of men and women 'seeking new ways of living the Gospel in today's world' who maintain three religious centres on Iona and the nearby island of Mull. Their principal focus is Iona Abbey, which takes up to 50 residential guests a week during the summer season, as well as welcoming thousands of day-visit pilgrims every day. The Iona Community was founded in 1938 by the late George Macleod who started the rebuilding of the thirteenth-century Benedictine abbey. The Iona Community has become a renewal movement with 200 full members and 15,000 associates spread throughout the world, sharing a common morality and principles for daily living.

Iona is now a major pilgrimage centre. It is a small island and most of the religious sites, including the Abbey, are within walking distance of the jetty. Part of the spirit of place so obvious on the island results from the fact that it is car-free. Day visitors stay, on average, around two hours, depending on the weather and whether they plan to walk round the island or have just come to see the Abbey. Relatively few stay overnight (but all available on-island accommodation is fully booked in summer). Some are members of coach parties, some are travelling alone or in small family groups (often as an excursion from the nearby island of Mull), and others are making a visit because of some association with the Iona Community. There is a high percentage of repeat visitors and many from overseas, especially the USA and Germany. Table 4.1 illustrates the seasonality of visitation to Iona. The island can only be reached by a short ferry crossing from the neighbouring island of Mull, operated by Caledonian-MacBrayne Ltd. The ferry carries only a handful of local people in the winter months but during the summer its business needs to cope with nearly half a million tourist visits, mainly day-trippers. Fifty times more visitors use the ferry in August than in January, yet the ferry size and operating costs remain roughly the same (although slightly fewer crossings are carried out in winter). No shelter or other facilities are available on the island for passengers waiting for the ferry (Fig. 4.2). The ferry company has recently introduced a larger ferry which carries 250 people on each crossing.

Table 4.1 Visitors to Iona in 1997 (source: Caledonian-MacBrayne Ltd, 1999)

Month	Passenger Numbers
January	591
February	865
March	3,860
April	9,019
May	20,435
June	24,426
July	26,139
August	32,187
September	17,812
October	9,687
November	2,986
December	842
Total	148,849

Figure 4.2 Visitors disembarking from the short ferry crossing to Iona

The island is an example of an extremely seasonal tourism resource. Although the Abbey Church is open throughout the year no residential facilities are offered out of season, although visitors can walk around the island. However, north-west Scotland is cold and wet during the winter and visitor numbers are low. The small size of the island (only three miles long and 1.5 miles wide) means that visitors are concentrated in very large numbers within a small space. The Abbey and its monuments are the focus of most visits and many tourists do not walk more than 500m from the ferry. During July and August most visitors come in coach parties whose presence creates heavy pressure on the only village, Baile More, with the rest of the island largely deserted. Visitors walking round the island are thought by farmers to disturb lambing, and also have an impact on island footpaths. However, they also underpin the entire economy of the island.

The lack of shelter or any clear orientation point on Iona could be remedied, but there are no plans for a visitor centre on the island. Facilities at the ferry embarkation point at Fionnphort on Mull are being improved and a new visitor attraction focused on St Columba has opened nearby. Uncontrolled camping on the island has become a problem since its ancient monuments provide attractive shelter from the wind, and it is difficult to see how better facilities can be integrated into such a small and sensitive landscape. Service provision on the island is unfocused, with its beauty marred by a plethora of signs in many different styles, confusing and not aesthetically pleasing. This is a result of uncoordinated private enterprise which could be improved by all relevant groups coming together to enhance the quality of the visitor experience. Problems also include difficulties with access for the disabled, and a desire to extend the season (smoothing out the visitor flow) without seriously increasing the overall number of visitors. Even within the seasonal patterns other concentrations can be observed – notably during the weekly pilgrimage walk that the Iona Community makes around the island between May and October, which can involve up to 80 people. All follow the same walking route crossing fragile areas of wet peaty ground, and unfortunately causing serious erosion currently being fixed by conservation volunteers. No formal footpaths exist within the Iona landscape which up to now has needed none, but in the future one solution seems to be for the National Trust and Iona Community to work together to formalize a footpath network.

An equally serious issue is how the spirit of place of Iona can be maintained in the face of this seasonal pressure. The founder of the Community, George Macleod, once described it as a 'thin place' where the presence of God could be clearly felt. Although it is impossible to be very specific, there do seem to be some attributes which islands such as Iona share with other similar sites and which contribute to their atmosphere, including:

- Relatively low visitor densities (compared with those for a built attraction)
- Panoramic views – visitors can see for miles
- Difficulty in reaching the island (necessitating a small element of hardship)
- A lot of unpredictable weather (the feeling of the presence of God)
- Wind, lack of pollution, cleanliness
- Evidence of cultural continuity (timelines)
- Spectacular natural environment which places people in their natural context.

In order to maintain this 'spirit of place' visitor flows need to be controlled, but this is far from straightforward. Visitor numbers cannot be reduced by de-marketing or reducing publicity budgets, since Iona as a destination is not commercially promoted although its accommodation providers may advertise. The majority of visitors to the island are either members of church-related organizations or visitors taking holidays in nearby areas of Scotland. It is not possible to develop counter-attractions on the island, since the site is unique. Some success has been achieved in reducing visitor pressure (and generating income) by starting a new museum/visitor centre at Fionnphort on Mull near the embarkation point for the ferry. It is difficult to see how an absolute limit could be imposed on the number of people present on the island at any one time. Local people, including accommodation owners and the ferry company, are clearly interested in maximizing revenue during the short season, since they need to subsidize the ferry service during the winter. One possibility is to actually *increase* the number of ferry sailings during high season (thus reducing crowding), although visitors will still cluster round the abbey and village. A combination of better signage and better information might disseminate visitors more widely throughout the island, if the footpath network could be rationalized and stabilized.

ENTRANCE FEES AND PAY PERIMETERS

Visitor flows can be controlled in various ways. In the case of sacred sites where an entrance fee is charged, access to the entire site may be restricted by the utilization of some kind of 'pay perimeter'. This refers to that portion of the site that can only be accessed after payment of a fee. In the case of a secular heritage visitor attraction, the pay perimeter is normally encountered after the visitor passes through some kind of visitor reception or information centre. Some sites locate their catering and merchandising exclusively within the pay perimeter to cater only for customers to that attraction; others locate them outside the pay perimeter for exactly the opposite reason – to broaden the customer base to include passers-by or those who do not wish to visit the attraction. Sometimes an attraction can have a nested series of pay perimeters. There may be an initial charge for access to the site and further charges for access to specific facilities or events within that site, such as a special exhibition or particular attraction such as a crypt, chapel or tower that can easily be divided off from the main facility. This also serves to control visitor flows as the numbers of visitors entering the secondary attraction will be much lower than those accessing the main attraction. Various commercial attractions, particularly theme parks, have now adopted the Disney model whereby the customer pays a single price for admission to all facilities within the designated pay perimeter (exclusive of catering and merchandising).

Some sacred sites designate a pay perimeter spatially located beyond an area where normal worship or prayer takes place – allowing both paying tourists and non-paying visitors access to the facility. But such arrangements are frequently resented. Some sacred sites make the payment voluntary. Lincoln Cathedral has recently adjusted its pay perimeter so that visitors entering the building are able to get an excellent overview and panorama of the nave for free. They are also able to enter a small chapel reserved for prayer, where the Blessed Sacrament is reserved, and gain access to the cathedral bookshop without charge, but cathedral catering is within the charging zone. Like all sacred sites, some areas are no-go areas reserved either for staff, administrative or storage use or for sacramental purposes where unlimited visitation is not encouraged. In order to implement a central charge Lincoln has removed the previous system of charging for admission to ancillary attractions such as Treasury or Library. However, if by chance these areas are closed to visitors yet admission to them is technically included in the entry fee, a cause for resentment is created. Moreover, instituting a charging system in a cathedral also means calculating what discounts or free access must be given to local people, how access for worshippers is maintained and how to provide visitors, who have now become customers, with value for money. At York Minster access to the main Minster building is free, but visitors are charged for access to fragile parts of the sites such as the crypt, foundations and central tower. The Minster attracts 3 million visitors per year but by this policy of selective charging the number visiting the more sensitive locations has been reduced to 170,000 – significant in reducing the levels of wear and tear in the stone staircases linking the Minster with its crypt tower and foundations. Exactly the same calculation was employed in pricing access to Tutankamun's tomb.

QUEUE CONTROL

Access to sacred sites seldom involves queuing but there are some notable exceptions – parts of Jerusalem, for example, or exhibitions held within sacred precincts. The principles of queue control were formulated for other aspects of the service industry, but are now well-established for cultural heritage sites (Shackley, 1998b). They include techniques such as 'snaking' the queue to apparently minimize its length, or posting information boards with projected queuing times along its route which are actually longer than the real anticipated wait. The visitor therefore reaches the end of the queue earlier than anticipated, and is less inclined to grumble. Other techniques for reducing the boredom of queuing and encouraging the visitor to remain in the queue, include diverting queuing people with entertainment (often music which may be either live or recorded), performance art or the provision of information. A common device is the introduction of sequential information panels along the route of the queue, which provide linked pieces of information and sometimes pose a question to which the answer is found on the next panel. An excellent example of queue management of a sacred site can be found in the 1998 exhibition of the Turin Shroud.

CASE STUDY: THE TURIN SHROUD

The Turin Shroud is a 14.5-foot linen cloth bearing the image of a crucified man; many believe that it was the burial cloth which wrapped the body of the crucified Christ. The Catholic Church never claimed the Shroud as a holy relic but treats it with reverence, careful to instruct the faithful that the Shroud must not be worshipped and that it possesses no special significance other than to reinforce the faith of individual believers. Radiocarbon tests done in 1998 indicated that the cloth was no more than 750 years old (probably made between AD1260 – 1390), but the results are not universally accepted by the scientific community. Despite doubts over its authenticity, the Shroud excites very high levels of interest and visitor levels to the 2000 exhibition were even higher than those of previous years.

The Shroud is undoubtedly one of the most familiar religious objects in the Christian world yet its status is somewhat ambivalent. Should it be considered a relic? Technically not, as it does not contain part of a saint. It is often referred to as an icon, with the term used here in the sense of a holy image, rather than a painting. It was publicly displayed again in Turin Cathedral (Italy) for eight weeks beginning at the end of August 2000. This is most unusual, since the cloth has rarely been displayed publicly more than once or twice a century and the 2000 exhibition, timed to coincide with the millennium and with a designated Holy Year, was the fifth since 1898. In September 1978 a major exhibition was held and the Shroud was displayed for five weeks, removed from its specially designed reliquary in the cathedral of St John the Baptist, placed behind bullet-proof glass and sealed in a nitrogen-filled case. Up to 100,000 visitors a day (3.5 million in five weeks) waited up to eight hours in line before getting near enough to view the Shroud from a distance of 20m. The streets of Turin became one big party, flooded with people and vendors selling food, drinks and souvenirs under colourful umbrellas. Every storefront in the city displayed the image of the Shroud, and many related books were produced. However, there were complaints of congestion, that the wait was too long and that the huge crowds destroyed the atmosphere of reverence.

Major improvements in managing the visitor flow were implemented before the next exhibition in 1998, which marked the 500th anniversary of the consecration of Turin cathedral and the 100th anniversary of the first photograph of the Shroud which paved the way for modern scientific research on the cloth. A visitor to the 1998 exhibition would have had no difficulty finding directions both to free parking and to purpose-built booths issuing tickets with reserved dates/times. A whole visitor experience had been devised, including the easy availability of tickets for Turin buses and cable car, and a lengthy trail laid out linking interesting features of the city, complete with guides, publications and adequate information. After obtaining his or her ticket the visitor entered a temporary theatre behind the cathedral to see a presentation about the Shroud, then joined the queue which was divided into groups of 75-100 people. Each group was moved along on a predetermined route. However, those without reservations could, if they were in the know, get almost as good a view by the simple expedient of entering the front of the cathedral. This did not permit getting quite as close, but did mean that the visitor was not time-constrained, nor part of a crowd. An atmosphere of reverence and contemplation was fostered in the cathedral by the use of the appropriate background music, and those in viewing parties close to the Shroud could hear the recording of a soft-voiced Italian nun describing the Shroud. For the 1998 exhibition the Shroud had a new 3-tonne bullet-proof case containing a temperature-controlled mixture of inert gas (argon) and steam, with oxygen volumes kept low at $0.01\pm0.1\%$. Visitors could choose platforms at three different levels, to view the Shroud from different heights between three and five meters. No flash photography was allowed, but the lighting used was of such high quality that good photographs were possible. A visitor limit of 4000 persons per day was implemented, with visit duration of just 2–3 minutes. Visitor comments included approval of the startling, eye-catching way the exhibit was presented, combined with applause for the sensitive way the cathedral had been restored after a major fire. New technology was utilized including live internet feed (although with a commentary only in Italian) so that the image was available to the entire world, on the web. And admission was always free, both to the actual viewing (in Turin) and the virtual viewing (over the web).

It is interesting to see how the management of visitors to an exhibition of the Shroud has evolved over the last twenty years. Any such exhibition is going to attract high levels of interest, with steady growth to be expected as a result of better publicity and greater mobility. Today, for example, Turin can be reached even from the UK by low-cost flights from several regional airports, whereas twenty years ago access for those coming from outside Italy would have been much more difficult. Despite the ambivalent status of the Shroud, visiting it inculcates a sense of reverence in the watcher, irrespective of whether it is authentic. To foster such an atmosphere without destroying the feeling by overcrowding in the relatively confined spaces of a cathedral is extremely difficult.

Additional complications are presented by the need to manage long queues of people and also, since their time in the exhibit is measured in minutes, to provide adequate information, distraction and supplementary attractions. The 1998 exhibition of the Shroud was a model of good visitor-management practice which avoided the complaints of crowding by visitors to the 1978 exhibition, employing a sensible mix of management strategies informed by contemporary advances in information technology and exhibition design. Visitor anticipation was built up by advance publicity, not only for the actual exhibition itself but for the new security casing for the Shroud, and for the striking way it was to be exhibited. The exhibit and cathedral were linked into a portfolio of activities within the surrounding area and excellent briefing information was obtainable in advance. Despite the large visitor numbers, good queue management techniques avoided a feeling of crowding and kept the queue moving forwards and properly informed. The pre-booking arrangement had the effect of reassuring the visitor that he would definitely get a good view of his objective, with the supplementary possibility of spending longer with the Shroud (albeit at a greater distance) by visiting a second time and sitting in the main body of the cathedral. Adequate preliminary information was available and good lighting and presentation maximized the impact and enjoyment of the experience for visitors, despite its brevity. Exactly the same approach had been taken some years earlier in London with the redesign of the Jewel House in the Tower of London, where the opportunity to see the Crown Jewels is one of the most popular tourist attractions in London. This also had previously had problems with overcrowding and the redesigned exhibition needed to cater for a consistently high level of visitor flow. Previous design flaws had meant that visitors who merely wished to pass through the exhibit for an overview of its major pieces were sometimes prevented from doing so by crowds clustering around the cases, obscuring their view. The new exhibit utilized information boards before the visitor arrived in the Jewel House, and a moving walkway to take visitors past the exhibition, together with standing places at some distance away for those who wished to remain longer. The Turin Shroud exhibit utilized many of the same principles. However, by not charging admission it avoided accusations that profit was being made from a holy relic, and (theoretically) permitted universal access at least to those pilgrims able to make the journey to Turin. Even those unable to do so are catered for by the website, although whether or not a virtual visit ensures the same degree of sanctity is an interesting area of controversy. This is a topic much on the minds of many church people with the increasing popularity of 'virtual churches' (Zaleski, 1977).

VISITOR CAPACITY

The concept of managing visitor flows is inextricably related to the idea that sacred sites and buildings have a certain optimum visitation level. Once that level is exceeded, the quality of the visitor experience is diminished and the physical fabric of the site may be adversely affected. This is usually referred to as the 'carrying capacity' of the site and can be measured in various ways. The idea of carrying capacity recurs in tourism literature (Wall, 1983: Graefe *et al.*, 1984; Westover and Collins, 1987), and is attractive to the managers of cultural heritage sites and major buildings. The underlying theory states that if it is possible to calculate the optimum number of users for a resource, then it should also be possible to devise a management strategy which restricts visitor access to that level, no more and no less. Utilizing carrying capacity as a site management tool involves one of three basic ideas: controlling visitor numbers, expanding resource capacity, or some combination of the two. But applying this idea to sacred sites runs into problems as the capacity of the site may not be directly connected to its size, but limited by its function in the eyes of the worshipper or visitor. To take an open-air example, it is a relatively easy matter to calculate the optimum number of walkers along a footpath before it begins to erode (its physical carrying capacity), but far more difficult to calculate the utilization level at which visitors will perceive the footpath as crowded (its psychological carrying capacity). However, there are certainly situations at sacred sites where a fixed-volume visitor capacity can be useful, usually calculated as the maximum number of visitors which the site can cope with before serious conservation problems develop. The pyramid of Chephren at Giza, for example, recently opened after a year's closure for conservation, has limited visitor numbers to 300/day for this reason. Within the Church of the Holy Sepulchre in Jerusalem the tiny Chapel of the Angel, which contains the stone on which the angel sat to tell of Christ's resurrection (Matthew 28:1) is so small that only four visitors can enter at any one time. A guardian stands outside to shape the waiting visitors into a line and adjust the flow of visitors into the chapel according to demand, restricting the time each is allowed to spend there in especially busy periods. The whole church is thought to have a theoretical maximum annual capacity of 750,000–1m visitors per year, but 4.5m visitors were expected during the year 2000 with no plans for flow management. A suggestion made by the Director-General of Israel's Ministry of Tourism that the solution to overcrowding was to create a second exit was not well received by church authorities.

Many so-called visitor carrying capacity calculations are merely guesstimates devised by site managers based on an overall impression of the maximum number of visitors that might be welcomed without causing damage. Such calculations also involve an estimation of the potential ways in which visitors could be limited to that level by devices including queue, price and volume control. However, a proper estimate of carrying capacity is based not only on physical factors such as avoiding potential damage, but also on social factors such as perceived crowding and the threshold number of visitors per unit area over which the site is perceived as crowded. Does the crowding of visitors in the Sistine Chapel in the Vatican diminish or enhance the quality of the individual visitor experience? It certainly has an adverse effect on the paintings, and the existence of the crowds means that it is difficult to stand still and get a good view. Moreover, the Chapel is extremely noisy, despite periodic attempts by stewards to limit the sound. On a busy day it is almost impossible to remember that the site is a place of worship, rather than a museum, since it is treated as just another art gallery by most of its visitors. Visitor capacity calculations are difficult as perceptions of crowding vary with the individual. Moreover, a building or site at which a major festival is being staged will have a far greater perceived capacity for absorbing crowds than one which is reserved for the practice of quiet prayer or meditation. Carrying capacity calculations should be just a means to an end. Outside the sacred site their utilization gets much simpler.

It is relatively easy to determine the carrying capacity of visitor facilities such as accommodation, car parks, lavatories, restaurants and shops, all of which have definite fixed capacity constraints. Visitor flows to such facilities can be measured so that adjustments can be made when demand exceeds supply, for example by the opening of an extra car park or provision of supplementary toilet facilities. But the capacity of the sacred site itself is usually fixed, with very limited possibilities for opening supplementary areas to reduce pressure. There are exceptions to this generalization. During the recent refurbishment of the Royal Chapel in Granada, Spain, it was calculated that the Palace was physically unable to accommodate the 500,000 visitors it received each year, and a decision was taken to double the floor space of the associated museum and enforce a daily admissions quota much more rigorously. Attempts have been made in cities with many sacred heritage attractions to establish their physical carrying capacity. Venice is the best known example (Borg, van der *et al.*, 1996) where the causeway which links the city to the mainland enables both measurement of visitor flow and control of visitor access. Similar examples have already been seen on islands where visitor access can be controlled. By contrast, it is very difficult to control access to an individual building with multiple entrances and no pay perimeter, since the public expect free and instant access and the management has no mechanisms such as ticketing or price control to assist in limitation.

Other methods to control visitor flow include temporary site closure. (Some sites are regularly closed one day per week or at certain times of the year, for maintenance.) At Giza one Pyramid is closed annually so that repairs can take place without interruptions from visitors, a procedure facilitated by giving advance warning of the closure to visitors. Not only does this allow conservation work to be carried out but gives the site a short holiday from visitor pressure. Another equally draconian method, the provision of an alternative product, has been tried at some cultural heritage sites. The best example occurs at the cave of Lascaux in south-west France, where the site had to be closed because of the damage being done by visitors to the fragile palaeolithic paintings. A replica was constructed, and has proved very popular with visitors, but this option is not available for sacred sites since the sacredness of the site rests in its authenticity. Diverting visitors to other, equally sacred, sites is a perfectly legitimate means of managing visitor flows. It is the basic principle behind the linking of sacred sites into recommended routes that introduce visitors to sites that they might not have been aware of and reduce pressure on the most frequented sites, both at the same time. Flow within sites can be controlled by ensuring that visitors are all part of a guided tour, the routes of such tours being added, subtracted or otherwise changed at different times to adapt to perceived congestion or visitor pressure. Tour group numbers can be increased or decreased as necessary. The opposite approach is to disperse visitors over a wide area to reduce both access and crowding. Many sacred sites have such low levels of on-site interpretation that the pressure on visitors to take part (and pay for) a guided tour can be intense, if the visitor wishes to maximize his or her experience.

Different groups of visitors move around sites in different ways. Pocock (1996) looked at visitor flows around Durham Cathedral and identified three different patterns. Overseas visitors moved relatively quickly around the building and utilized a guided tour, making short standing stops before places of particular interest. Local groups took a more leisurely approach to their visit and were generally addressed by bedesmen (vergers) rather than professional guides. They often spent time seated in particular areas receiving longer and more anecdotal commentaries. The third category consisted of individuals or couples whose progress round the building conformed to the recommendations of their guidebook which they consulted before each move, the rest of the visit merely confirming the written with the visual. The writer noted (Shackley, 1998c) similar differences between the ways in which visitors to cultural heritage sites in Damascus, Syria, managed their visit. Particular problems in managing visiting flow exist where the site has a fixed capacity but there are strong religious reasons for not limiting visitors, as the following example will demonstrate.

CASE STUDY: ST KATHERINE'S MONASTERY, MT SINAI

Figure 4.3 St Katherine's Monastery, showing the fortified walls

St Katherine's Monastery is an impressively fortified site dating from the fourth century and located at the foot of Mt Sinai in Egypt (Fig. 4.3). It covers the site of the Burning Bush, where God spoke to Moses, and has religious significance for Jews, Christians and Muslims but forms a small Christian oasis in a country with an increasingly significant fundamental Islamic element. Today, only 25 Greek Orthodox monks remain, follow a life of prayer which starts at 4 a.m. with matins. The dressed granite walls of the monastery are 3m thick in places and rise to a height of 20m, enclosing a multi-level labyrinth of living quarters, 12 chapels, an icon gallery, a refectory, a hospice and a major church. The monastery is especially famous for its library, considered second only to that of the Vatican in Rome in historical significance, and also noted for its collection of 2000 icons, constantly in demand for exhibitions.

Until relatively recently the monastery's few visitors were admitted via a wind-up basket chair cranked up over the walls, but by 1997 the site was attracting over 100,000 tourists each year (Grainger, pers. comm.). In theory the monastery is open 9–12 a.m. five days a week, though always closed on

Fridays and Sundays as well as major feast days (sixteen days during 1997). Tour operators are notified of feast day closures in an annual list circulated by the monastery office. In practice 'closed' is a misnomer. Even after official closing time visitors are still admitted via the side gate and visitors staying in the monastery hostel have unlimited access except between 9 p.m. and 4 a.m. Visitors enter through a small door in the north wall and can only walk in a small area around the main St Katherine's Church, built AD 542–551 in memory of Emperor Justinian's wife, and with twelve enormous pillars covered in icons (Baddeley and Brunner, 1996). Its magnificently carved doors, dating from the sixth century, are now being abraded by careless visitors ignoring 'do not touch' notices. A silver plate in the chapel shows where the original Burning Bush was supposedly located but its descendant can be seen outside, although extensively vandalized for cuttings.

The monastery now expects around 1000 visitors per day on a regular basis, but this number can be doubled on a very heavy day. Because of these large numbers and relatively short opening hours the monastery becomes extremely congested and visitors often leave after less than 20 minutes (Shackley, 1998d). Many complain that the crowding makes it impossible to

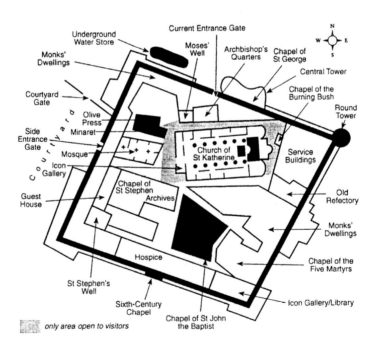

Figure 4.4 Areas open to visitors at St Katherine's Monastery

see the icons and detracts from what should be a spiritual experience. No entrance fee is charged. The church becomes rapidly congested – there are frequently in excess of 100 visitors inside. The busiest time is mid-morning, when tour buses bringing day-trip visitors from the coast tend to arrive. Large groups of visitors (up to 80 at a time) still continue to enter the monastery by the side gate after the closing bell has rung. The majority of visitors arrive in tour parties of 20–80 individuals, accompanied by their own guides. Relatively small numbers arrive individually, or in small groups. This contributes to congestion in the parking area below the monastery, which seldom contains fewer than 5 coaches, 10 cars and assorted minibuses. Some wealthy or VIP tourists bribe coach and taxi drivers to drive them right up to the monastery walls, rather than stopping at the car park and police checkpoint 300m away, polluting the ancient walls with diesel fumes and engine vibrations.

Although the actual time spent inside the monastery is short, visitors usually sit outside or climb on the rocks and take photographs for an average of 30–40 minutes, and this is allowed for by tour companies who usually schedule a visit for a 2-hour slot. Other options, such as the purchase of a camel ride from local Bedouin in the 'camel park' outside the walls are less popular – during the period of observation (Shackley, 1998d) only 0.5 per cent of visitors opted for a camel ride, although many went for a walk along the start of the trail leading up Mount Sinai. Relatively few visitors arrived with a guidebook or seemed to have much previous knowledge – most just relied on their guide. Those not arriving on guided tours frequently came after official closing hours or inappropriately dressed. Apart from the dress code the most frequent complaints were about congestion, poor lighting and inadequate lavatory facilities. Dissatisfaction with over-crowding is also becoming apparent at travellers' websites.

The coast of the Sinai peninsula is Egypt's premier tourist destination outside the Nile Valley, with rapid development of resorts taking advantage of its offshore coral reefs and splendid beaches. The historical sites of southern Sinai make an attractive alternative destination for visitors making a day trip from the coastal resorts, and if the present visitor trends continues more than 3 million annual visitors could be arriving at the southern Sinai coast by the year 2017. This has horrific implications for the demand for visits to St Katherine's. Day-trippers from the coast now constitute the majority of visitors to the monastery, although the site also offers accommodation in its hostel. A substantial number of religiously-motivated pilgrims come on a day trip or short visit. Many visitors apparently have a long-standing ambition to visit the site, yet may stay there for a far shorter period than they anticipate because of the overcrowding. Others take the view that the overcrowding is compensated for by the lack of commercial development, with some purists wishing that all commercial activity, including the bookshop and Bedouin-run refreshment stands, be moved away from the monastery. The latter certainly contribute to general litter levels but most of the garbage is deposited by local visitors, who seem especially careless and ignore litter bins, leaving discarded bottles, bags and plastic containers all over the monastery walls.

St. Katherine's monastery is one of the most important religious sites in the world, a node of spiritual life connecting a complex network of sacred and religious sites. It functions as a centre of scholarship and a destination for pilgrimage. It is a refuge for the spiritually distressed, and a home for an active monastic community who play a vital role in local temporal matters as well as on an international religious scale. Most of the standard solutions to visitor congestion cannot be applied here. For example, opening the site for longer is impossible because of its effect on the monastic life of the community. Nor can it be opened for more days during the year, because of the need to ban day-visitors on church Feast Days. Visitors could be allowed access to a more extensive area of the monastery rather than being confined to such a small space, but this impinges on the life of the community. Nor can the poor quality of the experience be compensated for by encouraging visitors to stay longer, as this just adds to the congestion. And the problem is made worse since visitors do not expect the site to be congested. Most arrive anticipating a quiet, desert location conducive to an atmosphere of great spirituality and are horrified by noisy coach parties. When expectations are not met by reality, a poor quality of experience is the result. Catering for the different motivations is not difficult as visitors staying in the monastery hostel have access to the site at all times, without the crowds, but the same is not true for the religiously-motivated day tripper. The members of the monastic community are not of like mind about their visitors although all view the idea of limiting numbers by instituting charges as incompatible with the aim of the community. All realize that the problem is increasing, but many see that their duty to offer hospitality to guests, whether tourists or pilgrims, may require the sacrifice of quiet. Moreover, the existence of a Christian monastery like St Katherine's in a Muslim country is protected by its position as a major tourist attraction and revenue generator. But none of the revenue accrues to the monastery that needs cash to finance conservation work. Unfortunately, many of the conservation problems such as noise, traffic fumes and vibration are caused by visitors, but these problems have not been helped by several small earthquakes. The most likely solution to these difficulties, currently being explored as part of an EC-funded study, is the construction of a visitor centre at the entrance to the valley with access to the site only by shuttle bus. This has many advantages, notably that local Bedouin people can obtain employment and a market for their crafts, but also that visitors in their pre-visit stage will obtain proper information, enabling them to maximize their time at the site. The use of a shuttle bus could minimize congestion but will not be popular with visitors. It is a notorious fact of visitor management that visitors expect to be transported right to the door of any attraction, even if this is not practical or logical. The plan has many advantages and reduces impact on the cultural landscape outside the monastery as well, but it is difficult to see how the monastery will profit financially unless some partnership is formed with the visitor centre. The current projections for increased visitor numbers suggest that the monastery will very shortly be swamped, with irrevocable damage to fabric and reduction of the quality of visitor experience to an absolute minimum. The impact of this over-visitation on the spiritual life of the community is already devastating, and the monks have become managers of a huge tourist attraction rather than the prayerful guardians of a sacred site.

MANAGING ACCESS AND MULTIPLE USE

Coping with visitors to a nodal site which acts as a focus of a sacred landscape is always difficult. The proposed shuttle bus to St Katherine's will require additional decisions: who is to be exempt, for example – disabled, elderly, VIPs? How can the ride to the monastery be made into an educational experience, with the visitor being made aware of the archaeological and historical features of the sacred landscape? A similar discussion has been carried out at Stonehenge in the UK, which has terrible parking and access problems and offers miserable interpretative facilities. One solution recently proposed is the construction of a visitor centre and shuttle bus for exactly the same reasons, with the objective of making the visitor become aware of the significance of the site as a node in a landscape, rather than as an isolated structure. Managing access to sites is, as has already been noted, facilitated if the site is very remote, but even at some remote sacred sites visitor pressure has necessitated special flow-control measures. A good example comes from the 43 km Inca Trail which provides walking access to Machu Picchu in Peru. The great Inca site of Machu Picchu is located at a height of 2430m in a place of extraordinary beauty. The site fell into ruin after the Spanish conquest and was not rediscovered until 1911. Many identify it with the famous 'Lost City' of the Incas, to whom it was probably a major sacred site. It is usually reached by train from Cuzco, with buses meeting the train to take visitors up the steep climb. Plans for a cable car were opposed by UNESCO as inappropriate for a World Heritage site.

The site can also be reached by a walking route, the Inca Trail, whose visitors have now reached 40,000/year, an increase of 800 per cent over the past decade. Despite attempts to control visitor impact both the fabric and atmosphere of the trail are disintegrating under sheer weight of numbers. The trail takes walkers 3–4 days to reach Machu Picchu, passing through a stunning combination of Inca ruins, magnificent views and ecological variety within the 325 sq. km of the Machu Picchu Historical Sanctuary. It can only be walked in one direction with the exception of a short stretch approaching the site itself. The route was originally part of an Inca sacred way and has become something of a contemporary pilgrimage as well. Visitors can walk the trail individually (permit cost US$17) or in organized groups (cost US$70–150) accompanied by guides and porters. To cope with rapidly-increasing numbers a shorter additional trail from Km104 has recently been opened (cost $12), starting at the Inca ruins of Chachabamba and connecting with the main trail at Winay-Wayna. The growth in visitor numbers has destroyed the original 'spirit of place', and the nature of the existing visitor experience is often recorded as unsatisfactory. Pressure to increase visitor numbers still further comes from commercial trekking agencies in Cuzco and local communities employed as porters. Physically, the fabric of the trail is damaged by heavily-laden porters wearing out the steep Inca masonry stairs and pathways, combined with damage to ruins from climbing and lighting fires. Social impacts include theft and mugging. The only solution seems to be restricting visitor numbers by a quota booking system, but this is unlikely to be implemented since hiking the Inca Trail supports a huge range of businesses in Cuzco as well as providing considerable local employment.

In many ways the visitor management issues faced by the Inca Trail and Machu Picchu encapsulate the issues raised earlier in this chapter. As has been discussed, the severity of visitor management problems increases in direct relationship to visitor numbers. Moreover, it is not always possible to utilize the most appropriate method of controlling visitor flows because of some extenuating factor. For example, at St Katherine's Monastery price control combined with some kind of pre-booking and queuing system would clearly be superior to the current ad hoc arrangement which results in severe crowding, yet the policy of the site manage-ment does not permit it. Visitor flows are also easier to control if the site has a firm perimeter (whether or not this functions as a pay barrier). Efficient means of controlling visitor flows require a great deal of careful planning and, more often than not, the development of co-operative partnerships between sacred site managers and those involved with the management of external visitor facilities. The queue management system at Turin would not be so successful if it had not been combined with improvements in local transport and the provision of easy access to a range of other attractions. A smaller but equally good example comes from the Cistercian Monastery of Santes Creus in Catalonia, a masterpiece of Romanesque art, linked by the so-called 'Cistercian Tour' to two similar sites. The site has been recently redeveloped to aid interpretation, and a new visitor flow route calculated. Before the refurbishment in 1995/6 visitors went directly to the Cloister (the highlight of the tour) and were then allowed to wander through the rest of the monastery, of less architectural interest. Today, the visit starts in a newly-created interpretation facility then continues through the rest of the monastery, culminating in the famous fourteenth-century Cloister as the climax of the tour. Visitors are not compelled to follow this route, but if they do not they will lack the key to interpreting the site. Visitor management calculations allow for 4800 visitors per day (600 per hour), divided into groups of pre-determined size (Moldoveanu, 1998). Some rooms are used for an explanatory presentation and a reception courtyard has been partially covered to provide coolness and shade in summer, with new facilities such as toilets being constructed. An enclosed area under glass contains the reception desk, ticket office, shop and a throughway to the exit. Controlling visitor numbers plays a major role in these new arrangements which are designed to encourage visitors to give the site maximum attention – easier if it is not overcrowded. The initial explanation is a multimedia presentation designed for a very diverse audience who may not be familiar with the world of the Cistercians. The room becomes dark after the presentation with a light on the exit door, encouraging the visitor to walk through. A secondary highpoint is the Scriptorium, which is used for the second part of a display of beautiful images focused on manuscripts. The whole experience keeps the visitor moving, and makes sure that he or she has sufficient background information to appreciate the site while minimizing crowding and providing visitor facilities that do not detract from the feeling engendered by the whole experience. The presentation is scholarly yet interesting, and the use of lighting, in particular, creates different moods in different rooms and encourages the visitor to keep exploring. The site manages the flow of its visitors without the experience becoming overly theatrical, and still manages to convey a special flavour of Cistercian monastic life. But in order to achieve such a result considerable investment was needed and a radical vision, not features that all sacred sites can emulate. Indeed, the raising of capital, strategic planning and product marketing are major weaknesses at sacred sites which are not commercial visitor attractions, issues discussed in the next chapter.

CHAPTER 5

Managing, Marketing and Planning

As has already been discussed, the nature of the visitor experience at a sacred site can be divided into stages of anticipation: the journey to the site, the visit itself and the return home. This, in many ways, reflects the standard way in which any service 'product' is consumed by its 'customers' (although these are not terms often used in association with sacred sites). The consumption process is also divided into three stages: pre-purchase, purchase and post-purchase, with each stage being characterized by product attitude formation, the effects of situational factors, and consumer satisfaction or dissatisfaction (Solomon, 1996). Although such terminology has a very commercial feel, it is still relevant to sacred sites. This is true even when the 'product' is a visitor experience rather than an item of fast-food, and when the consumption process is spiritual rather than physical, often without any money changing hands.

The visit to a sacred site begins with a potential consumer being stimulated to want, or need, a particular experience (which could be a tour, pilgrimage or attendance at a festival). The initial stimulus can be generated from many sources, only one of which is access to specific information about a particular site. Other potential stimuli might include the unexpected availability of disposable income, changes in social or religious beliefs, peer pressure or a perceived need for healing. The consumer then searches for information and processes it, considering the benefits, costs and risks associated with the potential 'purchase' in the light of his or her personality and expectations. The influence of friends, family and others within a shared worship, social or belief system may be very significant here. This culminates in the actual 'purchase', which may be the commercial purchase of a particular tourism product or just acting on a decision to visit a particular site. One interesting characteristic of tourism as a service industry, including religious tourism, is that its products are intangible. The pilgrim who has bought a visit to Compostela or a trip to Lourdes may have nothing to show for his or her expenditure before the visit, except a ticket. Even after the visit the only tangible residues of the purchase may be a guidebook and some photographs. However, the intangible memories may be very significant and include perceived spiritual benefit, actual healing or other aspects of personal development. This may seem a poor return for very considerable expenditure, perhaps a substantial slice of annual disposable income. This contrasts with expenditure on consumer durables such as a house, car or washing machine whose products can be seen and touched immediately after their purchase. Moreover, in religious tourism the length of time between the date of purchase and actually consuming the product (by taking the trip) can be months or even years, unlike other service industries such as fast-food operations whose products are consumed within minutes. During the time between purchase and consumption the purchaser reflects on his or her decision, acquires more information, and generally forms a very precise set of expectations and views about the quality of experience which he or she is anticipating. If these expectations are not met, or the experience is below the quality anticipated, the visit is seldom repeated, the trip will not be recommended to others and the purchaser is an unsatisfied customer. The decision to purchase a tourism product is taken on the basis of expectation, with a high uncertainty factor. To my knowledge, no specific studies have been undertaken on the purchasing behaviour of visitors to sacred sites. However, the major influences on purchasing behaviour are likely to be relatives and friends who have made a similar visit, as well as the perceived spiritual needs of the individual and practicalities such as cost.

What is the core product of a sacred site? The main benefit to the consumer/ visitor is intangible and subjective, including atmosphere and spiritual experience. Surrounding this is a tangible product bought to satisfy needs (provided by visitor services such as catering or accommodation). Additionally, there is an augmented product including all additional benefits. Within the world of secular visitor attractions the greatest challenge to site managers is usually trying to optimize visitor numbers in order to minimize adverse impact, and maximize the possibility of generating income. Since they usually wish to recover a substantial percentage of operating costs from visitor–related revenue, there is usually a direct correlation between visitor numbers and visitor revenue – at least in the private sector. In public-sector attractions, which may be non-profit-making, the greatest management challenge is often to create profitable public and private sector partnerships, as well as to develop an efficient network from the different administrative organizations relevant to the attraction. A World Heritage Site, for example, may not charge for access and therefore require subsidy from the relevant government department or Ministry charged with conservation and heritage management. On the other hand its visitors and tour operations may come under the control of another Ministry, perhaps of tourism. Theoretically, on a national level, revenue received from the tourism industry will be recycled through government accounting processes with part of it ring-fenced as funding for heritage management. In practice there are constant complaints from heritage managers that they are starved of the resources required for site conservation, presentation and management while simultaneously being pressured by tourism organizations (in both the public and private sectors) to allow more and more visitors. Moreover, in such situations the greater part of the revenue received by a site may go to the private sector. The situation with sacred sites is very similar, although their management is complicated by the need to cater for diverse customer bases including tourists and worshippers whose requirements may be very different. Life is usually made additionally difficult by not-for-profit motivations that compete with the need to generate revenue for the management and conservation of expensive historic buildings. Additional complications are provided by the fact that many religious sites and buildings (at least in the UK) do not fall within the public sector and may thus have very little access to government funding.

ECONOMICS OF SACRED SITES

Maintaining heritage costs money, and managing sacred sites is usually a steadily growing open-ended financial commitment of which only a minor part is borne by the users ('customers'). Continuous maintenance is expensive, as many sites are less than optimally organized and resourced for the functions they are expected to perform in the modern world. This is not universally true – in the face of financial pressures some sacred sites have discovered hitherto unprecedented uses for their buildings. Gloucester Cathedral, for example, is being used as a location for a film version of the popular children's book *Harry Potter and the Philosopher's Stone*. Gloucester apparently won the contract with Warner Brothers after beating off stiff competition from Canterbury and Salisbury, and it is likely that the fee will be substantial. A certain level of moral flexibility will be required from the Dean and Chapter since the Harry Potter books have been criticized for stirring up an unhealthy interest in witchcraft. Gloucester was also the location for the BBC's adaptation of Joanna Trollope's novel *The Choir* in 1995, which used congregation members as extras, and cathedrals are regularly used for concerts, plays, flower festivals and many other events. Utilizing sacred sites as a backdrop can have unfortunate consequences. In September 2000 the five hundred-year-old Intihuatena stone at Machu Picchu was severely damaged by its temporary conversion into a beer bar by a New York advertising company (McGirk, 2000). The contoured granite block is known as the 'Hitching Post for the Sun' and was used by Inca astronomers to predict solstices. It formed an essential element of Inca mythology and is the centrepiece of the Machu Picchu site. During a film shoot by the J. Walter Thompson group a 1000lb crane crashed down on the stone and chipped a fragment off the edge, to the fury of Peruvian archaeologists. The film crew apparently sneaked their heavy equipment into the Sanctuary at dawn, in violation of their permit. Staff at the production company now face criminal charges and up to four years in prison.

In a sacred building such as a cathedral, as with any other heritage site, large sums of capital are tied up as an investment in a product of the past. It is difficult to put a monetary value on such heritage, although it does earn money directly and indirectly, and sacred sites were not created for economic reasons, nor is the generation of income the major reason for their existence. Weiler (1998) quotes a Canadian study which estimated that a building restoration at a heritage site delivered 27.8 jobs for each million dollars invested, compared with 12.8 jobs for the less labour-intensive work on new buildings. Part of the reason that historic buildings are so expensive to maintain (and this includes many sacred sites) is precisely that any conservation and repairs are such a specialized business, usually requiring specific materials only available at additional cost. In secular heritage attractions such as museums, castles or stately homes which act as foci for a local tourism industry, their capacity to generate revenue compensates, at least partly, for high maintenance costs. This is not true for sacred sites whose capacity to earn money for themselves is limited, although their existence generates a lot of money for associated private-sector operators.

Sacred sites are operated by institutions or organizations which differ in type, ethos and working practices from the commercial firms who may control their marketing and product development. The management of sacred sites becomes more complicated if different sets of interest are involved. All such sites throughout the world are the foci of tiers of public- and private-sector interest, which can vary from the volunteers directly involved in their day-to-day management, through to UNESCO's World Heritage Committee if the site has been placed on the World Heritage list. There will be national, regional and local governmental organizations, NGOs, charities, pressure groups and other organizations concerned with the site. These represent the interests of local people, the religious establishment, planners at regional and national levels, tourism, resource management and a host of others. A sacred site which sees its primary function as providing space for worship may find itself being promoted for quite different reasons – the excellence of its catering facilities, for example. Considering sacred heritage as a product encounters problems, since by comparison with other elements of the service sector it lacks integration. There is seldom any linear agreement between resource-use through production to 'sale' and subsequent 'consumption' by visitors or worshippers.

It is almost impossible to derive econometric equations that have a sensible measure of the economic value of a sacred site, even though direct values can sometimes be arrived at (via entrance fees), but these are a fraction of the indirect value of the site. Sacred sites are literally priceless and function as a public good. Moreover, consumption of sacred sites is not restricted to those who pay for them, and much consumption is compulsory in the sense that the site is a definitive use of space. Anyone living near a major temple, shrine or church consumes it visually whether they wish to or not. The benefits of the presence of such sites are in many ways collective, but accrue to a mélange of public- and private-sector interests outside the boundaries of the site, which provide visitor services or benefit directly or indirectly from visitors. And it is often extremely difficult to define the product. Visitors to a sacred site may marvel at its architecture, its aesthetics or its craftsmanship. They may have a sense of identification with its function or the people or tradition who made it. They may receive a spiritually or educationally enriching experience but which of these is the product? The product of a sacred site is an experience, and the nature of that experience is influenced by the cultural tradition of the visitor and by the way the site is presented to the consumer. Thus, the nature of the product depends on the nature of the consumer, meaning that traditional language about production management becomes meaningless. The place itself, and the experience it produces for the visitor, is the product.

Everywhere in the world, the cost of maintaining sacred sites is ruinous. Such sites are literally priceless and impossible to value using conventional economic methods (Bizzaro and Nijkamp, 1996; Stabler, 1996). Usually, it is only possible to gain a simple overview of the differential between the cost of maintaining the resource and the income which it generates. Table 5.1 illustrates this for the English Cathedral of Southwell Minster.

The cathedral costs nearly half a million pounds a year to run, with a shortfall of £120,000 each year. In order to avoid cuts in the services that the cathedral provides (in both senses) this money has to be generated by raising funding from regular worshippers, and from local people within the small market town where it is located. One current funding appeal is trying to find more than 150 people prepared to donate £50 each month by covenant which, after tax refunds at 22 per cent, would bridge the funding gap. This is not impossible since Southwell is a

Table 5.1 Income and expenditure at Southwell Minster, Nottinghamshire (source: Southwell Minster published fundraising data, 2000)

Expenditure		Income	
Item	Value (£)	Item	Value (£)
Clergy Costs/stipends	116,000	Church Commissioners	133,000
Ministry Support	55,000	Investments	73,000
Music Foundation	76,000	Property	34,000
Church Services	7,000	Shop	47,000
Administration	39,000	Fees and Concerts	15,000
Education/Library	17,000	Irregular giving	26,000
Gifts to charity	14,000	Visitors	47,000
Vergers and upkeep	75,000		
Heat and light	8,000		
Upkeep of fabric	17,000		
Churchyard/exterior	8,000		
Insurance	11,000		
Funding campaign	6,000		
TOTAL OUTGOINGS	449,000	TOTAL INCOME	375,000

relatively affluent area. Alternative methods to generate revenue include starting to charge admission to the building (but this is opposed by the Dean and Chapter), increasing the revenue from the Minster Shop or encouraging more concerts and festivals. A less attractive option is to reduce expenditure by eliminating some expensive item such as the music budget. However, most cathedral worshippers and visitors regard the organ and choir as an integral part of their experience. Removing it would inevitably have a negative effect on their experience, reduce congregations, make the cathedral less attractive to visitors and generally remove a vital element which contributes to the 'spirit of place'. Although the Minster makes regular funding appeals these are almost exclusively for fabric, and usually for specific projects. People will give money towards a stained-glass window (especially when their names are recorded in some splendid donation Roll of Honour) but not for the wages of the window cleaners to maintain it. Anyone who has ever managed a science laboratory or scientific research project knows that the likelihood of getting funding for new equipment is far greater than the chance of getting funding for the people to work it. On a sacred site there is little option but to look to visitors as a source of revenue generation, but in order to do so the site has to be maintained and presented to the highest possible standard in order to maximize the experience quality for worshipper and visitor alike. Only then will visitors part with cash that can be diverted into management funds. The principle of Catch 22 applies here, since visitors do not readily part with cash if the site is poorly maintained, and without good maintenance the site cannot attract visitors. Nor are visitors generous with donations. York Minster attracted 2.5 million visitors in 1986, raising £359,000 (an average of 14p/visitor) to help offset annual maintenance charges of £600,000 (Ryan, 1991). A generally accepted figure for visitor revenue in English cathedrals today is around 25–30p per visitor. It is scarcely surprising that many have resorted to compulsory admissions fees, although these are almost universally resented, with their imposition deterring substantial numbers of visitors.

MARKETING SACRED SITES

It is just as difficult to define the market for the product of a sacred site as it is to define the nature and components of the product itself. Markets will always consist of different, and sometimes conflicting, segments. For some sites overseas visitors will constitute the major visitor segment, whereas others have a primarily local appeal. Most sites, however, can distinguish two major categories of visitor: (a) those who are there to worship, pray, meditate or otherwise reflect on the sacredness of the site, and (b) those who are visiting primarily as tourists. However, these categories overlap and the nature of the experience of category (b) visitors may fall into the category of worship if they are affected by the nature of the site. There are also intermediate categories that one might almost describe as business tourists, those concerned in some way with the management or marketing of that or similar sites, or those attending to perform some service function. Category (a) visitors are very likely to pay multiple visits to the site and to be part, in some way, of an organization connected with it, which can vary from a major religious tradition (e.g. Islam) to a small sub-group ('The Friends of ......'). The category (b) market for sacred sites in the Developed World, where cultural tourism may be a more significant motivator than pilgrimage, is difficult to distinguish from the market for other cultural attractions such as museums, theatres or historic buildings. Numerically, of course, it is salutary to remember that in terms of visitor numbers the well-managed Christian sacred sites of the Developed World only attract a fraction of visitors of the more informally-run Hindu/Buddhist/Islamic sites of the Developing World. Market research in the area of sacred sites is almost non-existent, largely because most sites are keen to build up category (a) visitor numbers and manage the development of category (b) visitors to balance conservation, worship, and revenue-generating functions. Not all sacred sites keep records of their visitors, and even when these are kept they may be unreliable. Only recently a major monastic site in England found that it had been over-estimating its visitor numbers by 30 per cent for many years. The previous estimates had been based round a 'census' taken by an elderly monk who walked round the site once a day counting visitors. He then multiplied the result by 6 (the number of hours that the site was opened) and returned that as the annual visitation. Only when a firm perimeter was established for the site, combined with accurate recording of visitor numbers, origins and arrival times, could an adequate database be obtained. It was found that the previous method of counting had overestimated visitors by 75 per cent.

Managers of sacred sites always wish to attract more 'worshippers' (category (a)) visitors, since that represents the traditional 'market' for the site, and the religious tradition which it represents. Most sites allocate funding for such missionary activities and develop a programme of activities to stimulate such demand, although they would seldom see this as a marketing exercise. Some sites are even beginning to cater for what is known in the trade as suppressed demand, namely people who would like to visit the site but are unable to do so for reasons of time, money or access. A classic contemporary way of marketing a site to such visitors is by the establishment of a website presence which can on occasion be interactive, and sometimes linked to other visitor facilities such as email shopping for souvenirs, or to a list of service times and driving directions to facilitate a future visit. There is also a huge area of potential demand which might include, for example, people attracted to a particular religious tradition but unwilling or unable to take the crucial step towards membership. However, attracting such individuals to a site is not strictly the business of site managers, but rather of the religious leaders of the sect or tradition that the site represents.

Conventional marketing of sacred sites is generally focused on category (b) visitors, the cultural tourists, who are not only a major potential source of revenue but also represent possible converts to category (a) worshippers if their visit is especially satisfactory. Both types of visitor may arrive in groups of different composition. In some cases the category (a) worshipping-customer base may be highly gendered. In the Christian tradition it is predominantly female, but in Islam it is predominantly male. Groups of worshippers seldom include a high percentage of young people or families with young children, but groups of tourists may be composed quite differently. This may not be the case for special events at a sacred site and it is difficult to generalize as each site holds a special appeal for a particular category of worshippers. A Shinto shrine in Japan or China with a reputation for helping fertility or assisting childbirth, for example, may attract disproportionate numbers of young women or couples. By contrast a staid Catholic pilgrimage centre such as Walsingham in England attracts mostly middle-aged or elderly people of relatively high educational levels and with adequate disposable incomes. 'New Age' sites can have a most diverse customer base, as we have already seen at Machu Picchu. Stonehenge at midsummer eve attracts a motley crowd including Druids, hippies, police, photographers and archaeologists. Most sacred sites are keen to attract as wide a range of tourists as possible (within the resource limitations of the site), particularly if they are concerned that a visit to the site may positively affect the likelihood that the visitor may eventually become an active participant in the tradition which it represents.

Marketing of a sacred site is almost always product-led rather than customer-led. It has a particular product (or series of products) which are offered to customers, rather than asking the customers what they want and devising a product that may be attractive. This is obviously because the site represents a particular religious tradition with relatively fixed ways of worship or prayer. However, most sites do offer a range of products to suit different segments of the market. Buildings may incorporate areas for quiet prayer as well as areas for active worship, cater for different religious traditions or try to develop a programme of services held at different times to accommodate customers from different backgrounds. The building may also serve merely as a shell for worship by a number of different religious traditions. This is frequently true at open-air sites but also true at many sacred sites shared between different religious traditions, such as sites within Jerusalem. However, most sites have regular programmes of events, festivals and services that are staged regardless of the wishes of the audience. A classic example might be the English parish church faced with a drop in the size of its regular worshipping congregation. The usual way of dealing with such an issue is to try some form of direct marketing (perhaps a mailshot to houses in the parish advertising Christmas services) but radical alteration of the product (the type of service on offer) is considered only as a last resort. In England at present it is calculated that more than 50 million tourists visit parish churches each year, compared with congregations of worshippers which total around 5 per cent of that number. Sacred sites in the western world are certainly becoming more receptive to the needs of their particular markets, but this can sometimes be more in response to legislative change than a desire to facilitate access. Provision for the disabled and socially disadvantaged is improving, as are levels of safety and child-friendliness.

The issue of 'brand loyalty' at sacred sites is an interesting one since, if the management is driven by religious priorities, it should be encouraging visitors to sign up to a belief tradition rather than to affiliate themselves to a particular site. Strong brand loyalties do develop – people attend the same church, mosque or synagogue all their lives for reasons of custom and tradition, proximity to home or family, or special affiliation with the site or its leaders. They may constitute a powerful pressure group opposing change. Any vicar who has attempted even a modest rearrangement of pews in an English church knows that this can arouse strong passions including threats of non-attendance and loud, angry scenes. Category (b) visitors, (tourists) are largely unaware of the in-fighting that takes place within sacred site management since they see only the results, not the process. They may complain about the absence of certain facilities whose presence would seem logical to them (such as a toilet in a much-visited church) without realizing the complex logistical and historical reasons that may make it difficult to provide one. In practice so little is known about the way in which believers are recruited to many religious traditions (apart from obvious studies of conversion or inheritance through family), and few or no sites make systematic attempts to contact regular but lapsed worshippers to find out why they no longer attend. Exceptions here occur in the Christian tradition where electoral rolls in English parishes, for example, provide a means of tracking those who no longer attend and encouraging them to start coming again. But this may never be done since it is so costly in terms of time and human resources.

Sacred sites do have competitors, and here again the idea is encountered that the site management is duty-bound to encourage adherence to the tradition, rather than their particular site. Competitors may be sites of the same religious tradition or other tradition, but this is an issue that will usually affect category (b) visitors and not category (a). Nor are the competitors for sacred sites always other sacred sites: a tourist visitor to a particular tomb or temple is unlikely to be motivated exclusively by a desire to visit only a site of the particular religious tradition that it represents, and can be easily deflected to other cultural or historical sites. In terms of marketing, sacred sites are unique in that they do less advertising than almost any other visitor attraction, partly because of lack of money and partly because large numbers of visitors may not be desirable. But the principal reason is usually that advertising is unnecessary since marketing is done by word of mouth or through non-commercial sources. Competition from other attractions is unlikely to be significant in pricing strategies (as it would be in the commercial world) since many sacred sites are free or just encourage donations.

COMMODIFICATION

The sacred inspires reverence, awe and commitment that may be enhanced by a process of journey to a sacred place. By contrast the profane is ordinary, mundane, lacking religious significance. However, secular things can become sacred through a process of transformation. There is a grey area here about how secular commodities acquire sacred status. The purchase of a book in the bookshop attached to some major sacred site seems somehow to invest the book with part of the sacredness of the site, as though this is infectious. Souvenirs bought at a sacred site acquire the same property even when the site has become commodified. The process of commodification creates tradeable commodities from resources, in this case sacred sites. This often happens with questionable taste, as in the development of items of religious *kitsch* which dominate the retail environment among most Christian sites. However, one man's *kitsch* is another man's piece of sacred property. The resources of a site (its appearance, legend, particular features) can be commoditized by interpretation and packaging onto everything from mugs to tea towels. There seems to be no limit to what can be commodified, including water from the River Jordan, sand from the desert of Judea, even cans of air from the Holy Land. Commoditization can also be very profitable. The Vatican sells special Papal blessings under licence to pilgrims in authorized shops around St Peter's Square. These, described as 'spiritual souvenirs', retail for around 18,000L upwards and are sold in the form of certificates bearing a picture of the Pope. In January 1999 the Vatican increased their cost by 25 per cent. Pilgrims complained, but the Vatican replied that by increasing profits it hoped to devote more funds to the poor, adding that it hoped that the price rise would be paid by retailers rather than pilgrims.

Religion establishes, shapes and codifies cultures with the result that cultural values can be abstracted from religious practices, documents and artefacts (Kluckhohn, 1949). This works in two ways, more and more elements of sacred culture are being commercialized, or commoditized, and more and more of what would have been regarded as profane commercial commodities are being 'sacralized'. This is particularly true in American culture and not unconnected to the popularity of televangelism and the dominance of right-wing Christian religious organizations where money and consumption are revered as key symbols in an increasingly secular set of beliefs. It is interesting to speculate where the sacred resides in such communities (O'Guinn and Belk, 1989). There are immense areas of overlap. To some extent contemporary consumers sacralize consumption (Belk *et al.*, 1989), and many consumers approach shopping malls and religious theme parks in the spirit of pilgrimage (Turner and Turner, 1978). This raises the issue of how sacredness is related to retailing, an issue discussed in the following case.

CASE STUDY: RELIGIOUS MARKETING AT HERITAGE VILLAGE, USA

In the 1980s Heritage Village, located near Fort Mill, South Carolina, was one of the most popular visitor attractions in the USA. It consisted of a 2300-acre, $200m complex attracting 6 million visitors per year, which around 1987 was the third most popular themed attraction in the USA, after Disney World and Disneyland (McNichol, 1987). It was the headquarters of the PTL televangelism organization (PTL stands for 'Praise the Lord' or 'People that Love') which subsequently fell into disrepute after its leader Jim Bakker was jailed for sexual transgressions and embezzlement. Management of the site then passed to another televangelist, Jerry Falwell. The site was the subject of a detailed case written by O'Guinn and Belk (1989). In the late 1980s Heritage Village was easily the largest religious theme park in the USA, its product a unique blend of religion, broadcasting, shopping, recreation and entertainment. The Theme Park included a church, hotels, campgrounds, auctions, a Passion Play, dinner theatre, television studios, water park and a replica of the Old City of Jerusalem. It was designed as a contemporary version of heaven with heavy product emphasis on beauty, luxury and shopping in an environment where the customers could openly confess their particular brand of the Christian faith. It was an intersection between traditionally sacred religious activities and the traditionally profane activity of shopping. In the 1980s the increased popularity of televangelism in the US was related to a religious polarization within American society between a humanistic 'new age' movement on the left and neo-fundamentalist Christianity on the right (Roof, 1983). The latter proved particularly attractive to lower- and middle-class families opposed to what they saw as the increased liberalization of American society, and attracted by nostalgia for a 'purer' past. The rousing sermons delivered by televangelists often claimed that America had become less prosperous as a result of secular humanism, with a return to godliness resulting in the ability to consume more. Many members of this new Christian right wing consider wealth and conspicuous consumption desirable as evidence of God's favour. Indeed, the evangelist Falwell declared (1980: 11–12) 'ownership of property is biblical. Competition in business is biblical. Ambitious and successful business management is clearly outlined as part of God's plan for his people'. This attitude partly accounts for the success of Heritage Village as a religious theme park, and for its emphasis on consumption as a spiritual activity. The visitor was welcomed with copies of the Village newsletter 'Heritage USA Herald' as he or she went through the gates of the Park into an environment deliberately landscaped to be different from the world outside. A landscape without billboards, with a mixture of forest and parkland with old-style split-rail fences and a reconstruction of the childhood home of Billy Graham. The centre of the Village is a complex including the 504-room 4-storey Heritage Grand Hotel, Main Street Heritage USA (a Victorian-themed shopping mall) and the entrance to Heritage Island water amusement park.

The shopping mall had been designed to create an other-worldly atmosphere with no natural light, and artificial carbon dioxide clouds at the top of its blue-lit cathedral ceiling. The perpetual twilight aims to detach the visitor from reality, conveying a heaven or dream state (Pilbrow, 1979) enhanced by the fact that the artificial trees are covered in miniature lights, rather than leaves. Visitors were dominantly charismatic Pentecostals whose position outside (and to the right) of mainstream American Christianity served to bind them together. Visitors interviewed by O'Guinn and Belk (1989) commented that the atmosphere helped them to feel the presence of God and that they were unafraid to pray, be overtly Christian, buy Christian books or records or lay hands on friends without being stared at or laughed at. Visitors saw Heritage Village as the real world, an oasis or island in a world increasingly hostile to their beliefs. It allowed them freedom for the open expression of their religious beliefs and its extreme cleanliness added to the idyllic image by promoting a sense of order in contrast with the chaos of the world outside.

Although the shopping mall was central to Heritage Village, all its surroundings were designed to reinforce this feeling of nostalgia, isolation and group solidarity. Needless to say the site hosted great gatherings on the fourth of July. Its lake, water slides, pools and artificial streams were also intended as reminders of Christian purification and healing rituals associated with water (including baptism). Indeed, the hotel swimming pool and hot tubs were used for total immersion baptisms. Souvenirs on sale in the mall included a plastic Crown of Thorns complete with red blood, a crib with a praying Santa and other Christian *kitsch* (Dorfles, 1969; Pawek, 1969). Partners (members) of the PTL movement who payed a subscription of $1000 each got three free nights in the hotel and a 10 per cent discount in the shops. Merchandise also featured books and records about Jim and Tammy Faye Bakker, together with a range of Tammy Faye cosmetics. In addition to spending lavishly on souvenirs and food, visitors to the site were also encouraged to donate money 'as evidence of faith and obedience to God's law' with the reasoning that such evidence of faith would yield material dividends in terms of increased prosperity. The overall message of the facility concentrated on reinforcing group identity and values and encouraging commercial activity, both as an act of worship and to demonstrate faith. The Village was centred around a personality cult of the PTL televangelist movement.

The Village is an excellent example of a blend of commercialism justified by religious activity, in a manner repugnant to many who do not happen to believe in the values being promoted. A deliberate attempt had been made to artificially create a sacred environment, by combining perceived freedom of religious action with the encouragement of consumption as a religious activity. Here, shopping had been sacralized. The appeal to nostalgia and the attempt to create a world where the consumer could feel physically and psychologically safe was, of course, deliberately manipulative. The artificially-created sacredness was used to add to the perceived value of the consumption experience. It tried to make shopping a mystical activity. Other writers (e.g. Zepp, 1986) have noted similar though less extreme tendencies in shopping malls where community bonding is fostered through a 'democracy of consumption', albeit in a secular context. The focus within Heritage Village was shopping, not religion, with the church taking second place to the mall. It begs the question of where the sacredness resided at the site. In many ways Heritage Village offers the opposite experience to a pilgrimage which traditionally involved dangers and hardships on the way towards a religious goal. Here the goal has been reached by eliminating any problems from the environment, by transformation through retail therapy with 'the ersatz Victorian luxury of the mall and hotel making a contradiction to the humility and asceticism of the traditional pilgrim' (O'Guinn and Belk, 1989: 234). Luxury and self-indulgence are encouraged by the creation of a metaphorical heaven. It is the ultimate commodification of religion, promoting a message that greed is not only good, but that it demonstrates God's favour.

ORGANIZATIONAL ISSUES

The effectiveness of the management and marketing of a sacred site is related to three principal factors:

- the nature of the religious tradition that it represents
- the type of site (its shape, structure and characteristics)
- the political structure of the actual site management.

Many sacred sites, for example, have rigidly hierarchical clerically-dominated management structures which may have functioned in the same way for thousands of years. Such structures are largely unaffected by modern management trends, with the exception of their peripheral activities (often financial). Some sacred sites seem not to be managed at all, and merely exist in a management vacuum where things happen by custom and nobody is too bothered with achieving specific targets. Sacred sites which do not have formal management structures tend to be managed by religious (priests, lamas, mullahs or other clerics), rather than secular administrators. It is thus inevitable that their priorities will lie in the encouragement of worship, rather than in the management of visitors. The managers of small sacred sites within a very large religious tradition (for example someone who is managing a small shrine within the enormous Roman Catholic Church), are nearly at the bottom of a management hierarchy which starts with the Pope and includes hundreds of thousands of sites and millions of worshippers. Management styles in such organizations are often dogmatic and authoritarian, with religious leaders issuing orders and directions that are to be obeyed, rather than debated. The corporate culture of such organizations is unlikely to be entrepreneurial (although there are exceptions), but is very likely to be conservative, bureaucratic, defensive and risk-averse with a strong dislike of change and caution about venturing too far into the commercial world. Of course there are exceptions to this rule, and in some well-run organizations marketing and finance are professionally controlled. Such organizations will typically devolve decision-making functions about facilities management and event timetabling to a series of committees, whose recommendations are then set before the senior manager (usually a cleric) who will be supported by a small but very senior and predominantly clerical management executive.

Senior managers on sacred heritage sites are almost exclusively male, although females are often to be found in charge at departmental level, but usually in service departments such as marketing or visitor management rather than liturgical or sacramental roles. Happily (in the opinion of some), this situation is changing within a number of organizations. In the Church of England, for example, the so called 'stained-glass ceiling' of cathedral management has been penetrated by the appointment of female Deans and many female Canons, although most Chapters are overwhelmingly male. Unlike other visitor attractions the individual responsible for managing the site will usually have no management training whatsoever, and may be deeply opposed to the very idea of management for religious, social or ideological reasons. Financial management is a weakness almost everywhere, and sacred sites are usually, if managed at all, managed as non-profit organizations with charitable status, in areas of the world where this has any meaning. Partly because they are seldom cash-rich and also wish to be inclusive, sacred sites generally place excessive reliance on volunteer staff. Many theocractic organizations leave matters such as the hiring, firing and training of lay staff to lay people in the (usually correct) assumption that they are likely to be more experienced and professional. However, every sacred site is in the business of maximizing the quality of experience that its visitors receive, and can therefore ill afford to neglect the effective utilization of human resources. But in practice, implementation is limited. On the credit side, the people employed at, assigned to, or merely associated with, a sacred site are usually not primarily motivated by financial concerns. The result can often be low levels of staff turnover which may not always be a good thing, as the same ill-assorted and poorly trained team can remain in place for a very long time.

It is possible to illustrate this by reference to Southwell Minster, whose financial plan has already been noted (Table 5.1). Its organizational structure is led, as in all English cathedrals, by a Dean, an experienced priest expected to act both as spiritual leader and facilities manager. He has a salaried staffing base of several dozen people and several hundred unpaid volunteers, involved in everything from visitor services to flower arranging. All Deans have insufficient financial resources to manage their large cathedrals and are required to establish ties with innumerable different organizations and to be ready to pronounce on everything from the flower rota to major fund-raising activities. The Dean of any cathedral functions as chairman of a Board officially known as the Chapter, which consists of his or her permanent salaried staff (called Canons Residentiary), together with a selection of unpaid lay and clerical members. Clerical employment in cathedrals carries high status within the Church, although this is unrecognized outside, but cathedral staff still receive low stipends by comparison with their equivalents in secular employment. However, their stipends are higher than those of their colleagues in parish ministry and they have total job security. Most have degrees in theology and particular professional interests, such as education or music, but few have any formal management training. Nor do they have a clear career structure, and the procedures for appraisal, reward and discipline are very undeveloped compared with those in the secular world. Their jobs are demanding, requiring high levels of communication skills and the ability to be cheerful, manage crises, deal with people in difficulties and handle the numerous, and frequently conflicting, demands of visitors and worshippers. Cathedral lay staff may, with the exception of specialists such as organists, accountants or architects, have few recognizable qualifications and there are few training opportunities. Most, such as vergers, are trained on the job. Recruitment and disciplinary procedures are arcane; many vacancies are not publicly advertised and most managerial decisions are taken in camera with little consultation. The management structure is still dominated by a clerical hierarchy.

It is both highly centralized and informal (often reliant on verbal communications rather than memo, procedure manual or standing orders), as well as risk-averse and change-resistant. However, times are changing. Management issues within the Church are receiving increasing attention as procedures are being upgraded, helped by the formation of organizations such as MODEM (Managerial and Organization Disciplines for the Enhancement of Ministry) and the development of MBA courses in church management. Most cathedrals are becoming increasingly professional in the way that they are run, largely because of the appointment of laypeople with managerial competencies to their Chapters and Councils. Qualified laypeople are also utilized to run visitor services, shops and catering outlets and are frequently involved in departments concerned with education, conferences/events and conservation. However, it is not uncommon to find that each of these functions is line-managed by an untrained cleric. Some cathedrals favour a more market-based approach with subdivisions of their visitor services dealing with coach parties, school parties, individual visitors, etc. but only a few are function-based and divided into traditional business-management lines such as human resources, finance and marketing.

SERVICE DELIVERY SYSTEMS

Even if they may be unaware of the terminology, sacred sites do generally have some form of management system which controls their operations and aims to balance the supply of services with demand from worshippers and visitors. Sites do not exist in a vacuum; they form part of a complex network of organizations which supply them, for example, with human resources, food for catering outlets, souvenirs, goods such as furniture, clothing (uniforms, vestments) and specialist services. The latter can include anything from textile conservation to the restoration of musical instruments and major architectural works of a highly specialized nature. Other suppliers provide education and training services, as well as material for on-site museums or visitor centres. Sacred sites also have intermediaries, people who interface in some way between the site and its visitors/customers (Swarbrooke, 1995). Intermediaries include tour operators, tourist information centres, group visit organizers who have to sell the attraction to group members (such the organizers of a pilgrimage), or travel writers in the media who provide information to the public which may condition whether or not someone chooses to visit. Dissonance may be created when the commercial objectives of an intermediary are not the same as those of the site manager. The role of such intermediaries is to provide correct factual information (opening times, facilities, relevant rules and regulations) but they also exist to convey the message of the site. Today, many sacred sites have a web presence that may be a significant provider of information for Western-world customers (and for some customers may even replace a visit. But a web presence is unlikely to be significant in affecting levels of local demand for a Hindu pilgrimage site in India, for example, although it may contribute to the numbers of international visitors such a site receives as well as to the level of background information available. To a certain extent guidebooks are also intermediaries, since they provide base-level information for visits.

Any sacred site has two types of visitor: first-timers and repeat business. Many worshippers (category (a) above) fall into the latter category and it is the first-time visitors who are more reliant on the information provided by travel intermediaries. Regular visitors have fixed expectations and relatively static levels of satisfaction with their visit, which may be adversely affected if site managers tinker with facilities in order to attract more category (b) or tourist visitors. Standard marketing strategies are unlikely to impact significantly on their levels of visitation, except by attracting them to special festivals and events or encouraging them to increase their participation levels in the worship or maintenance of the site. In practice most sacred sites have a 'hard core' of worshippers who, although theoretically encouraging mission and wider participation levels, in practice constitute a clique that is quite difficult for new members to enter, especially since its conventions are unwritten. However, many such sites operate schemes (formal or informal) where new members of the worshipping congregation are encouraged to attend social functions with the aim of making them into regular attendees, and also getting them to contribute cash and time to the site, often through formal or informal 'Friends' or supporters' schemes.

The real challenge comes with tourist visitors who have never been to the site before, and are not attending as potential worshippers. Can the quality of their visitor experience be so high that they are encouraged to become either regular visitors to this site or else members of the tradition that it represents? This is the aim of most service-delivery systems with sacred-site management, although it is usually articulated in terms of mission rather than management (in the Christian tradition). However, this is not a universal aim. Many religious traditions (Judaism, for example) do not proselytize, so that visitors to a significant Jewish site, such as the Wailing Wall, would not be considered as potential converts. However, it might be hoped that the presence of the devout, and the fact that the tourist is watching overt acts of worship taking place in sacred space, might make the individual more disposed towards thinking about the presence of God. Other sacred sites, such as those originally associated with the classical civilizations of Europe, belong to religious traditions that are no longer practised, removing the motivation of conversion. Still another category of site is highly specific to certain ethnic groups (such as Native American or Aboriginal sites) where conversion is not possible but the nature of the desired experience would certainly include an encounter with the numinous, in a general sense.

Sacred sites can be exceptionally successful at attracting large numbers of visitors even if they have no discernible management to speak of, make use of no modern interpretation techniques, have minimal visitor facilities and are extremely difficult to reach. In management terms they break all the rules for success, because their visitors may be motivated by quite a different set of factors from those of visitors to any other segment of the heritage attraction market. Sacred sites can be managed on a shoestring, sometimes entirely by voluntary donations, employ no permanent staff, submit no accounts, be located hundreds (and sometimes thousands) of miles from their target population and yet still be successful. The secret is the quality of the visitor experience, and that may be unrelated to the quality of the visitor facilities. In a Buddhist pilgrimage round Mt Kailash, for example, there are no facilities at all. The pilgrimage attracts phenomenal quantities of both new and repeat business, is completely unmanaged and yet provides the pilgrim with what will undoubtedly be the most significant level of spiritual experience of his or her life. However, it is also uncommercialized. As soon as visitors start to be asked to pay for the experience they demand better facilities, and expect value for money.

The quality of the visitor experience is obviously affected by the provision (or lack of provision) of various facilities. For example, churches in England come under the Disability Discrimination Act 1995 that makes it an offence to offer to disabled people a worse service than to the able-bodied. Despite the cost, churches now have to take 'reasonable steps' to make provision for the disabled and be fully compliant with the Act by 2004. Provision must be made for everything from hearing impairment to emotional instability, and this may involve far more than just a wheelchair ramp. The quality of interpretation also affects the experience. It may come in the form of storyboards, leaflets, guidebooks or guides, and often needs to be provided in several languages. However, the availability of information does not necessarily mean that visitors will read it, and they may ignore information contained there if they do not like it. This applies particularly to warning signs (e.g. Fig. 4.1). It is not necessarily true that visitors who are on a sacred journey such as a pilgrimage will have read so much as a guide book. Many prefer to leave everything to the guide and some, of course, cannot read. The writer was once asked by a pilgrim standing in a queue to enter the Church of the Holy Sepulchre in Jerusalem what his line of fellow pilgrims was waiting to see, and it was clear that the enquirer had done no preparation whatsoever. Interestingly, the same line contained two deaf pilgrims communicating to each other with sign language and making extensive use of a guidebook as they were unable to hear the guide.

STRATEGIC PLANNING

Various strategies are used in planning at sacred sites. Some are quite simple (like the idea of carrying capacity already referred to). Other methods include tools such as a SWOT (Strengths, Weaknesses, Opportunities and Threats) analysis, and LAC (Limits of Acceptable Change) calculations. In producing an effective management plan for a sacred site two points need to be borne in mind. First, it is necessary to establish a proper framework for management and, secondly, management plans will consist of several interrelated resource project plans. Clearly, creating an integrated framework will ensure consistency of approach between all departments in a complex site and encourage co-operation between stakeholders. It should also make the best use of the resource, may suggest ways to generate additional revenue and provide a firm basis for refusing undesirable projects that do not accord with the management philosophy. However, although this sounds reasonable for, let us say, the expansion of facilities at a major pilgrimage shrine in western Europe where appropriate expertise is available, it will be impossibly idealistic for a domestic pilgrimage destination in the wilds of central Asia.

Only a tiny minority of sacred sites carry out any form of strategic planning, partly because of the nature of their premises and management, partly for religious reasons and partly because of lack of resources (in terms of both finance and experience). Such planning that is done is often crisis-led, often resulting from an imbalance between demand and supply, or from some architectural reason such as the need to close part of a sacred building for conservation. A planning strategy may be forced by the need to plan for some specific event, or to cope with a change in financial resources or management structures. Such planning always includes three elements:

- identifying strengths and weakness in the light of the particular planning need
- identifying threats and opportunities
- allocating resources more effectively.

These may have the result of helping the site management assess their mission and look at likely future utilization trends, and it may guide the day-to-day operational management of the facility. Many simple planning methods based on common sense are used by commercial organizations and are available to provide the basis for a strategic planning exercise, including a SWOT analysis. However, these are seldom adopted without emendation, although the methods utilized may be based on them, consciously or unconsciously. A SWOT analysis is the simplest of tools, listing Strengths, Weaknesses, Opportunities and Threats which face the site, its visitors and its operating environment related to one particular issue. Such projects result in a snapshot in time that will need to be modified as circumstances change. But any strategic planning exercise requires an accurate database, which should include, for example, information about site visitors and their profiles as well as about non-visitors. Up-to-date visitor surveys are also needed, showing their opinion of the site, together with information about the operation and how it works, and an understanding of likely macro-environmental factors which may change. None of these may be available.

CASE STUDY: SWOT ANALYSIS OF A PAPAL AUDIENCE IN ROME

A simple SWOT analysis can be applied to a problem in visitor flow management, in this case the difficulties associated with managing large numbers of pilgrims and tourists to the regular open-air public audiences given by Pope John Paul II in the Piazza San Pietro in front of St Peter's Basilica, each Wednesday morning during the summer. Visitors fall into several categories:

- members of pilgrim groups with pre-booked tickets obtained via their local church or pilgrimage organization and sharing a primarily religious motivation
- members of other groups pre-booked by the same system, whose motivation probably combines religion with an element of cultural sightseeing
- tour parties without audience tickets who have timed their visit to St Peter's to coincide with the weekly audience in the hope of seeing the Pope
- other individual and group tourists.

SWOT analysis – visitor management strategy

Strengths   St Peter's Square is a self-contained space that can be delineated by barriers. Pillars and portico provide viewing spaces. Broad access roads, good viewing potential. Crowds unlikely to be violent. Weather often good; if not can shift audience to interior of basilica or audience hall. Many years of experience in crowd control.

Weaknesses Crowds volatile, sometimes hysterical. May contain elderly or disabled people and numerous internal groupings such as pilgrim parties and wedding groups. Large numbers (50,000–150,000) arriving in very short period. Need security, policing, visitor facilities such as toilets. Three police forces involved. No nearby parking.

Opportunities Highlight of visit to Rome for most people, especially pre-booked pilgrim parties with tickets. Opportunity for mission, enforcing sense of commitment to church and community. Stimulates religious fervour, impress visitors with power and majesty of the church and the vastness of St Peter's.

Threats Security of Pope. Theft and mugging of visitors. Crowd could get out of hand (panic, crushes). Square gets hot producing heatstroke and sunburn. Sometimes people get hysterical. Need for large amount of visitor facilities (such as toilets) in operation for a relatively short time.

In practice the event, as with all Vatican events, usually proceeds smoothly as its choreography has been rehearsed over the centuries and the procedures to control the crowds have been carefully thought out by utilizing the above process,

Figure 5.1 St Peter's Square, Vatican City, at the time of a Papal audience

although by custom and experience rather than the selection of a particular management strategy. Managing such large numbers of visitors is assisted by the fact that the visitors are on the whole highly co-operative, willing to go along with security procedures and highly conscious of the religious significance of the event, which makes rowdy behaviour (as opposed to religious enthusiasm) a rarity. Before the audience commences the square is blocked off with solid (but permeable) internal barriers to prevent crowd crushing. The centre of the square is laid out with thousands of plastic stacking chairs for pre-booked and ticketed individuals, but anyone is welcome to stand outside the central area and observe proceedings from a slightly greater distance. Thus no one is excluded, and the opportunity of giving even a casual visitor a glimpse of the Pope (albeit from a considerable distance) can be taken. Barriers are also erected between the pillars of the portico. Each archway has a pre-installed X-ray scanning system through which all bags must be passed, plus an X-ray system through which the visitor walks, just the same as at an airport. The cost, of course, is very considerable as up to thirty such systems may be in use at any one time, although they are deactivated after the Papal Audience and merely left in place for the next event. Any visitor, booked or not, wishing to go into the square must pass through this security net. Policing such an event actually requires co-operation between the three forces involved, the secular *Carabinieri* Italian Police who control crowds outside the square and on access routes, the Papal Swiss Guards who have both a ceremonial function and act as bodyguards for the Pope, and the Vatican security force. Such a high level of security is essential in view of the fact that the Pope has already been the subject of a public assassination attempt. Additional security is provided by guards on nearby rooftops. The pillars are also utilized to disguise the provision of several dozen portable toilets, quietly installed and tastefully coloured under the shade of the colonnade, together with several clearly signposted first aid posts. After the audience the X-ray barriers are deactivated and the barriers blocking off central road access are quickly removed, enabling the crowd to stream rapidly out of the piazza into the access roads in a remarkably short time. No car or coach parking is permitted near the piazza, nor may coaches drop visitors off, which reduces traffic congestion. However, it also means that coaches must park some distance away (usually in coach parks in the Via delle Fornaci or in the roads to the north-west of the Vatican walls). Wheelchairs are readily available for those with walking difficulties. The huge numbers of pilgrim groups converging on the square can present a problem for guides, often solved by adopting a group identity symbolized by a hat, t-shirt or scarf (usually in bright colours) worn by all members of the party, and a large and obvious umbrella, sign or banner acting as a focus for the group. Organized groups are encouraged to be seated well in advance of the Pope's arrival, although visitors to the standing areas are allowed in during the audience which takes the form of a Papal progress though the crowd with the Pope on his electric car accompanied by clerics and security, followed by an address (in several languages) and a blessing from the throne. The platform and Papal throne are raised on the steps of the basilica providing good sightlines for all, and huge video screens are provided (rather like those at a pop concert) to give people seated too far away a close-up view.

For the visitor the experience is a powerful and moving one. Being in Rome may be the ambition of a lifetime, enhanced by membership of a sea of tens of thousands of people of faith, and the opportunity to receive a blessing from the Pope. It strengthens faith, enforces on believers the power and majesty of the Church, impresses even casual tourists with its splendour and impeccable organization. Group bonds are reinforced and everyone is given the opportunity to be in the presence of one of the world's most recognizable figures.

An alternative to implementing a SWOT analysis is the useful management tool known as LAC (Limits of Acceptable Change), particularly relevant for sacred sites since there is seldom consensus, even among site managers, about what limits there should be. LAC was developed by the US Forest Service in the 1970s and, although primarily used for natural sites such as national parks, is becoming increasingly popular for the management of cultural heritage. It is based on the principle of 'Alternative Dispute Resolution' – getting all stakeholders involved in decision-making on an equal basis, so that site and visitor management decisions taken are acceptable to all. This is not always easy, as the management of sacred sites is, as we have seen, frequently very hierarchical and dominated by clerics (of whatever description) and with low levels of 'lay' involvement. LAC techniques ensure that a rational approach to planning is adopted with all agencies and individuals involved needing to specify their objectives for the site in question. It also promotes management for quality (a foreign concept at sacred sites where management is often highly whimsical, crisis-driven and dominated by the decisions of a small ruling caste). It requires public involvement and a dynamic, rather than a static, base. The process for developing a resource management plan may be summarized as follows:

- select indicators for the management parameters that concern site management at a given time and at a particular location within the site. Such indicators might be, for example, the extent of fabric erosion due to visitor pressure, the need to control graffiti, duration of visitor queues or visitor crowding. Selection of the indicators provides a way to tell the management team how well it is doing with regard to a pre-determined and agreed aspect of the site management – in effect, it is establishing desirable benchmarks.

- establish standards for each indicator that set some limit of acceptable change and agree the response to be set in place once these indicators are reached. Visitor impacts are inevitable. Any site that welcomes visitors will be gradually changed by them (and, in the case of sacred sites, it is implicit that a visit will also change the visitor in some subtle, spiritual way). However, it is necessary to set limits on those changes. If the queuing time to enter a particular exhibition is too long, what can be done to shorten it? Reduce length of guided tour? Add new storyboards to visitor centre? Open new tour routes? Design an alternative exhibition to take the pressure off?

- monitor conditions constantly and, if acceptable limits are exceeded, introduce prearranged management changes that bring the resource back within limits. Managers of sacred sites are often not good at receiving feedback and tend to take action only when a problem has been brought to their attention, either in the form of a complaint or when maintenance personnel have noted some difficulty. Few sacred sites regularly monitor sensitive areas on a regular basis, most relying merely on chance observation to detect a problem. Most would argue that the trained staff and expertise are not available but in the case of large Christian sites in the Western world this is not true. Not all indicators need to be monitored at the same intervals. Wear and tear on a floor could probably cope with a monitoring regime weeks apart whereas queue problems and crowding might need monitoring on a daily basis.

The efficiency of any strategic planning is directly related to the training and expertise of the management team, as well as to the recruitment and training of staff. And, ultimately, everything depends on available cash. It is a great deal easier, as any heritage manager knows, to obtain funding for some solid problem in conservation like repair of a few flying buttresses than to obtain help with running costs. But ultimately, if the site is to be used and developed sustainably, generating maximum quality of experience for visitor and worshipper alike, it is necessary to consider everyone's interests, not to regard the management of visitors as a secondary function interesting only because the visitors potentially contribute revenue or problems. One of the greatest sources of visitor revenue at sacred sites comes from the staging of particular festivals and events, and this is a topic dealt with in the next chapter.

CHAPTER 6

Pilgrimage, Festival and Event

In addition to providing normal day-to-day service for worshippers and visitors many, if not most, sacred sites have to cope with quite different operational logistics at particular times of the year. The disruption to 'normal' routine may be quite minor (as in the provision of extra services in a Christian church at Easter or Christmas). It may also be very significant, as in the staging of events to mark the turn of the millennium throughout the Christian world. Festivals and events may be categorized in several ways. The staging of festivals and events may be a purely local business, principally involving the worshipping community augmented perhaps by a few extra members in productions such as the staging of a flower festival or the celebration of a saint's day at a particular shrine or temple. However, any festival or event is likely to attract extra non-worshipping visitors (category (b) in the previous chapter), and may require the provision of extra visitor services which can be anything from a few extra chairs to accommodation for several thousand people. Festivals and events may last for a single session, perhaps an act of worship, or for days, weeks or months. They may be staged regularly (perhaps on an annual basis), irregularly (to mark a specific anniversary or major time division such as the new millennium) or spasmodically (determined by some religious anniversary or secular pressure). Many are one-off events. The managers of a sacred site could decide, for example, that for one year only they will host a series of religious plays, but may never repeat the experience. Other sites have a well-established seasonal round of festivals and events, and still others host particular special events in response to commercial, as well as religious, pressures. Special events also differ in the amount of travel required from their attendees. Clearly, all events require some travel even if it is only from home to site. The catchment areas of even local festivals can be surprisingly wide. Travel writers are often entranced by the great festivals which take place in Asia, both by their size, the length of time over which the festival has taken place and the enormous lengths to which people will go to reach them. Dalrymple (1998), for example, wrote about the Tamil town of Madurai which houses a great temple to the goddess Meenakshi. He noted that some people had walked for almost two weeks to attend an annual festival at the site which has been held there for 64 generations of priests, whose lineage is recorded. This would make its beginnings contemporary with the ceremonies of ancient Greece. The publicity that such festivals thus receive in the Western press often results in an influx of overseas visitors that, if it gets too great, can alter the entire character of the festival.

For some events the journey forms part of the visitor experience and, although it culminates at a particular site, may take considerably more time than the visitor spends at his or her eventual destination. The journey, effectively, becomes the destination. The most obvious example of this phenomenon is a pilgrimage, where both route and final destination serve as equal motivators for the decision to travel. The pilgrimage becomes a linear event, to be compared with a nodal event (such as a festival staged within a particular building). The destination in a linear event can be a single building or site (such as the Ka'bah shrine at Islam's most sacred site in Mecca). It can also be an entire sacred landscape, such as that surrounding Mt Sinai or the Celtic sites on the island of Lindisfarne, or even an entire urban centre, such as Jerusalem.

FESTIVALS AND EVENTS

Festivals and events can be staged for many different purposes, not all of which are overtly religious. Indeed, some may be blatantly commercial, such as the utilization of a sacred site as a backdrop for filming or for the staging of a concert or play. The secular producers of such an event may be considering the site just as a stage set enhancing their production by its special characteristics. However, the site management may have a hidden agenda including the hope that those who view the finished production may be sufficiently moved by the spirit of the site to attend a regular function, or make a repeat visit. Specific events may be staged to reinforce the solidarity of a particular group, such as an annual pilgrimage to the shrine of a particular patron saint, but they may also be offered to 'show off' the characteristics of a particular site such as its wonderful acoustics, perhaps by utilizing it as the background for a concert. Sites may be used to 'show off' the skills of their worshipping communities, which could be agricultural (as in harvest festivals), or to act as a showcase for local, regional or national skills in embroidery, flower arranging, fine and performing arts. Such events open the site to a wider audience than the normal category (a) worshippers, and may have the additional benefit of increasing social cohesion by the co-operation needed to stage the event. A further motivation is often the generation of revenue, which can be very considerable. One value-added factor for such events is usually the educational opportunities which they offer, and some events are staged specifically for educational purposes, as the following case study demonstrates.

CASE STUDY: 'TIME TRAVELLING' AT SOUTHWELL MINSTER

'Time Travelling!' is a unique programme devised for children, utilizing the cathedral of Southwell Minster. It has now become the largest educational event in any place of worship, school or church in the UK, welcoming over 8000 children from more than 120 Nottinghamshire schools during the course of the year. Schools send a group (or several groups) for a day, with the programme being offered twice yearly for three or four days at a time. It requires a very substantial investment of time and resources, both in preparation and briefings before the event and in the co-ordination of the actual visits. More than 300 volunteers are involved, as well as a programme management team. This includes representatives of the cathedral staff plus teachers, students, an administrator and a project manager who spends much of his time accumulating funding from charities, trusts, sponsors, schools, individual churches and donors. The annual budget for Time Travelling! is around £30,000, increasing as the project develops.

Before the visit, schools receive comprehensive packs including lesson plans and ideas, badges, itineraries and details for the day. Each day is carefully planned, with a small army of up to 500 children arriving at the appointed hour and marching into the Minster via the great West Doors. All are looked after in small groups by a volunteer Pilgrim Guide, dressed in medieval costume, with the staffing base supplemented by 'floaters' who assist wherever required (Fig.6.1). The children's day begins and ends with lively Acts of Worship including prayers, songs and liturgy, followed by a sequence of 20-minute activities located at eight 'Activity Bases' at strategic points throughout the building. Activities may include a look at the organ, participation in a play, lighting candles, exploring the Quire or looking at the Roman mosaics. Children are encouraged to touch and question, on topics ranging from music and architecture to history and religion. The route for each group is carefully planned so that all children can experience a sequence of quiet and noisy events to engage their attention.

Figure 6.1 Schoolchildren at Southwell Minster on a *Time Travelling!* Day

During the closing worship at the end of the day each school is presented with a candle to take back and use in worship. Last year, it was found that 93 per cent of Time Travelling! children had never previously visited a church, with the programme thus offering a wonderful opportunity for mission. Some children have been motivated to join local church choirs after their visit, and many others have brought their families to visit the Minster and other churches, because they enjoyed the Time Travelling! experience. Many schools send several parties of children each year, with more schools signing up as the programme becomes better established. Its success has silenced critics who were concerned that Time Travelling! would present an unacceptable disruption to the life of the cathedral, since it is felt that this is a price worth paying for the educational and spiritual benefits which accrue. The success of the programme has led to steadily growing levels of support, and to new developments including Day Conferences for older children and school leavers.

The Time Travelling! event has a primarily local focus, with its customers being drawn from schools across Nottinghamshire. However, its success has spawned many imitators elsewhere. The sheer size of the project means that the cathedral is effectively closed for normal business during Time Travelling! weeks, but many regular worshippers have come to enjoy the sight of the building being full of interested and noisy children, once they had recovered from their initial shock. The programme is clearly resource-intensive, requiring input not only from the cathedral staff but also from an extensive network of volunteers, many of whom sign up for regular stints as Pilgrim Guides and all of whom receive appropriate training. A day in the Minster as a Time Traveller is only part of the programme, since it takes place after considerable preparation in the classroom and is followed by assessment and assimiliation of all that has been learnt. In addition to the educational benefits, children are clearly being introduced to a new environment and new concepts. For many it will be their first visit to a sacred site, but the fact that so many make repeat visits (often accompanied by parents and friends) indicates that the spirit of the site has made a powerful impression. The substantial investment of time and money would appear to be paying off in a wide range of benefits, not least of which is the extensive publicity that the site has received as a result of the programme.

LINKS BETWEEN TRAILS AND NODES

Time Travelling! is a good example of a specific event repeated at regular intervals, yet entirely contained within a single building. There are few sacred sites which do not offer single events, often on an annual basis, and many which link such events together in the form of some kind of trail, encouraging the worshipper or tourist to visit several sites, rather than concentrating on a single one. Movement towards and between the sites begins to become a significant part of the visitor experience. The desired benefits vary. Sometimes the establishment of linkages between sites is done for educational reasons, so that visitors can see architectural or historical clusters of sites and appreciate their spatial arrangements within a specific landscape. Sometimes linkages are developed for specific events, staged sequentially. Sometimes linkages have been present for a very long period of time, such as sites which form nodes along a pilgrimage route. Sometimes, deliberate attempts have been made to link sites together for commercial reasons or simply to encourage the tourist to visit lesser-known sites which may not be able (or willing) to promote themselves as a stand-alone attraction.

A classic way of doing this is to link sacred sites into routes either thematically (related to the history or significance of the site) or by the means of access such as walking trails, car trails, coach trails or bike trails. Some churches in the Norfolk Broads area of the UK are even linked by a boat and canoe trail. Church Trails are very popular in England, where more than 50 million visits are made annually to parish churches, not all of which are open to visitors on a regular basis. The development of a trail links the church building with local businesses which may provide accommodation or catering for visitors, as well as encouraging communities to find ways to keep their church open. Church tourism also provides opportunities for mission, since far more people will visit a church as a tourist than as a worshipper; and for revenue generation, since such visitors may well give a donation, pay for a guided tour or purchase some souvenir such as a postcard or a guidebook. It is ironic that just as worshipping congregations are declining in number, church visiting is increasing in popularity with new guide books (e.g. Jenkins, 2000) being regularly published. However, not all churches are accessible, many are locked and all are concerned about security, although ironically those churches most free from crime are those that are open during daylight hours and constantly visited. Visitors to churches can be tourists but are often local people, or family historians chasing memorials to relatives buried in the churchyard. People come to visit graves, or stop by for a moment of quiet or prayer.

FESTIVALS

There is a very considerable degree of overlap between what constitutes a festival and what constitutes an event. Even more overlap can exist between the sacred and the secular elements within either festivals or events, and with the different issues surrounding the study of pilgrimage. Moreover, festivals and events are not static but dynamic features of the social and religious life of a community, which evolve and change in response to both secular and religious pressures. Although they may serve as opportunities for mission and social cohesion, exactly the opposite may happen. A good example comes from the Greek island of Skyros which is a famous beach tourism destination, welcoming thousands of summer visitors each year. Skyrians have adapted well to changes, even when these included the toleration of nude bathing beaches and the necessity of locking churches to avoid theft, against local custom. The landscape of Skyros is full of little private chapels, some dating back to the sixteenth and seventeenth centuries, each of which is the focus of an annual feast on its Saint's day. This is the major social and religious event in the village calendar. The festival takes the form of a pilgrimage with liturgy, dinner, singing and conversation. Before the advent of the motorcar pilgrims stayed by the chapel all night at the time of the festival. Since most feasts took place in summer, some visits from tourists were inevitable. Zarkia (1996:169) comments on one feast which was usually attended by 50–60 people, which a local man decided to exploit by hiring buses for tourists, doubling the number of visitors. After the service the yard of the chapel was full of tourists wanting to take photographs, and eat free food and drink. The religious authorities felt obliged to serve their guests first (with

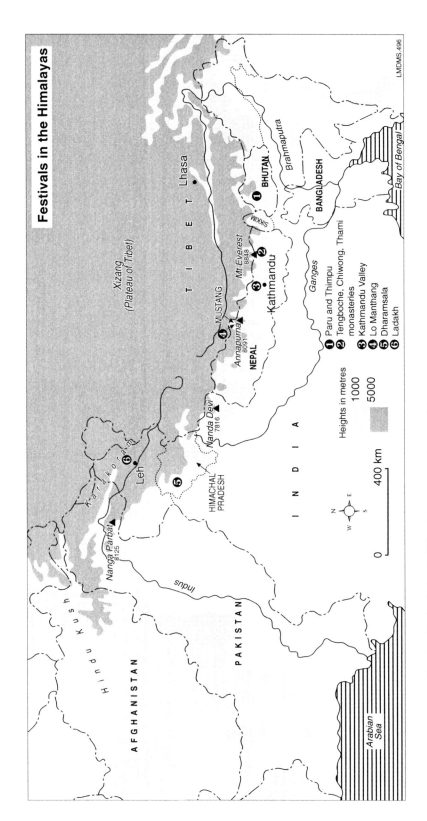

Figure 6.2 Location of major festivals in the Himalayas attractive to visitors

little left for locals) and the intimate atmosphere was spoilt by camera flashes and a tape player with rock music. A brother commented 'They sat there gazing, doing nothing. They did not participate, they did not understand the jokes. We tried to make them feel comfortable, but in vain. They didn't know the Orthodox ceremonies, they didn't understand what was happening and why. We were anxious to serve them, to look after the chapel, to explain this and that and our entertainment was spoiled' (*ibid.*). After the buses left things returned to normal. This pattern was repeated for three years, until the agent responsible was pressured by islanders to drop the idea which in any case had yielded little profit while spoiling a local tradition. The villagers still welcome Greek visitors, who understand the purpose of the festival, but it is interesting to see the evolution of their attitude towards non-Greeks when tourism converts the traditional host-guest relationship to a commercial one. The relationship had to be managed and the Skyrians did this by setting limits and protecting their rights to privacy (Zarkia, 1996).

Figure 6.3 A Buddhist house-blessing ceremony in north west Nepal

Not all local communities are in the position to limit visitors to festivals at sacred sites, and not all wish to do so. A classic example comes from the Buddhist monastic festivals of the Himalayas (Fig. 6.2) already referred to, which have become cultural products for sale to visitors. Such festivals have a primarily religious basis, but also create a social focus for scattered communities and maintain cultural continuity in remote and inaccessible areas. The festivals last for several days and typically include at least one day of ritual dances performed in the monastery courtyard by monks dressed in spectacular robes and masks, commemorating specific historico-religious events. These inevitably attract Western visitors, and some tour companies offer treks carefully timed to coincide with the festivals. With the exception of those motivated to visit *gompas*, the everyday tourist to the Himalayas has few structured encounters with Buddhism. *Gompas* are often shut, and even when opened may be in poor repair. Quiet, fusty monasteries are often poorly lit and full of the smell of rancid butter fat, and it is only by luck that the visitor might see an ancillary ceremony such as a house blessing, rarely encountered and often not explained (Fig. 6.3). Outside the monasteries *mani* (prayer stone) walls, prayer wheels and occasional pilgrims are reminders of the regional religion, together with *stupas* and wayside shrines or paintings.

The Mani Rimdu festival held in the Himalayan monasteries of the Sherpa country near Everest (Nepal) is particularly popular with visitors. The full Mani Rimdu festival lasts for nineteen days of prayer and community ceremonies, but it is the single day of masked dances that attracts visitors. The annual masked dance festivals of Bhutan (*tsechu*) are the only time visitors may enter many of the fortress-monasteries (*dzongs*), some of which were placed off-limits after complaints of inappropriate visitor behaviour at festivals. The impact of visitors on Himalayan masked dance festivals is directly related to their number, which itself is controlled by the accessibility of the site and the way the festival has been promoted. The longer the festival has been known, the more likely it is to receive large visitor numbers. The Tenchi festival of Lo Manthang represents one extreme where very small visitor numbers, difficult access and a short market availability (four years) have meant that the festival still preserves most of its original characteristics. The Mani Rimdu festivals of the better-frequented Everest region represent the opposite extreme where at the better-known monasteries (such as Tengboche near Everest) the festival audience may be composed of more than 80 per cent visitors. In Lo Manthang the figure would be nearer 1 per cent.

CASE STUDY: TENCHI FESTIVAL AT LO MANTHANG, NEPAL

The writer observed the Tenchi festival of Lo Manthang, the capital of Lo (Mustang), a Tibetan-speaking Buddhist kingdom in north Nepal, in 1994 (Shackley, 1996c). It lasts over five days in May/June, at a date determined by the Tibetan lunar calendar, and has many similarities to the Mani Rimdu events of the Everest area. It celebrates the slaying, by a famous Buddhist lama, of a demon who was causing problems for Lo Manthang in the thirteenth century. The first two days of the festival involve rites carried out within the confines of the monastery, but on the third and fourth days masked dances are held in the main square of the city. The dances, performed by monks, may last up to seven hours. The theme is always the triumph of good over evil, and the drama of the dances is punctuated by comic interludes,

Figure 6.4

Masked dances at the Tenchi festival, Lo Manthang

much in the manner of a Greek tragedy. Individual dances include the famous 'black hat' dance performed by monks wearing ornate hats, high boots and elaborate silk brocade costumes, accompanied by drummers (Fig. 6.4). The 'dance of fearsome gods' utilizes terrifying masks of angry deities, the 'dance of heroes' features yellow skirts and skull masks. Dances are usually performed by the younger monks and watched by the High Lama of the monastery, accompanied by senior monks and an extensive lay audience. A musical accompaniment is provided by traditional instruments including the long Tibetan trumpets, drums, pipes, gongs, cymbals and conch shells. On the fifth day the end of the festival is celebrated by ceremonies outside the city and involves the firing of volleys of arrows and ancient muskets.

In the four years since Lo has been opened up to visitors probably fewer than 30 tourists a year have had the opportunity to witness the Tenchi festival, whose precise date is not advertised (Shackley, 1996c). However, some tour companies are timing visits to Lo to coincide with it, but the volume of visitors is unlikely to increase significantly due to the cost of the trip (around $5000–7000 from Europe) and the extreme difficulty of reaching Lo Manthang which involves at least a four-day walk over mountain passes. Observed visitor concerns included:

- boredom due to incomprehension
- lack of any interpretative or visitor facilities
- the presence of too many visitors affecting the 'authenticity' of the experience
- erratic scheduling and timing making key events impossible to predict.

By contrast, concerns expressed by local people and monastic authorities included:

- poor visitor behaviour lacking cultural sensitivity
- inconsiderate taking of photographs
- best seats (and best views) being taken by visitors
- no revenue from visitors to help with the costumes and expenses of staging the festival
- visitors lacking reverence or interest in the festival's meaning.

Most visitors were initially entranced by the colourful dances but then bored by their length, a problem exacerbated by the fact that Lo Manthang is dry, dusty and lacking in any visitor facilities. By the end of the first day many visitors, even those who had trekked to the area especially for the festival, had given up and resumed their journey, with the remainder paying less than perfect attention. Without interpretation the dances become repetitive, breaks and characters are incomprehensible and many visitors are unable to cope with the lack of a proper timetable.

The issue of interpretation is critical here. Tour guides do not usually speak Tibetan and do not understand the meaning and plot of each festival and dance. Therefore, in order to understand what is going on a local guide or locally-produced leaflet is required. For religious reasons any such publication must be sanctioned by the relevant High Lama but the monastery itself is unable to fund production. The problem is not insuperable. During the 1980s a specialist tour company operating in the Everest area financed and wrote an explanatory leaflet for the Mani Rimdu festival at Chiwong *gompa* near Everest, to generate revenue for monastic funds.

Poor visitor behaviour may stem from ignorance or thoughtlessness, and is a great cause of local resentment. Isolated instances occur at almost every festival. Clough (1994) notes that two Europeans gatecrashed the High Lama's platform at a *tsechu* performance in Bhutan, but the monks were too courteous to remove them. The spectacular dances attract photographers who are intrusive in their quest for a perfect shot, and flash photography is often frowned upon. Many local people feel that photographing religious ceremonial is inappropriate, yet for the visitor getting a good photograph may be the motivation for his visit. Local people often resented the fact that foreigners assume that they could get the best seat, and were indeed actively encouraged to do so by monastic authorities who try, by this means, to enforce a contribution to funds as the price of a decent view. Some of the Everest area monasteries have taken this idea to its logical conclusion by issuing tickets. However, many visitors to Lo Manthang, including some who stated that the Tenchi festival was the express purpose of their visit, refused to make any contribution to festival expenses, claiming that the sum should have been included in the trek fee. The attitude of monastic authorities to visitors is also ambiguous. Most welcome increased foreign attendance principally for the chance of gaining cash contributions and the opportunity to display local traditions and promote Buddhist principles.

In most regions tourists can see only the 'front regions' of their destinations and the spaces specially prepared for them (MacCannell, 1973). However, festivals like Tenchi are not staged for visitors, thus providing an unusual opportunity to see the 'back space' (Goffman, 1959) where real living takes place. Boorstin (1964) noted that tourists often expect experiences to be arranged for their convenience and are frequently unwilling to accept uncomfortable local conditions. This is clearly the case in the Himalayas where the masked dances are often long, puzzling and boring after the first excitement has worn off. Start times are impossible to predict and the monks apparently break off whenever they feel like it, for tea to be served. Many of the associated ceremonies are held behind closed doors. The visitor who has been attracted to the dances by the chance of seeing something authentic is often dismayed by the fact that he does not enjoy it, with the discomforts and irritations not compensated for by interest in the proceedings. Although some monasteries make efforts to provide for the needs of visitors (roped-off areas where they will not be jostled, chairs, and access to good spots for photography), the festivals remain primarily local events at which visitors are tolerated but seldom really welcomed.

Many festivals are highly selective about those who may attend, and it is a common practice to exclude those who do not share the same worshipping tradition. The Jagannath festival at Puri in Orissa just south of Calcutta takes place at one of the four holiest sites in India and is highly exclusive. It features opportunities for local people and pilgrims to combine a social event with a pageant and display. On the day of the appropriate full moon all traffic stops and Christians are excluded from the site, which can welcome up to 1 million pilgrims. Each pilgrim is supposed to get two passes in advance for a few rupees, one to get inside the pay perimeter, which is cordoned off, and another for a seat. The associated procession involves three immense chariots running on two-metre-high wooden wheels, accompanied by chanting and singing, drums and cymbals, and needing four hundred men to pull the 100-tonne weight of each chariot. Sometimes pilgrims become so frenzied that they throw themselves under the wheels, which is considered to be a holy death. The procession takes eight hours to pull the chariots a mile to their final destination by the sea, where the festival continues for nine days. After this, the chariots are pulled back to the temple and destroyed, creating permanent work for 6000 people in the temple who spend the next year building chariots for the next festival.

ANNIVERSARIES AND JUBILEES

Anniversaries and jubilees can take many forms. Some sites celebrate an annual festival in the honour of a particular saint or deity, others may keep a festival in honour of the anniversary of a particular apparition, or the death or birth of a saint or martyr. Some anniversaries commemorate the completion of a particular building, the death of a patron or a particular historical episode. Some may be purely local, others national. For example, in 1997 England celebrated the 1400th anniversary of the landing in Kent of St Augustine, sent by the Pope to reconvert England to Christianity. More than 100 separate events were staged during the anniversary year, including a controversial exhibition at Canterbury of fragments of bone and brain tissue believed to be those of St Thomas Becket. The year-long programme involved a partnership between the Church of England and English Heritage, and was accompanied by the publication of a map of England's Christian Heritage which flagged up sites of particular historic or religious significance. The result was an increase in tourist visitation, but there was no effect on the size of worshipping communities.

By far the most significant anniversary or jubilee in terms of visitation to sacred sites was the events surrounding the turn of the millennium and the year 2000. In Catholic tradition a Holy Year, or Jubilee year, is a great event originating in Biblical times when the Law of Moses prescribed that the Israelites should hallow each fiftieth year as a jubilee (Leviticus 25: 10–14). Jubilee 2000 was especially important since it was also a celebration of 2000 years since the birth of Christ (if one discounts certain differences of opinion on when that event occurred). The Roman Catholic Church chose to mark the year 2000 by an extensive programme of pilgrimages, papal journeys and specific events whose purpose was widely advertised as 'to encourage holiness of life'. It anticipated that by the end of the year 25 million visitors would have come to Rome to attend a variety of religious events and concerts, financed by a partnership between the Italian government and the Vatican in much the same way as the British jubilee year was financed by the Church and English Heritage. More than a thousand separate projects were planned, with budgetary requirements reaching £1.2bn, but not all got off the blocks. However, the events in Rome proved popular, but difficult to organize in a relatively confined space. Estimates included the need for 7000 extra bedspaces at time of peak demand, and 8000 more police. Demand on other facilities could also be excessive – a day youth festival in Rome for 2 million young people in August required an estimated extra 15,000 portable lavatories.

The need to create visitor facilities for large events inevitably causes problems. During March 2000 there were complaints that the impending visit of Pope John Paul II to the Mount of the Beatitudes in Israel had converted it to the 'Mount of the Bulldozers' (Reeves, 2000), as a half-mile stretch of pasture at the foot of the mountain was flattened to create an amphitheatre in which the Pope celebrated Mass. Although the Israeli authorities said that the clearance was necessary for the 100,000 pilgrims expected to attend, cynics suggested that it just created an eye-catching background for the benefit of international television companies who broadcast the 3-hour service live. Israel saw the Pope's visit as a diplomatic triumph and exploited it to the full, with little regard for the environmental consequences. Local environmentalists complained that the event could equally well have been staged in a local sports arena without modifying the sensitive environmental area to create three parking lots for 2000 coaches. Despite claims that the area would be returned to its original state by the end of the year, it seems more likely to have literally paved the way for entrepreneurs to develop the land (Reeves, 2000). Nor was this the only problem faced by Israel during the millennium year, as the following case study illustrates.

CASE STUDY: NAZARETH 2000

The city of Nazareth, where Jesus grew up, is one of the three prime tourist destinations in the Holy Land, together with Bethlehem and Jerusalem. It underwent extensive remodelling as part of the Nazareth 2000 programme to improve visitor facilities, but the situation became highly political since Nazareth is a major Christian pilgrimage destination in a Muslim town surrounded by Jewish settlements.

Figure 6.5 Upgrading and pedestrianization projects at Nazareth

A recent study (Shoval, 1999) suggested that despite its importance, visitors to Nazareth stayed only between 1.5 and 2 hours. Of them, 85 per cent came on day trips, most by coach and with tightly organized itineraries that left little freedom for movement or taking in other sites outside their route. Moreover, Nazareth had terrible traffic and parking problems and had become virtually static during the peak tourism season. A day visitor to Nazareth spends around $14, compared with the $40 spent by a visitor who stayed in the town overnight, but 50 per cent of visitors spent nothing in the town, despite putting considerable pressure on its facilities. Much thought was given to how this situation could be remedied, partly to generate extra revenue for the town, but also to accommodate the anticipated increase in both day visitors and staying tourists in the year 2000. The plan involved a combination of trying to make the centre of the town (Fig. 6.5) more attractive by pedestrianization, building conservation, better signage and lighting and creating a road that carried the heavier traffic away from the centre. The sum of 30 million dollars was also invested in hotel accommodation outside the city centre where more space was available. The city managers wished to encourage tourists to stay longer and spend more, without altering the nature of the experience that they received at the sacred sites within the town and at the same time supplementing its facilities. Because few visitors stayed overnight, Nazareth after dark was deserted. Attempts were made to reverse this by making an attractive pedestrian area with interesting cafés and restaurants, well lit and attractive to people wishing to walk round in the evening. However, the need to offer more high-quality hotel rooms (only possible by the development of international-class hotels outside the city) militated against this plan. Hotels had a vested interest in retaining their clients in the hotel in the evenings to optimize revenue – easily accomplished if shuttle buses to the city centre are irregular. Nor did the new shopping precinct prove especially attractive to traders, which defeats the object since people do not wish to walk at night around boarded-up shops. There are still many beggars in the Old City of Nazareth, which Western visitors find disconcerting.

Nazareth 2000 involved the design of special tourist routes to link the sacred sites as well as financial help for new restaurants and other visitor-related businesses. The plan also involved potential charging of $500 for coaches with diminution of $100 for each hour stayed (therefore they could pay nothing), to encourage longer stays. However, this would have to be recouped from customers by raising tour fees. The availability of ample free parking actually made it easier just to come for a short time. There was also

Figure 6.6
Basilica of the
Annunciation,
Nazareth, with
contested
location for a
new mosque in
the foreground

the possibility of adding new attractions to persuade visitors to stay longer,
including a new museum and the 'Nazareth Experience', reconstructing a
biblical village. Nor was the charging of a city entry fee (to be used for
development or conservation projects) ruled out. Only 80 per cent of visitors
surveyed said they would still come if there were an entrance fee, but since
50 per cent spend nothing the balance would still be positive, although such
a fee would be opposed by churches. The Church authorities which control
sites such as the Church of the Annunciation oppose any tourism development that includes charging, since they feel that the Church should not
become involved in economic issues. The city council itself reached political
stalemate, with the situation not being helped by controversy over the

proposed building of a mosque within a few metres of the wall of the Church of the Annunciation (Fig. 6.6). Christian council members saw the Nazareth 2000 plans as helping the economic prosperity of the town. Muslims feared that tourism development would place increased stress on Christian/Muslim relations (already strained over the issues surrounding the mosque) and would make Nazareth more a Christian than a Muslim town, since most of the additional visitors would be Christian.

Not all the new developments were completed for the millennium, and the future direction of tourism in the city is still undecided.

In the summer of 2000 debate was still raging around these issues but the problems had not been solved. However, Israel received far fewer pilgrims during the Jubilee year than anticipated (partly because of perceived political instability) with the result that Nazareth now has an over-supply of accommodation. The case is interesting since it shows how closely the management of sacred sites and that of their surrounding visitor facilities are related. In this case the Church authorities who manage the Church of the Annunciation merely have large visitor numbers to contend with. It is the private-sector businesses outside that are not thriving, and unless some kind of partnership is forged between the two sets of interests it is difficult to see how the situation can be remedied.

PILGRIMAGE

Religions are not always happy with the consequences of possessing sacred places. As Davies (1994b) remarks 'there is a very real tension present in many religious traditions, deploring the fact that devotees may place more emphasis on the physical place than upon its spiritual significance'. The founder of Sikhism, Guru Nanak, opposed the use of pilgrimage to sacred places, arguing that genuine pilgrimage was an internal journey, a matter of the heart. It is ironic that one of the most important pilgrimage sites in India is the Golden Temple at Amritsar, which not only reflects the lives and works of some of Sikhism's early Gurus but is also is a concrete mark of the existence of Sikhism as a faith separate from Hinduism or Islam. The temple building itself is an expression of faith, as is a cathedral in the Christian tradition. Buddhism has similar reservations about pilgrimage. Buddha famously decried pilgrimage as a worthless activity: 'If the waters of the Ganges could truly wash away sin then all fish would go straight to heaven.' Yet Buddhists place an especial importance on pilgrimages to *stupas* and shrines. Major locations include the Lumbini gardens near Kapilavastu where Buddha was born, Bodhgaya which is regarded as the seat of the world, the Deer Park at Sarnath and various places where Buddhist miracles were performed. The Buddhist pilgrimage tradition started early when Fa-hsien travelled throughout the Far East in the fourth century in search of truth, documenting an enormous cult of relics before his return to China in AD 412. Local pamphlets were later produced devoted to particular legends of the area, providing historical material later incorporated into long guidebooks – a process similar to the way in which pilgrimage sites and guidebooks develop in all religious traditions. In Buddhism, pilgrimage is thought to produce great merit by discipline of mind, speech and body, with the significance of the activity enhanced if the pilgrim has the chance to receive religious instruction and ritual empowerment throughout his route. Auspicious timing is crucial because the pilgrim must be at certain locations at specific dates and times. The result is obviously large numbers of pilgrims at certain sites at specific times, when pilgrimage, festival, market and social functions interrelate inextricably. Pilgrimage may strengthen political as well as religious bonds. In Sri Lanka its Buddhist kings protected the relic of Buddha's tooth in the belief that the security and well-being of the kingdom depended on it (much like the ravens in the Tower of London). An annual public holiday is observed during which thousands make a pilgrimage to witness the relic being displayed in procession, on the back of a royal elephant. The Muslim pilgrimage to Mecca, the *hajj*, attracts more than two million pilgrims from 100 countries seeking repentance, purification and spiritual renewal in a ritual performed every year for fourteen centuries. It is also a major source of bonding between the different traditions and nationalities within the Islamic world.

Just as the journey is as important to the pilgrim as the destination, so may be the method by which that journey is carried out. Mt Kailash in Tibet is considered the most sacred mountain on earth by the world's 800 million Hindus as well as by Jains, Tibetan Buddhists and followers of Bon Po. The first non-Asian person ever to visit it was the Swedish explorer Sven Hedin in 1907, but although the region gradually begun to open to foreigners fewer than twenty had visited by 1984. Before 1988 it was never climbed and the correct religious ritual was to circle the mountain on foot. Buddhists and Hindu pilgrims walk round it clockwise, followers of Bon-Po go counterclockwise. The pilgrim trail is 32 miles long and mainly level, with the difficulty normal in any pilgrimage coming in actually reaching the site. Three, five or thirteen circuits *(koras)* are usual. Some pilgrims even do them in one day to save carrying food and shelter. Some, in long leather aprons and leather gloves, do the circuits by consecutive prostrations (*gyang chatsel*) that are thought to gain more merit towards the possibility of a better incarnation in the next life. One *kora* done in this fashion can take two to three weeks, with the pilgrim surrounded by an encouraging and noisy crowd and uplifted by religious fervour.

Pilgrimage is essentially a social activity. In Europe, there are three basic types of pilgrimage site (Nolan and Nolan, 1992), including:

- pilgrimage shrines (places that serve as goals of religiously-motivated journeys from beyond the immediate locality)
- religious tourist attractions in the form of structures or sites of religious significance with historic and/or artistic importance
- festivals with religious associations

Many shrines hold little interest for the casual tourist and many major religious tourist attractions are not pilgrimage shrines, resulting in the partial separation of tourist and pilgrim. Some major sites are both, such as Mont-Saint-Michel and Chartres Cathedral in France, all the major basilicas of Rome and sites like Cologne Cathedral in Germany or Westminster Abbey in London. Many European pilgrimage destinations are quite recent in origin, particularly those related to Marian apparitions. Medjugorje in Hertzgovinia is significant in eastern Europe, marking an apparation of the Virgin Mary in 1981. Although not yet acknowledged as authentic by the Roman Catholic Church, visits are not discouraged. Major nineteenth-century Marian apparation sites including Knock in Ireland and Lourdes in France. The levels of visitation to Knock in the 1970s resulted in the building of a modern basilica and international airport to accommodate pilgrims, a market dominated by Irish-American Catholics with little to attract the secular tourist. Lourdes, where the Blessed Virgin appeared to a young peasant girl, Bernadette Soubirous, in 1858 is probably the best known Marian shrine in Europe, especially famous as a centre of healing. The small provincial town of Lourdes now has one of the largest international airports in France. The girl was commanded to build a church, and the Virgin's appearance was marked by a miracle in form of a spring of pure water. The authenticity of the appearances is widely accepted, with the result that Lourdes has become a major sacred place where many come for healing to the waters of the spring. High levels of commercialization at shrines to provide visitor services often shock secular visitors but delight the religious. The crowded streets of Mont-Saint-Michel are lined with souvenir shops and full of people, commerce, noise and colour – exactly as they would have been in the Middle Ages. However, they lack the reverential monastic atmosphere that secular visitors sometimes expect. Anyone who has watched the feeding frenzy in St Peter's Square on the occasion of an open-air Papal audience when pilgrims come complete with team colours, banners, streamers and whistles before descending en masse on souvenir sellers is not likely to confuse piety with peace in a pilgrimage context.

Pilgrims travel for healing, and also for deepening and strengthening of faith. When people travel in groups there is often the sense of a depth of unity with one another. Within Roman Catholicism an important dimension is the merit to be gained through pilgrimage. The hardships of the journey, the devotion shown in shrines along the way and the opportunity to worship at the final destination are all significant factors in the visitor experience. In medieval times sacred pilgrimage sites were ranked in order of the merit to be gained from visiting them – two visits to St David's in Pembrokeshire, for example, equalled one to Rome. Canterbury remains the major pilgrimage site in England, where Archbishop Thomas à Becket was murdered in 1170 after a disagreement with King Henry II. Many miracles are recorded in relation to his shrine, and he was canonized in 1173. Chaucer's *Canterbury Tales*, written in the late fourteenth century, show how popular pilgrimage was at that time. Motives were varied. Some pilgrims hoped for physical healing, either for themselves or for others. Others made the journey to fulfil their part of a bargain made with God or the saints that might involve the granting of some wish in return for their journey. Others journeyed as part of a penance, still others to gain spiritual merit. Some wished to be associated with the saints of the past, acquiring insights about their perspective on life from visiting places where they had lived or died. Visits to Assisi in Italy, for example, were made to see the sacred sites associated with St Francis and his friend St Clare.

Although a pilgrimage can be simply structured as a journey from home to shrine, pilgrimages are frequently far more elaborate, involving the visiting of a series of sites and the completion of required rituals to attain the desired goal. This tradition occurs in all religions and may involve, as has already been noted, millions of people at a time. Each year, for example, more than one million pilgrims visit the city of Varanasi on the river Ganges, one of Hinduism's seven sacred cities. Varanasi also houses a community of more than 50,000 Brahmins who provide religious services for the devout, some of whom come on a traditional pilgrimage while others come there to die. The main attraction is the more than one hundred bathing *ghats* spread out over 5km of riverside. Five of them form a pilgrimage route where pilgrims must bathe in the prescribed order and on the same day. Another route goes around the city in a 50-mile path with stops for worship at 108 different shrines. The bathing *ghats* include shrines, pavilions and temples with several being reserved for the cremation of bodies, the most important being Manikarnika where Shiva is believed to be present to liberate souls from the cycle of rebirth. Floating bundles covered in white cloth float on the river, the bodies of children and those dying of high fever or (in the past) smallpox, which are not cremated. Varanasi is also a major tourist attraction for non-Hindu visitors with guidebooks recommending visits at dawn or dusk when good photographs can be obtained of pilgrims coming to bathe and drink the waters. The taking of such photographs is extremely offensive to religious Hindus. Tradition says that even when the water is dirty it never causes illness to a faithful person who drinks or bathes in it, despite the fact that the Ganges is one of most polluted rivers in the world. An equivalent destination in Europe might be the revival of interest in the Pilgrim's Road to Santiago de Compostela. In the Middle Ages the cult of Sant'Iago (St James) became an important element in medieval European ecclesiastical politics, with the result that Santiago de Compostela became the second most important pilgrimage centre in Europe. Later, it was also significant in the growth of Spanish nationalism as the country was reconquered from the Moors (Graham and Murray, 1997). Today, the ancient pilgrim route has been re-created both physically and symbolically as a symbol once again of a unified Europe, a symbolic representation of regionalism at a time when Europe is striving to acquire a new identity as the EC strengthens its hold.

Shrines can also go out of fashion for one reason or another. Today, one of the most popular modern pilgrimages in England is to the shrine of Our Lady of Walsingham, in Norfolk. The Virgin Mary appeared there in 1061 to the lady of the manor, and ordered her to build a replica of Mary's house in Nazareth. A priory was later built on the site, near to miraculous springs of water, and Walsingham became not only one of the leading British sites but also one of Europe's most important pilgrimage centres. It suffered centuries of neglect after the Reformation, but was rediscovered and rebuilt in the twentieth century and once again features as a major pilgrimage destination for both Anglicans and Roman Catholics. New pilgrimage destinations can develop and become extremely popular in a very short time, often with functions that overlap the categories of pilgrimage destination, festival and event. Taizé, for example, located in France 10km from the abbey of Cluny, is now one of the most popular Christian pilgrimage sites in Europe, specifically for young people. It houses an ecumenical international community founded by Brother Roger in 1940, which hosts weekly meetings and produces a huge output of music and prayer which has had a major impact on church music in post-war Europe. Every week of the year, Taizé is filled with young people aged 17–30 who come from all over the world, as many as 80,000 in a weekend. It is interesting to speculate about the reasons for its success. It is not an ancient site like Canterbury or Walsingham, but its mission is very specifically to act as a spiritual focal point for young people, offering an ecumenical message of peace and reconciliation. The success of the Iona Community is founded on very similar ideals. The Taizé community seems to exert astonishing pulling power, not so much from a deliberate plan but stemming from an authentic spiritual inspiration 'one of those thoughts from God around which a unity of life is forged' (Lena, 1993: 47). As sacred sites go it lacks landscape quality, being merely an assortment of odd wooden structures and tents grown up on the edge of the village. Its popularity has spanned forty years of immense change in the lives of young people, who today are searching for identity and a symbolic way of expressing it. The Taizé phenomenon is not settled nor institutionalized, and thus appeals to the young. Yet it is built on a monastic community whose members see themselves as such, not as youth workers. A new arrival at Taizé gets given a prayer which says 'you have come to Taizé to go to the living springs of Christ in prayer and silence. You have come to discover a meaning for your life, to find new vitality, to prepare yourself to take on responsibilities in your own situation' (Lena, 1993: 48). Taizé's liturgy is a created style which mixes material from both eastern and western Christian traditions, utilizing languages that follow or are superimposed on one another. It reflects a lost Latinity that underpins the simple, repeated refrains and invocations based on Gregorian chant. Taizé can be seen as the sacred equivalent of a youth festival such as Woodstock or Glastonbury, with a message which succeeds in reaching a wider audience via its published liturgy. Yet it is more than that, and in some way seems to assist its youthful pilgrim attendees to structure a personal faith by offering sayings and texts for reflection. It provides an opportunity to experience the Christian message shorn of its ideology and, significantly, not contextualized in a conventional sacred site.

At Taizé it is the nature of the message, rather than an inherent sacredness of the site, that attracts visitors, yet despite its architectural informality Taizé is regarded by many as sacred since it exercises a sacred function of providing facilities for worship, prayer and reflection. Other sites, such as Varanasi or Mt Kailash, are the foci of pilgrimage because of a sacredness inherent in their very landscape, viewed as the abode of the gods. Here, the pilgrim has the opportunity to become more than him- or herself. Still other sites facilitate the same process by assisting the pilgrim to focus on some particular characteristic, perhaps an appearance of the Virgin, the relics of a saint or a location commemorating some significant sacred event. It is easy to see the parallels here between sacred journeys and contemporary secular tourism – there was something of the tourist in medieval pilgrims and something of the pilgrim in modern tourism. For the pilgrim the experience is compounded of motivation, preparation, journey and arrival. For someone who is merely attending a festival or event at a sacred site (whether or not that event is secular or religious) the process is very much simpler. However, the underlying principle is the same in that something of the sacredness of the site, its 'spirit of place', contributes a unique character to any event which it hosts, bringing the visitor into fleeting contact with the numinous, whether he or she realizes it or not.

CHAPTER 7

Cultural Landscapes

As has already been mentioned in previous chapters, sacred sites need not involve built heritage. Indeed, many contain few buildings or have none at all. Sacred sites also vary widely in scale: some can be very large – sometimes whole mountains, or even entire regions. They may be groves of trees, springs, mountains or sacred lakes and are frequently a palimpsest of any one (or several) of these natural settings, associated with the remains of past and present human activity. These usually, of course, involve some element of ritual such as worship, prayer or pilgrimage for which the built heritage of shrines or temples may provide a focus. Such combinations of physical features with built heritage are often referred to as 'cultural landscapes'. The term came to prominence during the 1990s when UNESCO introduced it to the World Heritage list to replace a former category of 'mixed sites' (Shackley, 1998e) in addition to the two other categories of 'cultural sites' and 'natural sites' protected under the World Heritage convention. Several categories of cultural landscape are currently recognized by the International Council of Monuments and Sites (ICOMOS) (Cleere, 1995), including designed landscapes such as historic gardens, organically evolving landscapes and relict landscapes such as irrigation and field systems or linear industrial features which preserve historical or archaeological evidence of specific human activities. Another category is the 'associative landscape', of which the first to be inscribed on the World Heritage list in 1993 was Tongariro National Park in New Zealand, a mountain range sacred to the Maori people. UNESCO's operational guidelines (UNESCO, 1995) note that 'the inclusion of such landscapes on the World Heritage list is justifiable by virtue of the powerful religious, artistic or cultural associations of the natural elements rather than the material cultural evidence which may be insignificant'. Such landscapes provide a unique series of management challenges, since they contain a wide variety of natural and cultural sites that include elements sacred to different religious traditions. Their management is complicated by the fact that a cultural landscape is a place where contemporary communities may live, work and worship, rather than a deserted archaeological site or historical building. A cultural landscape is the result of a cultural evolution of, or in, the land (Haber, 1995). Landscape and culture both undergo constant dynamic changes, not all of which are predictable.

Cultural landscapes are mainly rural, yet certain townscapes would qualify under this category. Great cities such as Damascus (Shackley, 1998d), Rome or Jerusalem present townscapes of immense complexity, including hundreds of distinct sacred sites surrounded by visitor facilities and linked by cultural and pilgrimage routes. Smaller townscapes evolve round particular shrines, such as Bath in southern England whose status as a special or significant place is based on, and legitimized by, its hot springs, visited by over 2 million tourists each year, nearly half of whom visit the Roman baths, now administered as a heritage site. Bath's townscape includes the great Roman complex of springs, temples and baths which originally covered an area the size of two football pitches where religion, healing and recreation interacted. People still come to Bath with expectations of healing or some sort of spiritual experience (Bowman, 1998). The Roman name for the city was Aquae Sulis and in both Roman and pre-Roman Bath the waters seem to have been the focus for contact with the sacred. Many coins and objects such as lead tablets bearing blessings and curses, found on the two occasions when the Baths were drained for excavation, demonstrate an association between the substance and the sacred: throwing gifts, blessings or curses into the water established a direct line with the deity. Exactly the same phenomenon is seen in the universal custom of throwing coins into water as offerings. This may be logical in outside springs, but is less so in the artificial fountains found in the extremely secular landscape of a supermarket or shopping mall. Those who deposit coins are unconsciously retaining an ancient custom that exchanges a coin for a blessing.

The term 'cultural landscape' has most validity for sites where natural landscape features are considered to have a spiritual significance that may, or may not, be complemented by the presence of built heritage in the form of historical or archaeological sites. Mountains, springs, forests and rivers may all, in certain mythological systems, be 'power places' where power is received, or where power is needed to protect from spiritual danger. Such locations are often considered as places where the physical and spiritual intersect, and the description of the atmosphere of Iona as just such a 'thin place' has already been quoted. Mountains such as Mt Olympus, Mt Kailash and Mt Everest are significant in this way within many religious traditions, not just as elements in physical geography but regarded as part of the power structure of the spirit world. Caves represent another type of intersection, as do springs where water emerges from the earth (as at Bath). Major sacred sites evolve where more than one of these features occur, as at Muktinath in the Nepalese Himalaya, an important Hindu pilgrimage centre where jets of natural gas emerge in a cave near a spring in the mountains. Muktinath attracts not only Hindu and Buddhist pilgrims but also international visitors, since it is located on one of the major trekking routes just north of Annapurna. Visitors are not universally welcome at such sites. Many Native Americans believe that such sacred places should be left alone since visitors feed on the spirit of the mountain or area disrupting the spiritual harmony of the land (Opler, 1935). This would apply to the construction of buildings such as shrines, although other cultures believe that the sacredness of such sites can be made permanent by monument building. In some way the human institutions that created the monument are taking on the permanence of nature, with architecture and nature united into one landscape (Oechslin, 1984).

A cultural landscape represents part of a complex system of belief into which places were incorporated and explained in a way that had continued meaning to people, with that meaning orally transferred across generations. Many cultural landscapes also have political value by way of association with the mythic, and the following case study of Mt Sinai constitutes a good example.

CASE STUDY: THE CULTURAL LANDSCAPE OF MT SINAI

Within a 2km radius of the monastery of St Katherine the surrounding landscape includes 29 Christian and 6 Muslim sacred sites, including Mt Sinai itself (Gebel Musa) which, at 2285 m, dominates the area and is the site where Moses received the Ten Commandments. Mt Sinai has been a pilgrimage destination for thousands of years, with many pilgrims intending to climb it timing their arrival for either sunrise or sunset. At present anywhere between 30 and 500 people can be found sleeping rough on the mountain at any one time, causing great problems with litter, pollution and noise. This impinges on the quality of monastic life since the monastery is regularly woken by parties of trekkers ascending the mountain in preparation for a sunrise experience, accompanied by full-volume stereo systems. Two routes are available, the steep 3000+ 'Stair of Repentence' or the longer but easier 'camel path'. Motives for making the climb range from vague interest to a religious pilgrimage, and over the last two years trail-restoration programmes have greatly enhanced the amenity value of what was rapidly becoming a famously polluted trail. Future plans involve the installation of compost toilets and discouraging people from spending the night on the mountain (which has no facilities) in favour of a proper campsite just below the summit.

The immediate environment of Mt Sinai is an arid and forbidding landscape with a unique high-altitude ecosystem containing a surprising diversity of plants and animals, some found nowhere else in the world. The local Bedouin regard the whole area as sacred and have traditionally protected its fauna and flora. However, as has been previously noted this area of Sinai has become a prime target for day-visits from the resorts of the Red Sea coast. Some attempt is being made to limit visitor damage to southern Sinai by the designation of four Protected Areas (Shackley, 1999) including the 4300-sq km St Katherine Proctectorate which includes not only Mt Sinai but all the other archaeological, religious and cultural sites in the area including St Katherine's Monastery. The monastery itself forms only one node in a sacred landscape including the entire hinterland of Mt Sinai, and the great valley, Wadi Hebran, stretching from the foot of the mountain was the site where the Israelites camped while waiting for Moses to come down from the mountain. Today, the magnificent landscape is covered by a poorly-sited tourist village and various other developments of minimal quality.

Producing recommendations for the future management of the landscape is difficult since such a strategy must delicately balance the requirements and resources of the natural environment, local communities, incoming settlers and tourism. The area is still a living landscape for the Bedouin, playing an active social and economic role. It is also full of unexcavated archaeological sites, attributed landscapes, chapels on sacred places and sacred natural features. Pressures for both population and tourism growth in the area are substantial; the Egyptian Ministry of Planning aims at ambitious population growth targets for St Katherine which would triple the population of the town and double the tourist bedspaces, producing great pressure on the fragile archaeological landscape. A previous plan to establish a cable car up to the top of Mt Sinai has now been abandoned but there is still the possibility of increased hotel construction near the village of St Katherine. Many feel that further development of the Mt Sinai area is sacrilegious. Morrow (1990: 2) said, rather bitterly, 'Perhaps they will make the cable cars in the shape of calves and gild them. The golden calves can slide up and down Mount Sinai and show God who won.' However, there are underlying political reasons for developing the area, since Egypt feels that increased settlement provides some measure of security against a further Israeli occupation. Ironically, before 1967 when the area was under Israeli control development of the cultural landscape was tightly controlled. The subsequent tourist boom has produced employment and prosperity but the price would appear to be the desecration of the sacred landscape around Mt Sinai which is a non-renewable resource.

Not all visitors to Mt Sinai are pilgrims: many are tourists unaware of the many issues affecting the nature of the landscape through which they are travelling. In the Sinai area it seems probable that most tourists do not view the region as a sacred landscape, but rather as one discrete site (St Katherine's Monastery) surrounded by wilderness. Moreover, deserts are difficult to protect as to the uninitiated they appear devoid of life (Hobbs, 1996). Sinai is especially interesting since its landscape has a mythic quality exemplified by the search for the precise location of Mt Sinai (now with reasonable certainty identified as Gebel Musa). The landscape becomes a medium for symbolism, manipulation and transformation of the past. The Israeli occupation of Sinai was not just of political but also of religious significance, and the recurrence of the area in the religious mythologies of Judaism, Islam and Christianity has resulted in expectations that the area will have a powerful 'spirit of place'. The 'spirit of place' of Sinai is compounded of a totality of landscape quality, bleakness and emptiness, combined with reverence for locations of perceived divine or supernatural significance. To use a phrase already mentioned, Sinai is a 'thin place' where the power of God is sometimes felt even by unbelievers, although how long this will continue in the face of increasing development pressures is difficult to imagine.

SACRED MOUNTAINS

Mt Sinai is one of a series of sacred mountains that have prominent places in different religious traditions. Ancient Chinese beliefs include a visualization of mountains as pillars separating heaven from earth, with legends in Shamanism and early Taoism of sages and mystics living in mountain areas. The resulting cultural landscapes were regarded as sacred by association, access points to heaven and places where spirits and gods lived. In China a sacred mountain can be a single peak, a cluster of hills or a whole mountain range such as the Tien Shan in Shandong province. The Tien Shan were regarded not just as the mountain home of the gods, like Olympus or Sinai, but actually as a deity themselves, venerated as the most sacred mountains in China since the third millennium BC. The 7000 steps to their summit and their slopes were dotted with temples, inns, restaurants and shops to cater for the millions of pilgrims who came to visit the two temples at the peak.

Small hermitages and later great monastic complexes developed on Chinese sacred mountains with the arrival of Buddhism, with both Buddhist and Taoist mountains becoming primary pilgrimage destinations until the revolution of 1949. During the 'great leap forward' of the 1950s and the Cultural Revolution of the 1960s, religion in China was brutally suppressed and more than 90 per cent of China's temples and great cultural artefacts were completely destroyed. Since the 1980s, a less destructive attitude has permitted a modest revival in Buddhism and Taoism with some reconstruction of mountain monasteries, though often to very poor standards.

Sagarmatha, or Mt Everest, is perhaps the most famous sacred mountain, a World Heritage site and National Park which includes the highest peak in the world and several important cultural and religious sites. Caspary (1995) reviewed issues surrounding the management of the Sagarmatha cultural landscape, an area of 1244 sq km crossed by trekking routes and punctuated by villages and major sacred sites such as the famous Thangboche monastery. The latter is one of the few success stories of cultural tourism, as it was entirely destroyed by a fire in 1988, with subsequent rebuilding entirely financed by trekkers' donations. The area is one of exceptional natural beauty. Its Sherpa people, adherents of the Nyingmapa sect of Tibetan Buddhism, believe that all its constructed heritage such as *chorten, mani* walls, *gompas* and rock paintings are integral parts of the landscape. About 3000 Sherpas live in the National Park, which was relatively isolated until the early 1960s but is now visited by around 15,000 trekking tourists and anything up to 50 mountaineering expeditions a year (Wells and Sharma, 1998). Two thirds of the families in the park have direct income from tourism by working as guides and porters or selling clothing, food, lodging, handicrafts. There has been a dramatic expansion in construction within the sacred landscape. Locally owned and operated lodges grew from 7 in number in 1973 to 81 in 1991, with the main town (and tourist centre) of Namche Bazaar described by Wells and Sharma (1998: 239) as 'a scene of apparently unbounded small-scale capitalism'. A remote, poor, rural society had suddenly become affluent and cosmopolitan, with significantly adverse effects on the cultural landscape. Much publicity has been given to problems associated with tourism, especially tree-cutting for fuelwood, but today management controls have been implemented so that trekking groups must be self-sufficient in kerosene and local people require a permit to cut trees for house construction, although they can gather fallen timber. The actual extent of deforestation remains controversial but evidence suggests that tourists' pack animals damage the fragile high-altitude pastures. The region has been notorious for litter pollution with its main route nicknamed the 'Andrex Trail'. The park authorities blame this on tourists but have little political control since the park receives no tourism-related revenue. Moreover, since local residents were not included in the initial park-planning process, relations between the Sherpas and the park authorities are poor (except where Sherpas are appointed as park wardens).

Like Everest, the Annapurna area is also considered sacred. It is both physically and culturally one of the most diverse protected areas in the world. The Annapurna Conservation Area Project (ACAP) was started in 1986 to reconcile conservation and development by promoting local participation to enable the area to cope with its more than 45,000 trekkers per year. Activity is focused around only two trails, with environmental impacts resulting from uncontrolled development of shops and lodges within the designated Annapurna Sanctuary. The approach to management of the cultural landscape is quite different from that being used at Sagarmatha, involving a local approach to natural-resource management as opposed to a top-down imposition of regulations by outsiders. Special legislation replaced the original idea of a National Park with a multiple-use conservation area that delegated management authority to village level. It gave high priority to reducing the environmental impact of trekking and to increasing local revenues from tourism. ACAP collects and retains a visitor entry fee, unique in Nepal, and employs no government staff or funds (Bista and Heide, 1997) with the result that the Annapurna Sanctuary area is demonstrating dramatically reduced impact levels, combined with increased local employment.

SACRED GROVES

The practice of protecting patches of woods as sacred groves is ancient: groves of trees dedicated to the worship of the gods are mentioned by classical authors such as the Roman poet Ovid, who said 'here stands a silent grove black with the shade of oaks; at the sight of it anyone could say "there is a god in here!"' (*Fasti* 3:295). Throughout history respect was paid to sacred groves as places where spiritual beings were believed to reside, and such respect was manifested by a prohibition on ordinary domestic activities such as tree felling; gathering wood, plants, leaves; hunting, fishing; grazing, agriculture; or building. Some groves served as sites of worship, offerings or sacrifice and many of the legends surrounding them were collated by Frazier (1935). Today, sacred groves may be found in the near East, Asia, north and sub-Saharan Africa, and parts of native America (Hughes and Swan, 1986), presenting some interesting management challenges.

Good examples may still be found in India, where sacred groves still exist, although their importance is declining, including those studied by Chadran and Hughes (1997) in mountain villages above the western sea coast. There, almost every village used to have a sacred grove, ranging in size from a single clump of trees to several hundred hectares, and considered as the properties of the gods of the villages in which they are situated. Relics of these groves still survive, playing a vital role in forest restoration. These *kan* forests are natural tropical evergreen trees, used as places of worship with distinct borders. Rules for their utilization vary, but generally all consumptive use is excluded, and this is enforced by both the priests and the people of the village, acting together. There seem to have been two basic types of groves, a smaller category where no tree felling was allowed, and a larger variety used as a resource forest. Medicinal plants and leaves for fodder are gathered within the grove and village ceremonies held there or immediately outside, and the protection of the groves is enforced not just by human authority but by the god to whom it is dedicated, as well. Regulations are generally supervised by a village headman who might seek the god's permission before cutting a tree (a process which might also require an animal sacrifice). The sacred groves remain as relics of the original ecosystems of the areas where they are found, vital for studies of plant biodiversity. They shelter endangered species and enhance a supporting environment for others. Unfortunately, cultural factors are important in the dwindling of sacred groves, including the absorption of the local deities to whom the sacred groves are dedicated into the great gods of the Hindu pantheon. The result is usually the erection of a temple building with subsequent diminution in the size and significance of the groves, and associated relaxation of protection rules. The grove, which had functioned as a natural temple, is being replaced by a building that can often be constructed from wood cut from the grove that it is replacing. Transformation can be very slow. It can start with the marking of a sacred spring or tree with a carved relief or statue, gradually replaced by at first a small and then a larger temple. It is common to see tree-like designs used on such temples, and the trees themselves are often sold off to provide the raw materials. The process is an evolutionary one, as the sacred nature of the site is maintained but manifested in different forms. The paradigm shift represented does not diminish the sacredness of the site, but alters it. Other alterations can come from the adoption of the same sacred site by different religious traditions. In a curious way the function of sacred groves is mirrored in the world of science by Biosphere Reserves, their modern equivalent, where ecosystems are relatively complete and holy in the sense of possessing biological integrity or natural wholeness.

Some West African countries have flourishing sacred groves. The environment of Ghana is suffering from shifting cultivation and overgrazing, but its sacred groves are patches of relict climax vegetation that have survived, much like those of western India. More than 1400 sacred groves have been identified in Ghana, of two major types. Most epitomize the soul or symbol of a traditional protection source and are considered as final resting places of chiefs or dwellings of the gods. Some may be burial grounds, others fetish groves, and sacred groves exist within the fabric of almost all Ghanaian societies. Expressions of thanksgiving or sacrifices are offered, and sometimes festivals celebrating the prosperity of the community, which is seen to come from the groves. Groves are guarded by custodians who are believed to be chosen by the spirits through revelation to the elders after death of former guardian (very reminiscent of *The Golden Bough*). The rules and regulations binding the choice of guardian are irreversible, and it is believed that it is the gods who really appoint the management. Grove managers also become custodians of herbs and plants within groves, 80 per cent of which serve as watersheds or catchment areas that protect drinking-water sources (Tuffour *et al.*, 1992) and provide herbs of medicinal importance. All are protected by taboo, traditional belief and custom. Table 7.1 shows regulations related to the Malshegu sacred grove. Just as in India, the functions of groves can change

Table 7.1 Regulations relating to the Malshegu Sacred Grove, Ghana (source: Amoako-Atta, 1995)

Actions that are not permitted in and around the groves:

- No drumming or whistling on approaching the grove
- No person is allowed entry to the grove on Fridays
- No person is permitted to kill a crocodile, alligator or python in and around the grove and no person is allowed to eat any of these reptiles
- No entrance to the grove without the prior knowledge or consent of the guardian (in this case the fetish priestess or her designated representative)
- No person is allowed to use ebony as fuel wood for fire
- No cutting of trees from the grove
- Strangers access to and freedom of action in and around the groves is limited and subject to the directives of the custodian
- The fetish priestess as custodian of the grove is not allowed to marry during her reign, neither is she allowed to leave the confines of her room after midnight
- No person is allowed to enter the room of the fetish priestess wearing sandals, shoes, hats of any kind, or without an escort

Actions that are permitted or are mandatory in and around the groves:

- Cleaning the inside and immediate surroundings of the grove by the community under the supervision of the custodians is allowed on two occasions per year
- Sacrifices and rituals must be made twice a year
- Meat of animals, apart from crocodiles, alligators, pythons (which are the symbols of the gods) can be eaten by the people from the area

---

with the evolution of religious beliefs. Tuffour *et al.* (1992) quoted the case of the Boabeng-Fiema monkey sanctuary in Ghana which was full of monkeys in the late 1960s. However, it became a subject of great religious controversy when in the early 1970s a new sect emerged which regarded all monkeys as a source of evil, to be exterminated. A legal government conservation act was required to preserve the sanctity of the grove. This has worked to the benefit of local people, who now have a small but thriving ecotourism business based around welcoming tourists to see the monkeys. Ghana has demonstrated a consistently high level of interest in the protection of this and other sacred sites. In 1963–4 there was much concern about the likely flooding of sacred fetishes, shrines, groves and burial sites by the new Volta Dam. The government not only paid for the necessary libations to appease the gods and ancestors, but in many cases also paid for appropriate sacrifices and relocated fetishes in government vehicles, including the helicopter of the then president, Kwame Nkrumah. New sanctuaries were established and additional legal protection was given. Groves such as Malshegu have been protected and managed by villagers for more than three hundred years, constituting a cultural landscape of universal value. They demonstrate that traditional values, human settlement and initiative in conservation through religious beliefs can resist what seems to be the irreversible destruction and degradation of the biogeography of west Africa.

SACRED ISLANDS

Several good examples of sacred sites on islands have already been noted in this book, such as the Haida Native American site of Ninstints off the coast of British Columbia. Other examples are found with the Celtic Christian tradition of Britain, including Lindisfarne and Iona. It is also possible to identify places where virtually the whole island is viewed as a sacred place, for a combination of religious and ethnic reasons, depending on the cultural background of the visitor. Easter Island, or Rapa Nui, in the South Pacific provides a good example.

CASE STUDY: RAPA NUI (EASTER ISLAND)

Rapa Nui (Easter Island) is famous for its gigantic stone statues (*moai*) whose abundance and distinctiveness has generated many theories about how and why they were made and moved. 70 per cent of the island, and all the *moai* and associated archaeological sites, is included in a National Park, designated in 1996 as a World Heritage cultural landscape. Rapa Nui is a small

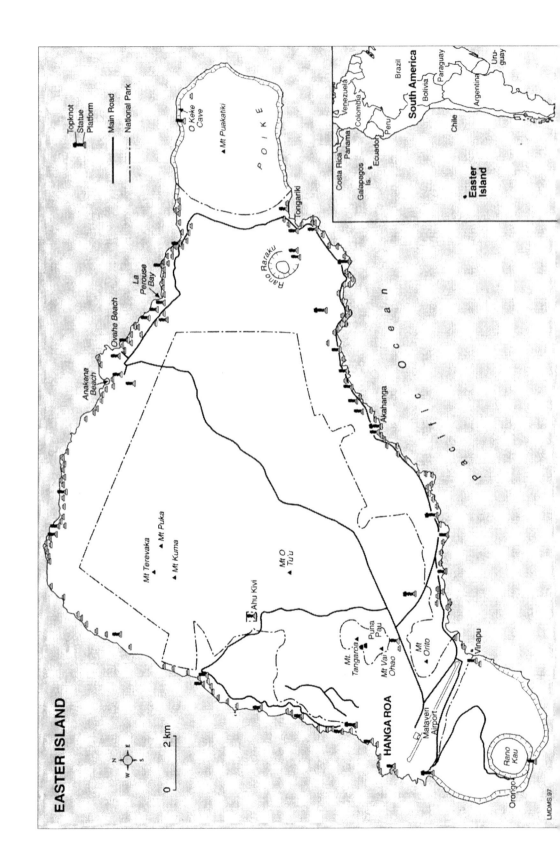

EASTER ISLAND

Topknot
Statue
Platform
Main Road
National Park

N
W — E
S

0   2 km

POIKE

O Keke
Cave

▲ Mt Puakatiki

Rano Raraku

Tongariki

La Perouse Bay

Oyahe Beach

Anakena Beach

Akahanga

Mt Terevaka ▲

▲ Mt Puka

▲ Mt Kuma

Mt O
Tu'u ▲

Ahu Kivi

Mt.
Tangaroa ▲

Puna
Pau ▲

Mt Vai
Ohao ▲

Mt
Orito ▲

Vinapu

HANGA ROA

Mataveri
Airport

Rano
Kau

Orongo

P a c i f i c   O c e a n

South America

Venezuela
Colombia
Ecuador
Peru
Costa Rica
Panama
Galapagos
Is.
Brazil
Bolivia
Paraguay
Uru-
guay
Argentina
Chile

Easter
Island

LMDMS.97

Figure 7.1 National Park boundary and location of major sites on Rapa Nui (Easter Island)

Figure 7.2 Stoneheads (*moai*) are the main attraction for visitors to Rapa Nui

island some 180 sq km (16,628 hectares) in extent which is home to around 3000 mainly Polynesian people (Fig. 7.1). It is the most distant inhabited point in the world from other dry land, 3700 km from mainland Chile and 4050 km from Tahiti. The large numbers of *moai* in what is today a bleak and inhospitably barren landscape have sparked many theories about the origins of the society that created them. Thor Heyerdahl (Heyerdahl, 1952) suggested that they were made by Peruvians, travelling from South America, on the basis of similarities in the stonework and his own Kon-Tiki voyage which replicated a journey from South America to Polynesia. Rapa Nui landscapes are bleak, grassy and windswept and the island itself is circled by dramatic cliffs, 300m high in places. Around 1000 *moai* seem to have been made around AD 700–1500, of which 200 once stood on coastal *ahu* platforms, facing inland and carved from volcanic tuffs with coral eyes and red topknots. A further 700–800, in varying stages of completion, were abandoned in the quarry or along the ancient roads between quarries and the coast (Fig. 7.2). Most of the erected statues came from a single quarry (Ranu Raraku), and were transported as far as 8km despite heights of up to 11m and weights of up to 82 tons. Abandoned statues include some true giants up to 21m tall weighing 270 tons.

Rapa Nui has been described as the world's largest museum, receiving more than ten thousand visitors each year. Visitor management is entirely in the hands of the Rapa Nui people themselves, working in partnership with CONAF (the Chilean forestry authority) who run the National Park, and SERNATUR (the Chilean tourism agency). Entrance fees of US$10 per person are charged by CONAF who return 60 per cent of these fees, an estimated $60,000/year, towards the management of the Park. About ten Park Rangers are employed, whose duties include generally watching the archaeological sites to prevent vandalism or erosion, answering visitor queries and giving directions. Few recent problems have been reported, although twenty years ago graffiti, souvenir hunting and climbing over the monuments had a deleterious effect. Nothing of the kind is visible today. Park management is unobtrusive, livestock are grazed within the Park and managed by mounted herdsmen but no one is allowed to live within the Park boundary except CONAF rangers. The only visitor facilities are the provision of (carved basalt) litter bins. At present no more than $122,000/annum is spent on archaeological heritage (half of that derived from admissions fees), only a fraction of the estimated $1 million required for statue stabilization and conservation. Many of the coastal *moai* and *ahu* exhibit extensive wind and salt-water erosion features, in contrast to the fresher, sharper *moai* in the quarries. Major issues relevant to the management of the island in the future include the need to generate more funding for conservation. Increasing visitor numbers also threaten the 'spirit of place' that is founded on the perceived mystique of the *moai* and their supposedly unknown construction techniques. This is helped by the bleak, treeless moonscape of the island that gives it an almost supernatural silence. Increased visitation will alter this. Park management is also having difficulties controlling local people who wish to sell souvenirs within the Park boundaries. Other threats to the sacredness of the site are provided by the possibility that visitor numbers may escalate if air transport arrangements are changed, perhaps by the abolition of the airline monopoly currently held by Lan Chile, or if the Polynesian liberation movement on Rapa Nui is successful in its attempt to gain independence from Chile.

The perennial fascination of Rapa Nui, underlying its inclusion as a sacred site, is the 'mystery' of who carved the statues and how they were moved. This is especially interesting because of the barren, desolate nature of the island which makes it difficult to imagine it as home to a thriving agricultural society capable of such megalithic construction. Similar 'mysteries' are constructed around any megalithic building project from Stonehenge to the Pyramids, and seem to reflect a general public reluctance to accept sound archaeological evidence when fantasy and the suggestion of extraterrestrial origins are more romantic. However, modern archaeological experiments suggest that even the largest statue could have been completed by around twenty carvers within a year, and required only a few hundred people with wooden rollers and bark ropes to move into a standing position. Pollen analysis confirms the existence of sub-tropical forests on the island at the time of the initial colonization by Polynesian settlers, but forest clearance was well under way by AD 800 and the final palm trees became extinct around 1400, about the same time as statue-carving stopped. The destruction of the forest and accompanying soil erosion and over-exploitation of all resources, including shellfish and seabirds, turned Easter Island into a desert. Cannibalism became common, streams dried up and wood was no longer available for cooking fires. Local chaos replaced centralized government and by 1700 the population had crashed, and rival clans had started to topple each other's statues. Some *moai* were seen upright by the first European visitors in 1773 but all had been torn down by the islanders themselves by 1864. Any *moai* standing today have been raised by archaeologists such as William Mulloy working at Ahu Akivi (Shackley, 1998e).

These prosaic explanations for the 'mystery' of the island do not deter visitors. The tourism industry now entirely underpins the economy of the island, with visitors coming from all over the world to sample its unique atmosphere, marvel at the statues and contemplate their ritual meaning. Today's visitor to Easter Island in low season may experience the cultural landscape almost devoid of fellow tourists, intrusive signage or facilities in a way seldom seen in National Parks. Even in high season such an experience can be repeated by judicious choice of timing. This possibility of being alone at the sites contributes to the success of the total visitor experience, and needs to be maintained in the face of increasing pressure. Despite the fact that local people took the decision to preserve the atmosphere by confining visitor facilities to the town of Hanga Roa, this is being eroded by the arrival of souvenir sellers at major sites, whose presence is largely ignored by officials. The archaeological heritage of Rapa Nui is no longer being affected by its visitors, but the quality of the visitor experience will deteriorate if the island becomes overcrowded. The island is an extremely expensive destination to visit, with the high prices charged being justified on the grounds that the visitor experience cannot be repeated anywhere else. The very lack of visitor facilities which makes the experience dramatic and strangely spiritual also means that the National Park has no means of generating additional visitor revenue. Maps, postcards, food, drink and tee-shirts must all be purchased in Hanga Roa, contributing to Rapa Nui private enterprise but not to National Park funds. It would be interesting to establish from visitors at what level they found the presence of other tourists irritating. Under normal conditions very low visitor numbers at individual sites could easily be maintained by co-operation between tour guides in Hanga Roa who could alter routes and departure times. At present almost all tours leave at either 10 a.m. or 3 p.m. and follow the same routes linking major sites. This means that on any one day at least half the tourists on the island will be lunching at Anakena and visiting the Ranu Raraku quarry in the late morning, whereas more creativity in route planning could ensure low visitor densities even with much greater numbers.

Easter Island exemplifies many of the issues involved in the management of cultural landscapes, especially those which either contain, or entirely consist of, sacred sites. There is a conflict here between a desire to allow visitors space and time to wander and marvel, and the need to make some money from their visit. In order for the 'spirit of place' to be maintained on Rapa Nui, the visitor experience has to take place, as far as possible, in a setting which involves only minimal contact with other visitors. Noisy contemporary tour parties inject a note of reality, and the 'sacredness' of Rapa Nui resides in its mystique, maintained only by ignoring well-argued archaeological evidence. The concept of a cultural landscape closely involves the spiritual and contemporary uses of a landscape with the management of its archaeological heritage. Many of its visitors see Rapa Nui as a potential metaphor for the fate of the world, devastated by over-population and poor resource management. The price the original inhabitants paid for the ways in which they chose to articulate their spiritual and political ideas was the creation of an island world which became a shadow of its former self (van Tilburg, 1994). The archaeological heritage of the island is of deep and fundamental importance to its present inhabitants, enhancing their cultural pride and supporting a new generation who are experiencing a renaissance of interest in their Polynesian past (a phenomenon also observed on Hawaii). The *moai* of Easter Island are not only links to the past but the kingpins of its future. They are artefacts which have curiously transcended their time frame (van Tilburg, 1994) to enter into modern consciousness and their rising again has spiritual as well as symbolic value.

Any cultural landscape is an integrated complex of cultural and natural resources, whose value derives from their physical quality, as well as from associated human endeavours and traditions. Many also have a significant resource value but all possess spiritual values for their visitor that cannot be quantified. Climbing Mt Sinai was the punishing reward of pilgrimage, a microcosm of the greater struggle already undertaken by the pilgrim to reach the site. In this final physical sacrifice the pilgrim escaped the ordinary world and become close to God. Similar ideas about approaches to holy landscapes appear in the traditions of many faiths, such as Mt Kailas for Buddhists, Jains, Hindus and Bon-Pos, Adam's Peak in Sri Lanka for Buddhists, Muslims and Hindus and the Tien Shan mountains in China for Buddhists. The devout visitor to a sacred grove, mountain or landscape is seeking a place where past and present meet, and even the tourist with no religious motivation may experience something of the numinous reflected in the very nature of the land itself. Pilgrims in sacred space describe universal reactions to sacred landscapes, whether that landscape is apparently unmodified by human activity or transformed in some way. Such a transformation can be physical, by the addition of shrines or other constructed heritage to mark a holy place, or perceptual by the beliefs and emotions of the pilgrims (Sumption, 1975; Tuan, 1978). The resulting landscape produces challenges which include the need to manage a large area in such a way that its spatial, archaeological and spiritual heritage is maintained for those who visit, those who live there and those for whom the area provides a focus for their lives.

CHAPTER 8

Political and Social Contexts

The nature of the visitor experience, and the ability of a visitor to obtain access to a sacred site, is controlled by many factors. Some click into operation even before the journey has begun, and are concerned with motivation and the availability of information. Others are intrinsically related to the journey itself, and might involve tour organization or the availability of travelling companions. Still others are site-specific, focused upon the issue of access. In earlier chapters this book has considered issues of access from a logistical angle, including queuing, pay perimeters, and the management of visitor flow. But there is another, and even more significant, factor governing the nature of access to a sacred site and that is the nature of the sociopolitical control over that site which may, or may not, be vested in the same group that controls its day-to-day operational issues. Such control may determine who may use the site, in what way the site may be used, and for what purpose. Many sacred sites are the foci of complex political or religious power struggles, since to possess such a site is a territorial and political statement. These kinds of debate go back a long way in recorded history – entire wars such as the Crusades were, after all, fought to determine which political and religious regime was actually to control the sacred sites of the Holy Land. And the situation was not so simple as a straightforward conflict between Christianity and Islam, having built into it sectorial disputes between different factions inside both camps. Problems can also arise on a very small scale with disputes over the ownership of different parts of the same building. The Church of the Nativity in Bethlehem is effectively under such multiple ownership. Of the fifteen lamps around the Grotto of the Nativity marking the supposed site of Jesus's birth, six belong to the Greek Orthodox Church, five to the Armenians and four to Roman Catholics, with the different interests of the Churches maintaining a precarious coexistence through an intricate worship schedule. And a dispute over the control of that particular church was, after all, one of the causes of the Crimean War.

Today, it is possible to find many contemporary examples of contested heritage, where people ask the question 'whose site is this?' , but where the answer is not as simple as the equation of ownership with the adherents of a particular religious tradition. Disputes over the control of sacred sites take place at different levels, and between different sects of the same religion. An example of the latter might be Shia and Sunni Muslims at Mecca. Many such disputes are settled peaceably and there are numerous examples of sites sacred to different religious traditions and political divisions being managed equably for the benefit of all, such as Muktinath in Nepal. But this is not always the case. In Tibet, for example, under the repressive political regime of China since the 1950s, access to the most sacred sites in Tibetan Buddhism is at best restricted and at worst banned, for political, rather than religious, reasons. This kind of contested sacred heritage can be examined at different scales. Some examples may be of purely local interest, others may involve regional, national or even international interests.

At a purely local scale the possession of a sacred site may produce marked sociodemographic changes within a community. Such changes relate closely to local political situations, and are frequently forced upon a community when visitor numbers to a particular sacred site begin to rise dramatically. Generally, the economic impact of this activity is very positive for a community (as long as revenue-generating visitor services are being run by the community, not by outsiders) but other types of impact may be less agreeable. The following case study looks at the way in which tourism to the island of Lindisfarne off the Northumbrian coast of the UK has completely altered the nature of the village socially, spatially and politically.

CASE STUDY: THE ISLAND OF LINDISFARNE

Lindisfarne, off the Northumbrian coast, is – together with Iona – one of the most significant Christian pilgrimage destinations in the UK and a major cultural tourism attraction. It was a centre of Celtic Christianity, with a monastery founded by St Aidan who came there from Iona. It is famous for the great illuminated manuscripts called the Lindisfarne Gospels, made in Lindisfarne by the monks around AD 698, but now in the British Library. St Cuthbert, Lindisfarne's patron saint, died on the island in 698, and the monastery which housed his community was sacked by the Danes and eventually abandoned in 875. Today, the island of Lindisfarne, roughly square in shape and about a mile in length, has become a major attraction for visitors who walk round the village and explore the ruins of the priory and castle and visit the Nature Reserve on the north side. The Priory ruins are the remains of a refounded Benedictine abbey, dissolved by Henry VIII in 1537, and the castle is small, just twelve rooms, focused around a stone-walled garden designed by Gertrude Jekyll. Lindisfarne is part of a cultural route known as St Cuthbert's Way, consisting of a trail of accommodation and visitor facilities linking Lindisfarne with Melrose Abbey and offering a central booking facility.

Although there is no accurate count of visitors to the island, it is rumoured to attract more than 500,000 visitors/year, but it seems likely that this figure is exaggerated. Vehicle access is by means of a causeway that is only exposed at times of low tide, meaning that a visit must be carefully planned in order not to be caught unawares. Most visitors come by car or coach, although in summer there is a twice-daily bus. The one-mile causeway takes the shortest route across the sands linking the island with the mainland, but the site of an older crossing known as the 'Pilgrims' Way' is shown by a line of restored poles in the sand. This foot-way is still sometimes used by pilgrim groups. Some 165,000 visitors/year (Adams, pers. comm.) head for the seventh-century Celtic Church of St Mary the Virgin, which has some Saxon features and was the home of St Aidan after his arrival in AD 635. No admission fee is charged and, for this reason, the church attracts twice as many visitors as paying attractions such as Lindisfarne Castle or Priory, and donations from visitors assist with its upkeep, and that of neighbouring parishes. The area around the church, priory and museum becomes extremely congested in summer, making it difficult to see the appeal that the island had for Celtic monks drawn to windy, spiritual and empty places. Tour groups spend, on average, around two hours on the island though individual travellers usually stay longer.

Visitors to Lindisfarne must walk a third of a mile from the main car park to the village centre. Its central car park is now closed (except for buses and disabled visitors) but a shuttle bus is available at a cost of £0.70 to take visitors to the castle and around the island. The centre of the island becomes congested, especially in high season, when it may be difficult to buy food or gain access to a toilet. Lindisfarne Castle (in the care of the National Trust) is located quite a distance from car parks, requiring either a long walk or the services of the shuttle bus. It has lower visitor numbers than Lindisfarne Priory (controlled by English Heritage), for this reason. The Priory is open all year and in 1998 attracted 76,251, reflecting an 8 per cent increase over the numbers in 1997. Its management thinks that this is a direct result of the promotion of Christian Heritage year.

Figure 8.1 Minibus transport for visitors around the small island of Lindisfarne

Fewer than 150 people live on the island, although it is difficult to estimate the precise number since not all are permanent residents. The island's inhabitants are therefore outnumbered 400:1 by visitors. Lindisfarne was formerly a fishing community, but now only 30 per cent of houses belong to local people. The remaining 70 per cent are rental cottages or have some religious purpose such as retreat centres. This small population is served by five hotels/pubs, three guest houses/bed & breakfasts, three coffee/tea shops and seven shops, plus a post office and the shop attached to the museum and a sandwich stall in the street to cater to excess demand. All are extremely busy in high season. On average, the visitor to the island can expect to have around 30–80 other people in their field of view at any time (Fig. 8.1). The large numbers of visitors destroys the spirit of place that people expect: in 1998 one commented to the writer 'I thought it would be flat and deserted like the photographs'. Despite this and other complaints, many say that the site still feels holy. There are generally around 20–50 people inside the church, whose vicar (a well-known poet and liturgist in the Celtic Christian tradition) is often on duty to speak with tourists. The church offers three services each day, usually well attended, and there are some 50 bedspaces in retreat houses on the island available to religiously motivated pilgrims.

It is an irony that an island which has for so long been a symbol of piety and tranquillity should now have had that atmosphere swamped by too many visitors. Burns (1995) comments that 'residents of Holy Island say they are being swamped by too much religion'. This spatial and social claustrophobia is enhanced by the small size of the island, and the fact that it is cut off twice a day by the tide. There are fewer than one hundred buildings on the island, together with a couple of churches, hostels and a small ecumenical conference centre. Many of the buildings were originally the residences of local people but have now been bought up for visitor use. Some are places where local ministers of religion live, others offer a pilgrimage focus for particular religious groups. The former fishing community of Lindisfarne has virtually disappeared, and has been replaced by the growth of service operations to cater to visitors. Not all of these are owned by local people (a great source of resentment). Moreover, the tourism business is seasonal and the villagers suffer congestion in summer matched by desertion in winter when many of the hotels and shops close. In 1995 the United Reformed Church wished to build a manse on the island for their minister, but met with stiff opposition from local people who took the view that there was more than enough clerical housing on the island already. Local resentment has been fuelled by the fact that the price of housing on the island has risen, so that a small cottage on Lindisfarne can cost twice or three times as much as on the mainland (and such cottages seldom come on the market). No affordable housing is available for local people who complain that the existing working community is being squeezed out by religion. The case of the United Reformed Church produced particular resentment since although the URC has a 103-year-old lease on its church on the island, the church has no active congregation. Planning regulations have also been relaxed to allow more houses to be built for retired churchpeople wanting a base for a religious community. However, feelings now run so high that some positive steps are being taken to redress the balance in favour of local people, notably with the development of Kyle Gardens, five energy-efficient homes owned and managed by the local community.

However, the inhabitants of Lindisfarne have little choice but to welcome visitors to the island since it constitutes a public place. Fortunately, the villagers themselves are not part of the visitor experience unlike the inhabitants of the ultra-orthodox Jewish *haredi* quarter of Jerusalem known as Mea She'arim. Here, the local people themselves have become a reluctant tourist attraction for visitors seeking a diversion after a surfeit of the Old City. Many of the male inhabitants of Mea She'arim have beards and sidelocks in the fashion of Jewish sixteenth-century Poland; some still wear a long black caftan and all have black Homburg hats. Women wear long sleeves and wigs, head scarves or hats. Tourists ignore the signs that women should dress modestly (defined as 'the same as the locals') which has frequently resulted in intruders being stoned. A similar fate can befall cars which try to traverse the area on the Sabbath, and Mea She'arim remains an excellent example of the politicization of religious views, with spatial implications. The population dynamics of Mea She'arim have remained totally unaffected by its increasing popularity as a tourist attraction, since tourism is transient and visitors do not interact with local people. This is in direct contrast to the situation on Lindisfarne, where tourism has resulted in a complete change in the socio-demographics of the island community. Not that such changes can be totally attributed to tourism – fishing villages everywhere in the north of England have seen similar changes, but not to such a great extent. The economic benefits of tourism are insufficient to make the villagers comfortable with the dramatic changes which have taken place to their way of life. Political control has passed from the local community into the hands of incomers. Resentment is incurred against the owners of holiday homes which may be visited only a few days a year, when local people are unable to afford housing. The questions being asked revolve around the issue of ownership of the island. Who owns Lindisfarne? This is purely a local matter, and it is encouraging that planners are taking steps to redress the balance by the provision, for example, of alternative housing. But there are other sites whose heritage is contested at a national scale, as the following case study demonstrates.

CASE STUDY: CONTESTED HERITAGE AT STONEHENGE

Stonehenge is in many ways the symbol of England, a World Heritage Site and one of the most popular visitor attractions in the country. Not all visitors would describe it as a sacred site, and such sacredness as it possesses stems from religious traditions separated from those of today by thousands of years, undocumented and leaving only the stones as their memorial. Yet most visitors, although frequently disappointed with their experience, can at least feel the power and mystery of the place. Who owns Stonehenge? The land on which it stands is owned by the Department of the Environment, but its management is entrusted to English Heritage, a State-funded quasi-autonomous quango established by Act of Parliament in 1983 (Golding, 1989). The National Trust owns 1500 acres around the site and the Ministry of Defence owns large areas of Salisbury Plain which are frequently used for military exercises and include a nearby Army camp. In practice, the day-to-day running of the site and its infamously poor visitor facilities is in the hands of English Heritage.

Visitors are unimpressed by the lack of parking, inadequate catering and merchandising and excessive regimentation. Today's visitors are not allowed unlimited access but constrained by barriers because of fears of vandalism, although exceptions are made for academics and 'those in the advertising industry with enough money to pay for privileged access' (Bender, 1999:122). Golding (1989) reported an earlier survey suggesting that only 18 per cent of visitors thought their visit was good value for money, despite the spectacular nature of the site. Mass tourists arriving by bus have a dwell time of only 25 minutes (50 per cent of which is taken up with food, souvenirs and toilets). Such visitors greatly outnumber individuals or small groups, and visitation to Stonehenge is highly seasonal with the site deserted during the winter and highly congested in the summer. A great debate has taken place for nearly a decade about the construction of a new visitor centre, which might involve closure of roads, additional impact on archaeological sites and the surrounding cultural landscape as well as an impact on MOD housing and access to military sites. Current plans for the centre are costed in excess of £15m. In addition to submitting to normal tourist visits, Stonehenge becomes a focus for eclectic ritual activity at certain times of year, particularly around the summer solstice.

Druids started to come to Stonehenge in 1905 but until 1970 they were quietly tolerated as exotic and good for tourism. Photographs of white-clad Druids worshipping at the stones at the summer solstice were commonly seen. However, the tolerance exerted towards the small and well-behaved groups of Druids was not extended to less acceptable groups such as the New Age 'travellers'. Such 'travellers', also referred to as hippies, held a Free Festival in the field next to the monument from the mid-1970s to 1984, when over 50,000 people attended. Bender (1999), writing an interesting book on Stonehenge, aptly described it as 'a tacky tourist trap . . . which once a year, at the approach of the Summer Solstice, becomes a gulag' (Bender, 1999: 114). In 1985 five hundred 'travellers' (an assortment of mainly young people moving around the country in old vans and buses) who had come to the site to watch the sunrise were arrested, and 200 vehicles impounded.

Objecting to access for travellers while allowing access to Druids implies not only religious, but social, selectivity. Druids are perceived as harmless eccentrics, hippie travellers are widely thought to use their New Age beliefs as a cover for a drug culture parasitic on the state. Moreover, Druids appeared in only small numbers and travellers came in their thousands. And yet the more charitable noted that many travellers, although undeniably using the solstice as an excuse for a party, also saw Stonehenge as a place for spiritual and other celebrations, forming part of a seasonal circuit of summer festivals. Their New Age belief systems saw it as a source of psychic forces, energy fields and a convergence of Ley Lines. Public opinion did not favour the travellers, and by 1985 the National Trust and English Heritage took out an injunction enabling police to move them on, resulting in the violent showdowns of 1985 and 1988 (Chippindale, 1986). Today, matters are much more relaxed and policing is less repressive, but Stonehenge is still promoting a view of the past acceptable to the Establishment and in line with modern conservative sensibilities. Its real heritage is both political and contested.

Stonehenge is a unique, readily-identifiable symbol that fascinates visitors because of its temporal remoteness and the many archaeological puzzles connected to it that remain unsolved. It is on the itinerary of almost every international visitor to Britain and there can be few humans in the English-speaking world who fail to recognize its image. Since site access is not free, the level of control is greater, as Stonehenge may be a sacred site but it is also a commercial concern. Moreover, control of the site is contested not only by different religious factions but also by different political organizations. This is the reason why construction of a new visitor centre has been so long delayed. None deny the need for it, demonstrated by the fact that Stonehenge no longer features on overseas marketing material for cultural tourism in Britain since the poor facilities at the site have become something of a national embarrassment. There are tensions between factions coming from different angles, notably between the charitable sector (represented by the National Trust), the public sector (English Heritage) and the military sector. These are supplemented by tensions between local people and visitors, since the most favoured solution for problems of visitor pressure will probably involve closing at least one segment of a main road important to the local community. The current interpretation of the site, which visitors read on story-boards and in brochures, concentrates on its position in the national past and national identity, with a political emphasis stressing the empowerment of organizations to make people work. Pictures of gangs of men heaving heavy stones, supervised by a more leisured ruling or priestly class, commonly illustrate such material. Some would see this approach as selective, and it is certainly gendered as very little mention is made of the role of women. Common views see the sacredness of the site associated with rituals connected with the worship of the sun or moon, or for the renewal of seasons, or from unsubstantiated associations with human sacrifice. Archaeologists have different opinions about the reasons for the construction of Stonehenge and its significance to Bronze Age societies, but most accept that the construction must have been, at least in part, connected with religious or ritual activities. It is equally reasonable to question what function the site is now performing. In many ways it can be regarded as both museum exhibit and product image for consumption, rather than as a sacred site. Very clear parallels can be seen here between Stonehenge and Easter Island (Rapa Nui, p. 133).

Because the religious tradition for which the site may have been constructed no longer exists today, its current utilization becomes both contested and politicized. Recent ritual users have included both members of the Society of Druids and the marginalized 'travellers'. Both these groups live (though in different senses) outside the accepted confines of society, both are derided and have become figures of fun since their rituals and beliefs do not fit comfortably into the mainstream of contemporary British thought. For many believers in 'New Age' ideas, including 'travellers', Stonehenge is an earth energy symbol. Just because such views come from a marginalized minority does not necessarily mean that they are invalid. However, access to the site is controlled by an Establishment which, though politically diverse, shows a certain social unity which has set clear boundaries over which set of people are acceptable users/worshippers at the site, and which are not. This is not a unique situation: the example of the great Borobodor temple in Java has already been cited, where both political and religious factors have resulted in the exclusion of a particular worshipping group from a site that clearly belongs to their own tradition. The religious heritage of such sites is contested when they become players in political or social games, to emphasize the dominance of certain cultural groups, traditions or nationalities over others.

A fine example of this can also be found in the United States at the Alamo in Texas, which has become a national symbol presenting a socially biased view of history, largely developed for commercial gain. It has become a sacred site in American mythology, viewed as the location where the first definitive step toward Texan independence from Mexico was taken by a group of Anglo-Americans who voluntarily sacrificed themselves in a noble stand for freedom against numerically superior Mexican forces in 1836 (de Oliver, 1996). However, the Alamo, as a managed showcase for general public consumption, is a twentieth-century creation. It is located in San Antonio, a city with twice the average percentage of Latinos (55 per cent) as other locations in Texas. The Alamo is currently a temple or shrine to Anglo ideas in a sea of Latinity. Visitors are encouraged to adopt a meditative and reverent attitude to the site that presents a solemn, almost sepulchral, image of place. The nearby cultural landscape includes mostly streets named after Alamo-associated persons such as Davy Crockett, and the fort's distinctive shape has become just as familiar in the world of American advertising as Stonehenge is in Britain. Nearby, a large mall has been developed with the cultural monument serving as a lure. The whole Alamo complex has become a shrine and focal point for Anglo-American culture in a city dominated by Hispanic immigrants. This is politically sensitive at a time when many Anglo-Americans feel threatened by what they see as a rising tide of Hispanic immigration. This modern political socialization is contextualized by commodities, and a consumer landscape translates the traditional spiritual pilgrimage into commodity form. The Alamo, once a battlefield, has now become both shrine and political statement.

POLITICAL CONTROL OF SACRED SITES

The previous examples illustrate some ways in which control over sacred sites may be politicized at a local and national level, with consequent sociodemographic implications. However, right from the beginning of recorded history it is possible to find instances where national governments have exerted political control over such sites, limiting either access, freedom of worship or freedom of speech. This can also result from religious and political confrontation between different groups within the same religious tradition, as in the confrontation in Mecca between demonstrating Iranian pilgrims and Saudi security forces on 31 July 1987. This resulted in over 400 dead and possibly ten times that number wounded, an extraordinary event in what has always been an inviolable sanctuary, for in Islam it is virtually unthinkable for one Muslim to raise his hand against another in the Holy City. The incident reflected religious and political divisions within Islam, and happened at a time of rising tensions in the Gulf, and Arab attempts to internationalize the war between Iran and Iraq (Kramer, 1988). It also expressed pilgrimage tensions that date back to Iran's revolution, an event that kindled intense rivalry between Saudi Arabia and Iran over primacy in the Gulf, and in Islam. In the 1980s there was no *hajj* which passed without some incident involving Iranian pilgrims, a conflict which originates in the great historical animosity between Wahhabism, the source of Saudi Islam, and Shi'ism. Distrust between Iranian pilgrims and their Sunni hosts dates back to the sixteenth century, originating in a dispute over the succession to the Prophet Mohammed (Kramer, 1988).

Fortunately, there are many examples of sacred sites that welcome visitors from any religious tradition. Muktinath, the site in the Himalayas, is regularly visited by the King of Nepal to perform *puja* on auspicious occasions and, apart from Pashupatinath near Kathmandu, is the most sacred place in Nepal for Hindus and Buddhists alike. But Hindu *sadhus* are the only people allowed to sleep at the site, which was once on the ancient walking route from Kathmandu to Mt Kailas in Tibet. It is in Tibet that the best example of a repressive political regime controlling access to sacred sites can be found. The idea of Tibet as a sacred destination is very attractive to the West because of its perceived exoticism and mystery, but it is also a sacred land for Tibetans (Bishop, 1989). This mystique was reinforced by the fact that Westerners were not allowed into Tibet, with the exception of a few adventurers. Myths about Tibet and a desire to visit its cultural sites explains the overwhelming interest in visiting the secret Tibetan kingdom of Lo (Mustang) when it opened to visitors for the first time in the 1980s. Until the 1950s Tibet was a theocracy, ruled by a Dalai Lama (a reincarnation of the Bodhisattva Avalo-kiteshvara, or Chenresi in Tibet, the deity of compassion) as god-king. State policy was implemented through a monastic network. A Marxist interpretation of this system would suggest that the piety of Tibetans reflected coercion by a priestly elite acting in its own interests, but in effect it was also a demonstration of patriotism. Trade and economic development followed sacred sites and pilgrimage where people gained karmic and political merit. Pilgrim donations to sacred sites ultimately supported the state and were fundamental to the economy of a country where Church and State were integrated (Nowak, 1984). Pilgrimage routes and destinations became conduits and nodes in an emergent infrastructure, with pilgrimage affirming both individual and group religio-political identity as Buddhists and Tibetans. This all changed after the Chinese invasion of Tibet in 1959, after which the country became a vanished homeland to thousands of refugees. Yet its loss cemented a national identity in a way that can be paralleled by the attitude of Jews towards Israel after the diaspora.

The Chinese invasion resulted in a wholesale slaughter of Tibet's monks and nuns, sometimes in the most depraved ways, and the almost total repression of individual Tibetans' freedom of worship. It is estimated that one million Tibetans have been killed since 1959, with the result that they are now a minority in their own country. Chinese is now the official language, and more than 6000 monasteries and shrines have been destroyed. Tibet has had famines for the first time in its recorded history, and its natural resources have been devastated. Tibet's capital, Lhasa, has changed a great deal in the 40 years since the flight of the Dalai Lama in 1959. With the exception of the area around the great Jokhang temple it now looks like any other drab Chinese city with traffic jams, advertising hoardings, high-rise housing, pollution and 100,000 ethnic Chinese immigrants. Human-rights groups contend that the few remaining monks and nuns who show any independence are still liable to be tortured. Lhasa's main attraction for international visitors is undoubtedly the Potala palace of the Dalai Lama, built over a sacred cave in a rocky hill. The first palace was built in AD 637 and incorporated into a major structure more than 1000 years later, when the present palace was begun in 1645 during the reign of the fifth Dalai Lama. It was only slightly damaged during Tibetan resistance to the Chinese in 1959 and not sacked by Red Guards during the 1960s and 1970s, unlike most other Tibetan religious sites. This was apparently achieved through the personal intervention of Chou En Lai. As a result, all its chapels and artefacts are well preserved. The huge 130,000 sq m building was not only the residence of the Dalai Lama and his large staff, but also the seat of government, a school and a major pilgrimage destination since it contained the tombs of past Dalai Lamas. Before 1959 it was visited by thousands of Tibetan tourists each day. The building itself is a marvel, 13 stories high (117m) including 1000 rooms and 10,000 shrines, all built without a steel frame or nails but with walls strengthened by infills of molten copper. Like Stonehenge and the Alamo it is one of the world's most recognizable structures.

After an initial clamp-down on all manifestations of Tibetan religion some flexing-out of Chinese attitudes took place in 1979, when a limited revival of traditional pilgrimage was permitted and the Chinese government granted between one and two thousand tourist permits a year for international visitors. Independent tourism to Tibet was only possible after 1984, and by then annual visitor numbers had reached 40,000 and Chinese officials saw tourism as a revenue-generating activity. Consequently, some rebuilding of major monasteries took place, not to make amends but to provide better visitor attractions, as well as an opportunity to present a political message to the West. The Chinese justification for their invasion was the view that Tibet had always been a province of China, and this political message included Tibetans as noble savages and Lhasa as a Buddhist Disneyland (Klieger, 1992). Westerners were not fooled and China has been under continual pressure about its Tibetan policies, with little success. International visitors tended to seek out indigenous Tibetan, rather than Chinese, guides (sometimes with unfortunate consequences) and neglected state-run accommodation in favour of simpler Tibetan establishments.Tibet is still a magnet for local visitors even though the Dalai Lama is currently based at Dharamsala in India. This has been helped by Western interest in Tibetan Buddhism (there are more than 250 Tibetan Buddhist centres in the USA alone) and the country receives a continuous stream of pilgrims, climbers, and trekkers. Political controls have therefore not been totally effective – in December 1975 the Dalai Lama performed the Kalachakra Tantric initiation ceremony in Bodh Gaya, India. Tibetans crossed the border in such droves that an estimated 20,000 people overwhelmed border posts and got straight through. Today, limited religious activity is permitted in Lhasa under the watchful gaze of Chinese security police, and Indian and Nepalese tour operators employ refugee Tibetans. Moreover, limited pilgrimage activity is now allowed from outside Tibet. Since 1981 strictly controlled groups of Indian pilgrims called *yatris*, who follow pilgrim trails through Uttar Pradesh and across the 17,000-foot Lepu Lekh Pass, have been allowed into Tibet. Every year, 200 enter the country, in batches of 25 accompanied by Indian physicians, to be met by Chinese guards and taken by bus to the sacred Lake Manasarovar which, for Hindus, symbolizes the receptive female aspect of creation, the *lingam*. In 1948 some of Gandhi's ashes were scattered here.

The Chinese invasion of Tibet has almost destroyed its indigenous religion, and the associated pogroms have had a significant impact on its population. However, the slight relaxation in Chinese attitudes has at least made its boundaries more permeable and permitted greater access to the surviving sacred sites. Changes in political boundaries affect access to sites and tourist flows. For example, if the relaxation of frontier regulations between Israel, Syria and Lebanon becomes genuine (as seems likely to be the case) all sorts of new possibilities are opened up for Holy Land tours which would then be able to start, as well as finish, in Israel. Nowhere has political control over sacred places been more bitterly contested than in the Holy Land itself.

Access to the Western Wall in Jerusalem (usually known as the Wailing Wall) has always been a political hot potato. At present the Wall itself is separated off by a railing from a vast open esplanade which gives a good view and enables large groups of people to assemble (under strict security). The Wall itself has the same status for Jews as a synagogue, and the esplanade is a popular place for Jewish groups and

Figure 8.2 Jewish worshippers at the Wailing Wall, Jerusalem

families to assemble for prayer and festivals, and even to hold Bar Mitzvah services (Fig. 8.2). However, access to the site was not always this good and before 1967 only a narrow alley divided the Wall from the nearest houses. All this changed when bulldozers moved in, giving the Muslim residents only three days' notice to remove themselves before their houses were razed to produce the esplanade as it is today. No consultation preceded this action, which simply resulted from the fact that political power resided with the Jews, who utilized it to take whatever action they wished. Access to other sacred sites in Jerusalem may also be restricted for religious reasons, with Temple Mount being a good case in point. Temple Mount contains the Dome of the Rock, the holiest Muslim site in Palestine, located on Mt Moriah which is the traditional site (sacred to Jews, Christians and Muslims) where the prophet Abraham prepared to sacrifice his son. It also marks the site where Solomon is supposed to have erected the First Temple in 960 BC to house the Ark of the Covenant which his father King David had brought to Jerusalem. The First Temple was destroyed in 586 BC, the Second Temple consecrated in 515 BC (and rebuilt by Herod in 20 BC) but destroyed by the Emperor Titus in AD 70 following the First Jewish revolt. The Second Jewish Revolt in AD 135 resulted in Jerusalem being razed to the ground, with the exception of small fragments like the Western Wall. A mosque at the southern end of Temple Mount marks the place where the prophet Mohammed tied his winged horse al-Burak after reaching Jerusalem, and where he prayed in the company of the Archangel Gabriel before ascending into heaven on a staircase of light and returning to Mecca before dawn. Temple Mount is always accessible to Muslim visitors, albeit with notional restrictions on dress, eating and smoking, widely ignored by many Muslim families who bring a picnic. Certain parts of the complex are off-limits to all visitors and the Mount is closed to non-Muslims during prayer times. It is, unfortunately, always closed to Jews. Under Jewish law (not always observed by non-observant Jews and denied by many Jewish fundamentalists), Jews are not permitted on Temple Mount in case they might accidentally find themselves on the site of the original Temple's 'Holy of Holies' which was forbidden to anyone except the High Priest. There is a second reason for their exclusion, stemming from the belief held by some Jews that since the extinction of the red heifer of biblical times, whose ashes conferred ritual purity as specified by the Torah (Numbers 19:1–10), all Jews are now ritually unclean and thus unworthy to enter the site. One Jewish sect is attempting to breed the animal to avoid this prohibition. A third, and more recent, reason for Jewish exclusion from one of their own sacred sites dates from 1990 when an ultra-Orthodox sect (Ateret Cohanim) caused a Jewish-Palestinian riot by trying to place a foundation stone for a new temple. Their action resulted in 19 dead and three hundred wounded. An Israeli statute was passed forbidding Jews to pray on Temple Mount, even individually and in silence.

Tourism is not an equal-opportunity activity. It is often claimed that the opening of new exotic destinations or forms of special-interest travel discriminate against those who cannot afford the price or cope with the journey, but this has always been the case. Access to tourism destinations has always depended on an individual's motivation, financial state, gender, religious persuasion and state of health. As has been discussed previously, access to many sacred sites is physically impossible for disabled or elderly people or those unable to walk. The Via Dolorosa in Jerusalem, for example, includes several sets of extremely steep stairs. It culminates in the Church of the Holy Sepulchre where the final stages of the journey include the ascent of an almost vertical slippery stone staircase (admittedly equipped with a handrail but not with a one-way system). However, problems with physical access which exclude certain groups can be remedied by investment in appropriate facilities. Other means of restricting access, which include social, political and religious constraints, cannot be so easily solved. Mt Athos in Greece presents an example where access is restricted by gender. The first monastery on Mt Athos was founded by St Euthymius of Salonica in the ninth century and, 200 years later, after many other monasteries and chapels had been added, the place had a bad reputation for monkish debaucheries with visiting women. The reigning Byzantine emperor therefore decreed that nothing female (human or animal) should henceforward come within its limits and that rule survives into the present day, relaxed only for cats. Today, the Holy Mountain is a self-governing monastic republic dedicated to the single-minded preservation of the Greek Orthodox Church, which has implemented a compulsory access code. Control over sacred sites may be exerted by religious groups, as in this case, for the exclusion or inclusion of specific groups. It may also be social, excluding or including specific groups whose presence is felt by a governmental elite to be inappropriate, for whatever reasons. In many cases religious and political motives are tightly interwoven. Situations can change. Governments fall, national religious affiliations change and society becomes more tolerant, with the result that site access codes are altered. But the emotive character of sacred sites always makes them a suitable focus for making political capital.

CHAPTER 9

Secular Sites

There is a certain category of sacred sites which present especially interesting management challenges, yet belong to no religious tradition. For this reason they can reasonably be described as secular, yet this is in many ways a misnomer. Although not sacred in the religious sense nor are they profane, and although non-ecclesiastical they may be perceived as holy by their visitors. In terms of management they are usually under civil, rather than clerical, jurisdiction. They all share one unifying characteristic, namely that they are locations of outstanding significance to particular ethnic, racial or social groups. They come in many shapes and sizes. Some are memorials to a particular event, mute witnesses to something of such significance that a visitor who journeys to its location is effectively making a pilgrimage. Generally, they are of (relatively) recent foundation and many share the distinction of playing a significant role in the lives of living people, unlike the shrines, temples and churches discussed previously which, although also significant to the living, are also archaeological sites encapsulating (sometimes literally) the remains and cultures of the dead. Secular sites, as defined here, are a part of our contemporary culture. This creates certain management difficulties because here we have sites that may form an integral element of the life of some social group, family or individual. He, she or they may feel passionate about the site and its significance in a manner which has not been blunted by continuous repetition over millennia. Everything about the site forms part of their contemporary life and culture, a witness to something of great emotional significance whose memorial has to be managed with the greatest possible sensitivity. This can create management dilemmas. Tinkering with the interpretation of an archaeological sacred site may cause academic discussion or even mild controversy, but altering the way in which one of these sites is preserved or presented may actively impinge on the social or spiritual welfare of a particular group of people. Similar difficulties occur in the museum world, where it is a well-known fact that exhibitions of artefacts from the recent past are, in many ways, much more difficult to curate than those of the archaeological past. Anything belonging to historical or archaeological time can be challenged, questioned and reinterpreted, whereas ethnographic material of relevance to some contemporary society has to be treated with great respect. Every member of a visiting group can contribute some view or opinion on how the object was used, drawing from his or her own memory and informed by his or her own prejudices. An archaeological object, even if less well documented, is likely to be less contentious. Exactly the same phenomenon is seen on secular sites: an excavation in a Saxon graveyard, for example, may yield interesting archaeological information but is without relevance to people living today (except in the rarest of circumstances). However, altering some feature of a war cemetery or designing a new war memorial will be highly contentious, not only because it affects the living but also because it may reflect on the memories and deeds of those recently dead.

Secular sites, then, come in a range of shapes and sizes; all are in some way contentious, but the category is heterogeneous. Some are simply memorials to a single tragic event (such as the Hiroshima Peace Memorial) which act as a pilgrimage focus, and a place of reflection and meditation. Another category includes war memorials, battlefields and graveyards of which the most contentious are the most recent, in Europe those resulting from the First and Second World Wars. Thirdly, there are sites and museums associated with shameful episodes in human history. This category would include West African sites associated with the slave trade, as well as the South African prison site of Robben Island where Nelson Mandela was imprisoned for nearly twenty years. This site, now a museum and World Heritage site, has become both a pilgrimage centre and a shrine to a living man. Parallels can be drawn here with the many sites associated with the Holocaust, and in particular with former concentration camps such as Auschwitz and Dachau that serve as memorials and a terrible reminder of man's inhumanity to man. All these 'secular' sites can become centres of pilgrimage, and many include shrines, chapels, memorials and places of more formal worship. Many are the particular 'property' of a specific ethnic or social group whose 'ownership' of the site may give rise to conflict with visitors of different views – a matter discussed below in relation to the views of different racial groupings at Slave Route sites. Visits to such sites by 'believers', members of the particular tradition which it represents or commemorates, reinforces the boundaries of the group. Visits by non-believers, who do not necessarily empathize with or understand the nature of the event commemorated or celebrated, are often encouraged for educational reasons.

Particular site-management methods may be required, especially appropriate for emotionally sensitive historic sites whose collective histories are seen as living proof or representation of the collective history and/or social experience of any distinct group of people. Many of the sites have become formal or informal visitor attractions identified with human suffering and mass death, which means that the visitor experience is likely to be highly emotional. There is a school of thought (Foley and Lennon, 1996, Otto and Ritchie, 1996) that sees emotion as central to the provision of service quality; but controlling the public expression of emotion by large numbers of visitors, sometimes in disparate groups, can be very tricky. Visiting such sites is sometimes referred to as 'dark tourism' or 'thanatourism' (Otto and Ritchie, *op. cit.*), with such visits being made mainly for remembrance, but also for educational reasons. The provision of visitor facilities which in any way resemble entertainment at such sites is very difficult, and can provoke strong reactions. This can result from the availability of inappropriate merchandise as well as methods of interpretation that are seen as in any way trivializing the experience, or minimizing the significance of the site to its primary controlling group. Differences of opinion about what is appropriate has resulted in minor conflicts, most recently between serious pilgrims and supposedly frivolous tourists at the sacred mountain of Sri Pada, Sri Lanka, but there have been many far more serious incidents pointing up the emotive potential of such sites.

People with an emotional attachment to historical sites which are prominent in their history and life experiences as an identifiable group visit such sites with the desire to experience the affirmation of these expectations. Their image of place will have been formed as a result of personal and group history and beliefs. They expect the management and use of such sites to reflect their long-held expectations, which are inevitably biased in favour of their specific group. Kiley (1995) comments on the visibly different reactions of tourists to Cape Coast Castle, Ghana, a former slave fort in west Africa, contrasting the reactions of African-Americans making a secular pilgrimage with those of 'ordinary' tourists: 'The returning members of this diaspora sometimes get even more emotional on entering the dripping dungeons. Some burst into tears, or babble in the imaginary tongue of their ancestors. On one occasion an American (i.e. an African-American) hid in the cellars and attacked a British vicar from another tour group.' The African-American visitors pictured the misery of the slaves imprisoned in the castle, and projected their presumed emotions into themselves. The emotions turned outwards, with the visitors venting their frustration and resentment on others who were not thought to share the experience or were felt to be in some way members of the group that had caused it.

It is worth considering this example in more detail, since Cape Coast Castle as a visitor attraction and pilgrimage centre illustrates many of the problems faced by managing this type of site. Cape Coast Castle was developed as a visitor attraction by the government of Ghana as a peg for its emerging tourism industry and, together with the neighbouring Elmina fort, was designed to attract both African-American and Western European visitors. The government of Ghana also co-operated with other countries whose histories were also formerly linked to the transatlantic slave trade in joint tourism projects, culminating in the UNESCO/WTO-sponsored Slave Route Project. Cape Coast Castle is one of the oldest surviving exit points for slaves. It has become a major pilgrimage destination for people of black African descent, 30 million of whom live in the USA. Slavery has been common in many communities, although at different levels of intensity. However, for most societies today slavery is no more than an historical event. But to some (and in particular to African-Americans) things are very different. In the past the slave castles of Senegal and Ghana were centres of historical discovery, but now governments are beginning to exploit the economic benefits of slavery as a tourism product. This is a highly sensitive issue and one may question whether it is ethically reasonable to present this aspect of cultural behaviour commoditized for tourism. Many parallels exist here between the kinds of tourism product being developed around the slave trade and those associated with Holocaust sites.

CASE STUDY: CAPE COAST CASTLE – VISITOR REACTION AND RACIAL TENSION

The site has a long and complex history, generating interesting arguments over which period (and version) of its history should be displayed for visitors. At any visitor attraction, sacred or secular, those who possess authority may determine the nature of displays and interpretation to suit their version or perception of history. At Cape Coast Castle (Ghana) the Ministry of Tourism reluctantly agreed to portray the total history of the castle, not just that of the slavery era, although they were under strong pressure not to do so. Estimates suggest that at least 10 million Africans landed on the Atlantic shores of America between 1619 and 1808 (the legal end of the trade), with many more being smuggled in illegally until 1860 when the trade finally ceased. But it is possible that six times this number of people were captured, and lost their lives in storage and shipment. The trade was characterized by the appalling treatment of slaves, with many dying from shock, fear, and brutality made acceptable from a Western religious and social perspective that considered black people as subhuman.

Cape Coast Castle was set up as a visitor attraction with substantial government and aid funding. Latest available figures (1994, quoted by Austin,

1997) suggest that nearly 20,000 visitors per year come to the site, of whom 70 per cent are local Ghanaians. African-Americans form the other significant visitor group. The site is partly funded through government subsidy with supplementary funds generated from entrance fees, leasing of on-site shop facilities and rental of the main courtyard for 'appropriate' cultural events. An entrance discount assists local Ghanaians to visit the site, justified on the principle of ability to pay, and also to encourage local people to patronize the site as part of their history. However, African-American tourists see this as discriminatory, since they claim the site is also part of their history as well. Active conservation work is being carried out at the site, generating constant complaints from visitors whose 'sense of reverence' is disturbed by work-men. The reaction of African-Americans is especially interesting since they demonstrate a strong emotional attachment to the site. Austin (1997) completed a detailed study of visitors, and noted that Ghanaians regarded all non-Ghanaians (including African-Americans and other black African people) as 'tourists'. Moreover, for around 10 per cent of the African inter-viewees visiting the site was purely a leisure activity, producing no emotional impact. The highest level of emotional linkage came not from Ghanaians but from African-Americans, of whom 90 per cent gave race involvement as the reason for their visit. Around 30 per cent were upset by the presence of visitors from different racial groups, while this was quite unimportant to Caucasians. Many became obsessed with the 'how' and 'why' of the slave trade. Some were unable to accept facts that did not agree with their preconceptions, including the clear evidence that part of the slave trade was run by black Africans who had sold their own people for gain. The African-Americans preferred to blame white slave traders. African interviewees expressed concerns over structural works at the site, especially the whitewashing of the slave dungeons and reopening of the exit tunnels to the slave ships, which had been sealed. The site management regularly white-washes the dungeons, re-creating their appearance as it would have been during European occupation, but others see this as beautification. Austin summarized visitor emotions as follows:

- Africans – surprise, sorrow, amazement and anger that the enslavement of Africans did take place and in the way that it did
- African-Americans – sadness, disgust, anger and hysteria, with many actually tearful or crying, especially in the dungeons
- Caucasians – some disturbed, others feel sorrow and guilt, but generally such feelings are carefully concealed.

Tour guides at the Castle were uncertain whether they were merely supposed to be portraying the history of the site as a slave fort, or giving a full interpretation of its complex history, a conflict resolved by tailoring tour content to group motivation. African-Americans were surprised and insulted that local people considered them as tourists, since they saw themselves as reluctant migrants now returning home, and expected to be treated as such. Site managers frequently have to cater for aggrieved people who insist on special tours, sometimes without white visitors present, and they comment that the main visitor motivation is learning, but with elements of worship and leisure. The site has a powerful 'spirit of place' that affects the visitor irrespective of his or her background, but the durability of the experience must depend on how fixed and blinkered visitor attitudes are. Visitors should not be given a sanitized version of events, even if those events are painful or shameful. Current moves by the Ghanaian government to market the site simply as a tourist attraction (which it is for visiting businessmen with time to spare) are seen as devaluing its message. Cape Coast Castle is a site of pilgrimage, remembrance and (for some) self-discovery. Such a promotion de-mystifies the site's emotional appeal which is, after all, a selling point uniquely attractive to a clearly identifiable market sector.

The case raises a number of interesting issues, notably the different pre-tour motivations and images held by different racial groups. African-American visitors (the main commercially significant target market of the site) resented the castle being described as a tourist attraction (Austin, 1997) because of the connotations of leisure. For them it is a shrine, a symbol of injustice, a focal point from where they derive their history and traditions. For Caucasian visitors the site presents an educational opportunity, which may or may not contain any emotive content. But such Caucasians are sometimes identified, by African-Americans, as the enemy and treated as such. Aggressive visitor behaviour may result – is this the responsibility of management? In what way could management deter such behaviour? Increased security is only one answer, racially segregating groups might be another which, although practical, would perpetuate exactly the kind of racial and social divides that contemporary society is trying to eliminate. Surely the solution must lie in the nature of the interpretation. The presentation of such sites for general visitation offers an opportunity for society to heal the wounds of slavery, giving both blacks and whites the chance to come to terms with it. It also serves as a vivid reminder of a shameful episode which it is hoped will never occur again: reasoning identical to that underlying the opening of Auschwitz, or the encouragement of tourism to the 'Killing Fields' of Cambodia. It is also undeniable that Cape Coast Castle presents an opportunity for people to know and learn their history, except that (just as at Robben Island, p. 170) there will always be an element of society that are not interested in doing so. The Castle's management has attempted to encourage domestic visitation by instituting a discounted entry fee. Unusually, such a scheme has met with resentment from international visitors who seldom object to paying more than local people on the grounds that they receive similarly favourable treatment at home. In this case the key to the resentment comes in the different meaning that the castle has for international and local groups. The management has two basic options, one of which is to withdraw all admissions charges and replace them by voluntary contributions, and the second of which is to introduce a new non-discriminatory charge. This situation can be paralleled in the great debate that took place in the UK during the 1980s and 1990s over the issue of admission charges to cathedrals. Although visitors to sacred sites that charge for admission frequently complain that charging for access to the numinous is inappropriate, the same argument cannot be advanced here. Nor can the Castle afford to eliminate charges. The best solution would seem to be to introduce a flat-rate charge, and top end load services for international visitors such as specialized guiding, expensive merchandise or better catering to recoup the lost revenue. A less acceptable alternative would be to bite the bullet and ignore international complaints on the grounds that these represent less than 15 per cent of visitors. However, it is the reaction of the African-American group here that is especially interesting, since they clearly see the castle as sacred ground and their visit as a homecoming, articulated as a 'quest for their roots'. Such a motivation is common in all sites associated with the slave route, including the Ile du Goreé in Senegal and the various sites in the Gambia that were associated with the best-selling novel *Roots* by American author Alex Haley. These sites have been commoditized to attract African-Americans who wish to commune with the past without the obvious intrusion of the present, and are therefore scathing of anything which interferes with their vision. This may include unpleasant historical realities and a disregard for the obligation to present a reasonably unbiased interpretation of the chronology of a complex building. The nature of their experience is adversely affected when something (or someone) at the site causes their vision to falter. But if the purpose of opening the site is to encourage reconciliation, and to educate all elements of society about their history, then dismantling precon-ceptions (however they have been acquired) should, perhaps, be the primary educational function of the site.

HOLOCAUST SITES

Slave forts such as the Cape Coast Castle act as historical reminders and educational devices for visitors. They can evoke intense emotional reactions even resulting in inter-group confict – precisely that element of history that they are trying to eliminate. Managers of such sites may be accused of trivialization, the unacceptable commodification of historical events or biased presentation and interpretation. The same is true for events surrounding the sites and museums associated with the Holocaust, to the extent that some writers have now coined the term 'Holocaust Industry' which they see as a widespread but unacceptable level of commercially-driven interest in the Holocaust, detracting from its social and religious horrors. Elements of this 'Holocaust Industry' include former concentration camps, memorials and museums, most of which attract very significant numbers of visitors. Films can also be part of the phenomenon. For example, many Jews see films such as *Schindler's List* as trivializing events and issues surrounding the Holocaust. For Jews today anti-Semitism is not just a phenomenon of the past but still occurs in the present, just as racial discrimination is not ancient history for African-American residents of the United States but something with which they must contend every day. Each year, more and more sites associated with the Holocaust are becoming significant visitor attractions at an international scale. Airey (1998) examined the phenomenon of tours by international visitors to the Kazimierz district of Crakow in Poland, an area which contained the former Jewish quarter where many Jewish buildings, synagogues and memorials have been restored. Many of its visitors are Jews who also visit the nearby concentration camp of Auschwitz-Birkenau, also a World Heritage site, but others are tourists with historical or cultural interests stimulated to visit the site by a film. Kazimierz provided many of the backdrops for *Schindler's List*, and is preferred by visitors to the actual location of the Nazi-created Jewish ghetto and concentration camp that are across the river from Kazimierz itself. Visitors are choosing the site which is familiar from the cinema, rather than the genuine location where the events portrayed actually took place. They are selecting a constructed over an authentic history and, in doing so, transferring the sacred nature of the site from its real to an imaginary location.

Several concentration camps have now been opened to visitors, of which the best known are undoubtedly Dachau and Auschwitz-Birkenau. Dachau played a crucial role in the development of the concentration camp system in Nazi Germany and was considered by the SS as a model, a prototype later developed into death camps such as Auschwitz in Eastern Europe. During the 12 years of its existence, between 1933 and 1945, more than 200,000 prisoners were kept there under dehumanizing conditions, with in excess of 31,000 deaths recorded. Its remaining prisoners were finally liberated on 29 April 1945 by American Armed Forces. After liberation the grounds became run down, and for many years the site lacked a formal memorial. In the 1960s plans matured for a permanent museum laid out by Comité International de Dachau and financed by State of Bavaria. The grounds were rearranged and the camps cleared of thirty barracks formerly used for prisoners but now in decayed condition, and two new barracks were constructed for educational purposes. Such activities gave rise to much criticism. Although few objected to the construction of a memorial to the dead, a debate developed between those who considered that the camp should be allowed to decay naturally, and those who wished to restore part of the camp to something approximating to its former state. The reason for the final decision to clear dangerous structures and erect modern copies was that it was felt that such a solution offered the best educational benefits. On the twentieth anniversary of liberation the site was opened, later to be supplemented by educational facilities and a library. The Dachau Memorial Site and Museum at the former concentration camp now attracts almost 1 million visitors per year, and is the major visitor attraction within the Munich metropolitan area of Germany. It is deliberately negatively marketed – hardly advertised, not marked on the official Munich tourist map and often featuring only in small print at the end of regional guidebooks. Exact visitor numbers are not monitored as entrance is free, with guesstimates of visitor numbers taken at the Museum, which is the major attraction at the site. Foreigners outnumber German visitors, the latter arriving in large groups whereas the former (mainly Americans) are usually individual travellers or families. The site receives many Israeli and Eastern European visitors. It has been interesting to note, in view of the negative marketing which suggests that the site is something of an embarrassment to Germany, that there was a gradual increase in the percentage of German visitors to Dachau following its opening. In the late 1990s some 40 per cent of visitors were German, reflecting a wider acceptance of Dachau as an historic site significant in the cultural history of Germany. This by no means diminished its stature as a pilgrimage and mourning destination for the relatives and friends of those who died there, as well as their co-religionists. A visitor survey suggested that the motives of visitors could be either personal, political, historical/educational or humanitarian, but were generally a complex mixture of all of these. Personal motives dominated with former prisoners, their relatives and friends, while political motives were more important for groups suppressed under the Nazi regime including Trade Unions, Jewish communities and other social and religious groups who often participate in rallies, lectures and exhibitions on the site. Some visitors are simply motivated by general interest in learning about the site, and others by the humanitarian educational programmes which are offered, including summer camps targeted at young Germans. Dachau is now a permanent centre for international youth meetings. The growing popularity of a site with such painful associations is embarrassing to a large segment of the local population who resent the flourishing and exclusive attention given to the site as a focus for the entire area. The name of Dachau has itself acquired a symbolic meaning (Mayo, 1988). Attempts have been made to redress a perceived lack of balance by negative marketing of the activities at Dachau during the Holocaust and by placing increased emphasis on the reconstruction of the activities of the Resistance and anti-Fascist organizations in the period 1918–1945. The strategy involves a stronger focus on the pre-concentration camp history of Dachau, often with the omission or downplaying of Dachau during its concentration camp period. This is aimed at reducing perceived negativity, utilizing arguments already introduced in reference to Cape Coast Castle. At Dachau, they are remarkably ineffective as can be seen from the rapid increase in visitor numbers. However, this is another example of a complex site which, as a result of one phase in its history, has acquired a symbolic value synonymous with human rights abuses on an enormous scale. Very few visitors to either Cape Coast Castle or Dachau will be aware, before their visit, of the earlier history of the site. Even fewer will care. Tinkering with interpretation and massaging site history to downplay significant events will have no effect on visitor numbers, nor will it redress the wrongs done there. Its only effect will be to indicate that the site managers are embarrassed by the site and unable to grapple with the presentation of its emotive history. Managing such sites is delicate, but it is significant that at Dachau the site is succeeding in attracting increasing numbers of German visitors, many from a generation to whom the events of the Holocaust are merely a shameful historical episode, from which many hopeful lessons have been learnt.

WAR MEMORIALS

Dachau commemorates the dead, and interprets the political and social events which resulted in their death, provides a focus for grieving and educates an entire generation about a significant historical episode. Commemorating the dead is a delicate issue. War memorials serve a similar function as political memories, not only as the foci of family or military pilgrimages but also as a remembrance of the futility of war, its waste and its stupidity. The more recent the war the more controversial the memorial, and none more so than the Vietnam Memorial in Washington, DC (Mayo, 1988; MacCannell, 1992). This was designed by a young Chinese-American architect Maya Ying Lan, and constructed in the form of five enormous Vs dug out of the side of a grassy knoll. It is faced in polished black granite and simply engraved with the names of the 58,022 Americans who died in Vietnam. The monument is possibly the most powerful war memorial ever constructed, and one of the most subtle. Too subtle for many, who felt that something more overtly martial was proper. The simple directness of its design in black – the colour of mourning – is striking, and has a hidden meaning: most of the US servicemen who died were African-Americans. The monument thus expresses a suppressed truth, and the literal and figurative convergence of its V-shapes and shiny surfaces permit reflection, in both senses of the word. When visitors approach they see themselves reflected in the monument as though being involved in the war. As they walk along the wall, as it gradually ascends, visitors see their reflections become bigger until at the top they see their own faces with the names of dead soldiers written across them. This gradual build-up increases the emotional power of the site, causing people to cry, and also to reflect on the meaning of the monument and, inevitably, on the war that it commemorates. The path round the memorial is one-way and, as the visitors walk on, the names of the dead pile up above their heads, written against the reflected sky. At the end, where the names of those last to die are listed, the polished surface breaks slightly to the right so that where visitors' reflections are the smallest and the listing of the dead the longest the entire memorial reflects itself, and the images of visitors reflect themselves also, meeting themselves in the list of dead. Despite its power and much critical acclaim there have been complaints that the monument is 'insufficiently representational'. These have now been addressed by the erection, in front, of three figures of bronze combat soldiers, which appear to be looking at the memorial. Mayo (1988) commented 'they appeared to me as if they have just paused to gather enough strength and courage to go over the memorial to find their own names' (p. 282).

War memorials can be big business for the travel industry. In the UK the Royal British Legion has a Special Tours Department which arranges group visits to war cemeteries, war memorials and campaign areas in Europe, Africa and the Far East. Many participants come to visit the personal grave of a friend, family member or fellow soldier. The anticipated age structure of the group may be inferred from the fact that each tour is accompanied by a doctor or nurse, and the widows of soldiers killed in either the First or the Second World War are charged a fraction of the normal rate, subsidized by the Ministry of Defence. As the battles which those cemeteries commemorate become part of history books and school syllabi, they gradually evolve from memorial to educational opportunity, with the best remaining an amalgam of the two. Nowhere is this seen better than at Ypres, where half a million men were killed and more than a million wounded during the summer of 1914. 'A more sacred place for the British does not exist in the world,' said Winston

Churchill in 1919. Ypres – Wipers in soldier and schoolboy slang, is, like Dresden or Hiroshima, a town whose symbolic significance in the history of war is ineradicable. A new Flanders Fields Museum has been developed in the reconstructed Cloth Hall. Here, a visitor receives not just an admission ticket but an identity card of one of the thousands of soldiers of his or her nationality (British, French, Belgian or German) who were going to die near the site. The card contains a photograph and the dates of birth and death of the soldier, and as the visitor goes through each section of the museum, the card can be inserted in a computer to discover the progress of the soldier at each stage of the battle. It is a brilliant piece of interpretation, telling the story of the war through the eyes of an everyday soldier rather than a historian. The museum makes an interesting use of interactive multimedia, creating at times an almost palpable sense of the fear that each soldier felt, the tremendous noise of constant artillery bombardments, and the stench of corpses. Displays are accompanied by the testimonies, poems and trench diaries of soldiers presented on interactive CD-ROM in kiosks in every section of the museum (Wullschlager, 1998). Ultimately, both the overall story and its eclectic asides are both a memorial to the dead and a warning to the living, appropriately located at a site whose name is virtually synonymous with the pointless slaughter of the First World War.

CEMETERIES AND CATACOMBS

Cemeteries and catacombs provide another category of memorial, varying in type from the ordered rows of white crosses found in wartime battlefields to the architectural complexities of Highgate Cemetery in London or Père Lachaise in Paris. Cemeteries perform multiple roles: they are partly memorial, they act as foci for grief, they may be of great historical or architectural interest and many have developed as pilgrimage centres because of some particularly famous person buried there. The management of such sites has a spatial element, since they may have evolved both vertically and horizontally over very long periods of time. There are also issues of conservation, though seldom problems with authenticity, and certainly issues of multiple use since many cemeteries have considerable recreational value as green, tree-lined open spaces popular for walks and even for picnics.

Highgate Cemetery in north London covers an area of 37 acres, where development was started in 1839. It was originally one of a loop of seven burial grounds built to cope with the rapidly-expanding population of Victorian London when existing cemeteries could not cope. About 167,000 people are buried on the site, in 52,000 graves, its most famous occupant being Karl Marx. The cemetery is a mixture of gravestones, memorials, mausoleums (some up to three storeys high) and catacombs, and its management has a chequered history of trying to raise funds for conservation. The Friends of Highgate Cemetery (FOHC) were formed as a registered charity in 1975, to start work to halt the decay of the site. In 1983 it was declared a place of outstanding historic and architectural interest and five years of formal restoration projects were started, financed by a partnership between FOHC and government. In 1985 the government department English Heritage started to assist FOHC in a continuing programme of repairs to buildings and monuments. Burials resumed in 1981, but the costs of running and maintaining the cemetery now mainly come from grants, donations and other FOHC fund-raising activities. The cemetery is divided into two parts, east and west. FOHC opened the eastern cemetery to visitors, admission being free to 'grave owners' [*sic*] and FOHC members and £1 to others. The western cemetery does not have such good access, although guided tours are run at £3 for an hour, and there are ongoing programmes of building and restoration. Karl Marx's grave remains a place of pilgrimage for those who share his political views. Flowers are always to be found on his grave which is, by an irony of fate, located opposite that of Herbert Spencer the Victorian philosopher who coined the terms 'evolution' and 'survival of the fittest'. The proximity has led to many quintessentially English jokes about Marx and Spencer. In 1983, the centenary of Marx's death, marchers came to hold a ceremony by his grave but got lost in the notoriously complex site. FOHC also provides an information service for those wishing to trace relatives that they think might be buried there since, in common with most cemeteries, there are only patchy official plans and records. Again, like many cemeteries, Highgate houses a wildlife project and provides a safe home for wildlife.

The Cimetière de Montparnasse in Paris has a similar range of attraction for visitors. It has the graves of Simone de Beauvoir, Alfred Dreyfus, Jean-Paul Sartre and numerous artistic figures. The Père Lachaise is probably more famous and significantly larger at 44 hectares and 100,000 burial spaces. It has received an extraordinary 1 million burials since opening, showing why cemetery plans are so seldom comprehensive. Some of the most famous graves are near the entrance in Boulevard de Menilmontant and limited map coverage is available, enabling fans to locate the graves of Oscar Wilde, the rock singer Jim Morrison, Marcel Proust and Frederic Chopin. All are visited by secular pilgrims, but their popularity varies. The colossal ornate tomb of Oscar Wilde gets a great deal of attention in the form of notes, flowers and memorabilia, whereas the small, clean marble tomb of Chopin seems seldom visited. The Père Lachaise has a series of guidebooks to help leisure visitors and pilgrims negotiate its maze of graves in their park-like setting (Le Clère 1990). It often figures in the top ten of cultural tourism attractions in Paris.

Similarly, the San Michele cemetery in Venice, in existence since the early 1880s, has also become a visitor attraction. It was once described by Jan Morris as 'wide and calm, a series of huge gardens, studded with cypress trees and awful monuments'. Originally it consisted of two separate islands, now joined, and cluttered with tombs. The cemetery dates back to when Napoleon's occupying force told Venetians to start burying their dead across the water, rather than in the town of Venice itself. The graves are on short-term lease with bodies in each row of graves allowed to decompose for 10–12 years. After that time they are dug up and cremated, with the ashes of occupants whose families can pay for reinterment being transferred to small metal boxes for permanent storage in smaller (waterproof) containers. This is an improvement – in less sensitive times, remains were dumped on the ossuary island of Sant'Ariano. The custom of temporary occupation of graves in areas of high water table is not uncommon – a similar situation is found in New Orleans. At San Michele floods present a problem, and coffins must be set 3.1m above the water line, rather than below ground. New occupants for San Michele are delivered by aquatic hearse or funeral gondola (also a tourist attraction) and the fifteenth-century church and convent on the island are on the tourist route linking the main city to the island of Murano, famous for its blown glass, by *vaporetto*. A design competition was held in 1998 for the best use of the last remaining space on the island, which will be developed to add 15 per cent more space to the cemetery as well as a new chapel and crematorium at a cost of £5–6m.

San Michele also performs different functions. For native Venetians it may house the graves of family members, but it is also a tourist attraction. Some cemeteries which play similar roles have to cope with huge numbers of visitors. At Arlington National Cemetery in the USA, 4.5m people arrive each year to pay homage to the American military heroes, presidents and other public figures who are buried there, and to their memorials in the grounds. In addition to this tourist traffic the site is also an active military cemetery with twenty new additions each day. The large visitor numbers necessitated the opening of a new visitor centre on 16 January 1990 near the entrance and metro station, which provides historical information and grave-site locations. It was constructed by the US Department of the Army at a cost of $18.7m and has a solemn, dignified feel, emphasizing the ceremonial approach to the cemetery down Memorial Drive. Arlington's most popular attractions are the graves of President Kennedy and his brother Robert, and the memorials to the battle of Iwo Jima and the space shuttle *Challenger*.

Special challenges are presented if the cemetery is located underground, in which case it is known as a catacomb. Some cemeteries include catacombs, as in Highgate, but the most famous catacombs are not necessarily purpose-built, nor exclusively used for burial. Paris has a series of catacombs constructed in late Roman times as gypsum and limestone quarries, 10–35m below the city. In the late 1700s they were used as a repository for overflow from overcrowded cemeteries, and visitors are allowed access with regular tours scheduled. The Catacombs of Rome are much earlier in date, beginning in the second century with excavation continuing until the first half of the fifth. At first they were just burial places where Christians gathered to celebrate funeral rites, anniversaries of martyrs and of the dead. They were sometimes used as places of refuge during the persecutions as Mass could be said there, but their wholesale utilization as the hiding places of early Christians was invented for novels and movies. After the persecutions, and especially during the time of Pope Damasus in 366–84, they became real shrines of the martyrs and the centres of a pilgrimage tradition that continues to this day. Christians preferred these underground cemeteries and rejected the pagan custom of cremation, wishing to be buried as Christ was buried because they felt that their bodies would one day rise from the dead. This created a great space problem, solved by the economical, safe and practical solution of catacombs which were cheaper and easier to dig than large patches of open ground, at a time when most early Christians were poor. Christians wished to be together even in death, which reinforced their sense of community, and the catacombs could also be used for meetings and the display of Christian symbols. Today, five of Rome's most famous catacombs (St Agnes, St Priscilla, St Domitilla, St Sebastian and St Callixtus) are open to the public, all under the control of the Vatican's Pontifical Commission of Sacred Archaeology. Guided tours are arranged in ordinary visiting hours with the possibility of special archaeological visits or the celebration of Mass. More than 60 catacombs remain closed to the public, totalling hundreds of miles of galleries. Thousands of pilgrims come each year to pray and worship at the graves of martyrs and to see the paintings and inscriptions which constitute an archive of the early Church and document the usages, customs, rites, beliefs and doctrine of the times. The Vatican is keen to emphasize that a visit to the Catacombs should not be merely sightseeing from ghoulish motives, but should constitute a pilgrimage of faith.

POLITICAL SHRINES

Not all pilgrimages of faith are made to sites that commemorate the dead. The examples quoted above include locations that enable people to remember certain historical events, to empathize with certain communities, to mourn, or to learn. But not all secular sites commemorate the past; there are some sites which have acquired sacredness not exclusively by their association with the previous events but by association with current events or living people. Of these, easily the best example is provided by Robben Island, off the coast of Cape Town in South Africa. Robben Island has become a worldwide icon of the universality of human rights, of hope, peace and reconciliation. Although linked inextricably in the public mind with Nelson Mandela, imprisoned there for nearly twenty years, it housed many others who gave up their freedom in the process of building a new and democratic South Africa. Another famous prisoner, Walter Sisulu, wrote 'the name Robben Island is inextricably linked to the struggle against colonialism, for freedom, democracy and peace in South Africa. Robben Island's notorious history as the place to which so-called undesirables of our society were banished . . . should be turned around into a source of enlightenment and education on the dangers of myopic philosophies, social and economic practices whose primary and sole objective is the oppression of one group by another' (p. 4 of Robben Island: nomination file for World Heritage Status Government of South Africa, 1999).

CASE STUDY: ROBBEN ISLAND: SHRINE, MONUMENT OR MUSEUM?

Robben Island is located some 30 minutes by ferry off the coast of Cape Town. It is an island some 475 hectares in extent with a complex cultural landscape of which the high security prison is the main attraction for visitors. Robben Island's history is documented as far back as 1488, and it contains many structures from the Dutch East India period, the succeeding English occupation with its churches and institutions to house lepers, as well as the famous maximum security prison. Within the prison, 'B section', the wing where the political prisoners were held during the 1950s–1970s, has been maintained in the state at which prisoners experienced it during that period. It contrasts with the orderly village of the warders elsewhere on the island, with its abandoned swimming pool and crazy golf course. Nelson Mandela spent nearly twenty years on the island as prisoner 488/64, and his cell within 'B section' is the prison's most famous attraction. The rest of the prison has been left as it was at the moment when it was transferred from the Department of Correctional Services to the newly-established Robben Island Museum in 1997. It has an air of abandonment and helplessness, enhanced by graffiti and the presence of small pieces of broken furniture. The prison, village and other buildings including a Muslim shrine or *kramat*, and Second World War bunkers and gun emplacements are located within a surreal landscape whose most prominent indigenous members are a large colony of jackass penguins, who co-exist with

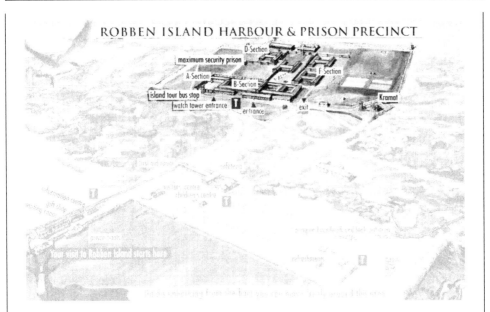

Figure 9.1 Visitor attractions and facilities at Robben Island, South Africa

introduced species including ostrich and European fallow deer. The rocky shores contain many wrecked ships and during the winter there are 8–10 days when seas are too rough for visitors to reach the island.

The change from closed-access prison to open-access museum came abruptly in January 1997, with the museum forced to open at a couple of weeks' notice as a result of political pressure. No formal planning had been carried out, and no visitor facilities installed. In 1999 Robben Island was declared one of South Africa's first three World Heritage sites, together with Greater St Lucia Wetlands and Sterkfontein fossil hominid sites. Currently, Robben Island Museum (RIM) is financed by both State and donor funding from overseas, sponsorship from the private sector and revenues from visitor services such as shop, ferry, post office and catering. At opening it was decided that the carrying capacity of Robben Island was 1200 visitors/day on the condition that the service infrastructure be upgraded. Visitors pay a fee of R100 (about £10) which includes the ferry trip, a tour of the prison and an optional tour of the island. The ferry departs from Cape Town's premier tourist attraction, the redeveloped Victoria and Alfred waterfront, with several trips a day. When on the island all visitors must stay in guided groups. Within the prison some of the guides are ex-political prisoners who can recount their own stories of prison life, greatly enhancing the quality of the visitor experience and generating an authentic spirit of place. Despite poor

Figure 9.2 A former prisoner, Lionel Davies, acts as a guide for visitors to Robben Island

visitor facilities there is generally a high level of satisfaction with the experience, especially for specific items such as the 'Cell Stories' exhibition that uses recorded voices and photographs to recount the story of inhabitants of different cells. Visits to the communal cells are also popular, but the star attraction is undoubtedly Nelson Mandela's cell, which has been preserved virtually as a shrine. Outside the prison the bus tour of the island also receives high marks, as does the Penguin Boardwalk near the harbour.

A recent extensive consultancy study by KPMG has been completed as part of the process of creating an integrated tourism development and management plan for the island (Keyser, pers. comm.). This is necessary as South Africa has experienced rapid growth in tourism in recent years, suggesting that visitor numbers to Robben Island are likely to rise steeply as well. In 1998 over 830,000 overseas tourists visited the Western Cape region, and Robben Island has the potential to become the cultural tourism anchor for its entire tourism product. In 1997 Robben Island received 300 visitors/day, with a total of 100,000 received during its first year of operation. This almost doubled to 188,000 in 1998, and increased to 235,000 in 1999. The highest monthly visitation of 32,000 was achieved in December 1999, in excess of 1000 visitors/day. Increasing levels of demand are likely and the greatest challenge to the island's management is to reconcile their desire to welcome visitors to a shrine to progress while still retaining a spirit of place and generating income. Not an unusual problem for a sacred site, but one made complex by the fact that its sacredness is so recent and, indeed, embodied in a living man.

Many of the difficulties experienced in managing a sacred site like Robben Island stem from the fact that it is inextricably associated in the minds of most international visitors with its most famous prisoner, Nelson Mandela, and is thus functioning as a shrine to the living. Mr Mandela himself is comfortable with his cell being opened to the public, but emphasizes that recognition should also be given to the thousands of other fellow-prisoners rather than concentrating on just one individual. The prison went out of use less than a decade ago, which makes at least one element of the cultural heritage of the island very recent indeed, within the lifetimes of many people who lived and worked on the island during its use as a prison. Many of the ex-political prisoners incarcerated there are now key political figures in the new South Africa, and some of the former wardens are now employed in its tourism industry. For many South Africans Robben Island is a prohibitively expensive destination to reach – its admission charge of R100 is more than the average local weekly wage – with the result that its visitors are predominantly from overseas. This somewhat negates its function as shrine and political statement and a new pricing structure is necessary to increase accessibility to all South African people, perhaps including off-peak tickets for domestic visitors. Another difficult issue is posed by the possibility that the island's tourism services may be extended by developing luxury VIP accommodation. For many people Robben Island is sacred ground, not to be profaned by conference accommodation with *en suite* bathrooms. For others the island is a potential money generator, and also an opportunity to present a symbol of reconciliation and peace for both past and present in the new South Africa. Establishing appropriate levels of catering, accommodation and merchandising within such a complex brand is very difficult. What is appropriate merchandise? At present the island souvenir shops sells teddy bears with prison tee shirts that are thought by many to trivialize the whole experience. Opinions also vary about whether interpretation of the island should encompass its whole history or just focus on one period, a dilemma already encountered at sites associated with the Holocaust and the history of slavery. Moreover, the entire concept of the island as a shrine to a living man will need reappraising after Mr Mandela's death, when the island is likely to become a major pilgrimage centre, far more significantly associated with his life than his birthplace or last residence. At present RIM is trying to be everything to all, and it has had a comparatively short lead-in time to develop a distinctive product with no time for planning before its opening. The next few years will show a new direction and vision. Increased visitation generates revenue, but also may degrade the environment and over-utilize its resources. Already, the prison itself is overcrowded at times, removing part of the atmosphere of desolation that forms part of the experience.

Robben Island may be compared with other sites that have unique symbolic significance in a universal context, and which may also act as the focus of a pilgrimage or perform the function of a shrine. Its situation is not necessarily comparable with other prison islands such as St Helena, place of final exile and imprisonment for Napoleon Bonaparte from 1815 until his death in 1821. St Helena has historical but not quasi-religious sacred-site status. Nor do other famous prisons such as Devil's Island, off the coast of French Guyana, used by the French as a high security prison whose most famous inhabitant was Alfred Dreyfus. Nor are there many similarities with the island of Alcatraz near San Francisco in the USA, which was closed as a prison in 1963 and is now open as a museum. Rather more relevant sites of secular pilgrimage include the Statue of Liberty at the entrance to New York harbour, which has come to symbolize the spirit of freedom offered by America to refugee immigrants. It is now a World Heritage Site, often regarded as an icon of freedom. So is Independence Hall in Philadelphia, where the Declaration of Independence and the American Constitution were signed in 1776 and 1787, respectively. These sites, together with Ellis Island, attract American visitors because of their historical significance and family histories, both reinforcing the concept of nationality and retaining memories of the homelands from which the immigrants came. Other secular pilgrimage sites include the Hiroshima Peace Memorial (Genbaku Dome) in Japan. The guidebook to Robben Island ends 'you have participated in a pilgrimage, a journey on Robben Island which, we hope, will inspire you to make the world a better place'. In many ways this is the mission shared by the sites considered within this chapter. All are sacred, in the sense that they have special, sometimes ritualized significance to a particular group of people. All are of immense symbolic significance in the history of the world. Many commemorate shameful historical events but some, including Robben Island, demonstrate a triumph over such inhumanities and a genuine move forward.

CHAPTER 10

Reflections

Earlier in this book the idea of pilgrimage as a sacred journey was considered, with associated issues of motivation, information, companionship and experience. The term 'journey' implies a spatial relationship between places, at least between the point of origin and the destination, supplemented in a pilgrimage by the fact that the route itself is an important component of the experience. There is also an extensive literature exploring the idea that the process of tourism itself represents a sacred journey (Graburn, 1989), as a result of its included rituals, ceremonials, human play, and cross-cultural aesthetics. Tourism can be seen as a special form of recreation, or play, which involves travel and 'getting away from it all'. It affords relaxation from tensions, and opportunities for reflection, whether or not those opportunities are realized in the context of a sacred site. There is also a long tradition in anthropology of the structural examination of events and institutions as markers of the passage of natural and social stages in life. This stems partly from Durkheim's (1911) notion of the contrast between the sacred (the non-ordinary) experience, and the profane. The alternation of these states, and the importance of the transition between them, was first used in the nineteenth century in various analyses of the almost universal rituals that emphasized the process of leaving the ordinary. The rituals, by sacralizing the process, elevate participants to a non-ordinary state where marvellous things happen, and the converse process of desacralization equates with a return to ordinary life. For a worshipper, such rituals might involve pre-departure preparation such as a ritual bath, the donning of special clothing, or the packing of a bag with worship-related materials such as scripture, prayer books or ritual objects. For the tourist leaving for a journey the stages are similar: before departure, complex plans are made to allow the individual to make the transition from home to holiday relatively painlessly. This might involve the making of complex domestic arrangements varying from pet care and medical provision to making a will. In the case of a journey this can be taking out additional insurance, making farewells to friends, almost a symbolic death. The tourist will leave home dressed in holiday clothes, with a carefully packed bag including items specifically holiday-related, such as reading material for the beach, sun creams or guidebooks. The return process will also be managed with equal care, and the most sensitive points in the process are the actual transitions from home and to home, where arguments and stress are most likely to occur as the tourist makes the transitions between normal and holiday states.

Time has a pattern, and the transitions between the stages are marked by formalities. The travel involved in tourism is more than geographical movement but is also a symbolically altered state. For Westerners who value individualism, self-reliance, and the work ethic, tourism is sacred in the sense of being exciting, renewing, and inherently self-fulfilling. Is it any wonder that tourists are disappointed when their chosen fantasies don't turn out as planned? Leach (1961) suggests that the regular occurrence of sacred–profane alternations provides a measure by which society has always divided up time. In all human cultures the year's progress is marked by a succession of festivals, representing a temporary shift from the profane to the sacred, and back. Within our own lives such festivals are marked from the domestic level (by birthdays) to national level (by Bank Holidays) with additional layers of formal, ritualized events produced by religious festivals and, in the West, by events such as Christmas and Easter which combine religion, holiday and family gathering. The holiday provides just another annual marker, a means by which the holidaymaker enters an alternative culture and becomes a different person (often with different cultural, ethnic and behaviour norms) when at his or her holiday location. We can therefore see many parallels between tourism, in a recreational sense, and visiting sacred sites. Indeed, MacCannell (1992) argued that tourism has become a secular substitute for organized religion, with interpretations of authenticity containing critical representations of good and evil which function as a religious text for modern man. This has generated an interesting supplementary literature in the sociology of tourism (e.g. Allcock, 1994).

It is interesting to compare these ideas with more conventionally religious definitions of sacred places. The following comes from a letter of Pope John Paul II concerning his millennium pilgrimages to the places linked together in the Christian history of salvation.

My meditation turns to the 'places' in which God has chosen to 'pitch his tent' among us (John1:14, cf. Exodus 40:34–5, 1 Kings 8:10–13), thus enabling man to encounter him more directly. At first sight, it may seem puzzling to speak of precise 'spaces' in connection with God. No less than time, is not space completely subject to God's control? Everything has come from his hands and there is no place where God cannot be found. Yet this does not take away from the fact that, just as time can be marked by *kairoi*, by special moments of grace, space too may by analogy bear the stamp of particular saving actions of God. Moreover, this is an intuition present in all religions, which not only have sacred times but sacred spaces, where encounter with the divine may be experienced more intensely than it would normally be in the vastness of the cosmos. In relation to this common religious tendency, the Bible offers its own specific message, setting the theme of 'sacred space' within the context of the history of salvation. On the one hand, Scripture warns against the inherent risks of defining space of this kind, when this is done as a way of dividing nature. On the other hand, the Bible does not exclude a cultic use of space, as far as this expresses fully the particularity of God's intervention in the history of Israel. Sacred space is thus gradually 'concentrated' in the Jerusalem Temple, where the God of Israel wishes to be honoured, and, in a sense, encountered. In the New Testament this concentration of sacred space reaches its summit in Christ who in his person was the new 'temple'. The mystery of the Incarnation therefore reshapes the universal experience of sacred space. (http://www.vatican.va/holy_father... I_let_30061999_pilgrimage_en.html) accessed 22 June 1999)

This passage contains a number of interesting issues. First, although the Pope is admitting that God can be found everywhere, He is also present in a special way at some locations where His presence has been particularly felt. This related closely to the typology of sacred sites presented in Chapter 1, which include memorials to particular religious and supernatural events, as well as locations which com-memorate the lives of those endowed by God by particular grace (in the Christian Church this would include all saints and martyrs). The Pope has defined sacred space as somewhere that the visitor can feel the presence of God, both part of normal time and space but also separate from it. The relationship between these ideas and their modern contextualization within the literature of tourism and visitor behaviour will be explored in the rest of this chapter.

SITE MANAGEMENT CHALLENGES – AN OVERVIEW

The definition of a sacred site needs to encompass five factors:

* how is the site recognized?
* who owns it?
* who has rights of access?
* what does the site mean to different individuals and communities?
* what is its relationship to both the living and the dead?

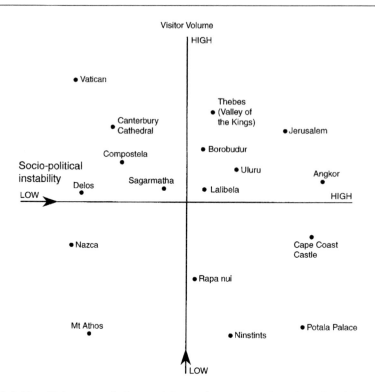

Figure 10.1 Classifying sacred sites – visitor volume vs socio-political stability

The word 'sacred' is derived from a Latin term which technically means 'restriction through pertaining to the gods', and implies that such sites come with inbuilt restrictions and prohibitions on human behaviour, and the observation of rules regarding them. These may not always be compatible with cultural tourism. It is frequently difficult to convey a concept of sacredness across cultural boundaries. In England, for example, the concept of sacredness is mostly derived from a Christian heritage which does not include a dimension of the sacredness of land, but this is diametrically opposed to the view of the sacred that might be expressed, for example, by a Native American. Fig. 10.1 plots the relative volume of visitors to a selection of sacred sites against the perceived degree of socio-political instability. Visitor volumes are clearly relative, and the term 'instability' is used here to mean anything from a distant threat from terrorism to disagreement between national government policies and those of a religious, social or political group with a vested interest in the site. Thus we see that a site with very high visitor volume and high uncertainty inevitably has management problems (such as Jerusalem). The Valley of the Kings (Thebes) in Egypt also has high visitor volume but a slightly less elevated uncertainty factor due to security improvements, whereas remote sites such as Ninstints in Canada not only have few visitors but are located in a politically stable area. However, this combination does not necessarily eliminate adverse visitor impact; at Nazca in Peru, for example, there are many worries about vandalism of the famous Nazca Lines. High uncertainty may also be created if the visitors are differentially motivated, and may thus react to the site differently. A classic example occurs as the slave fort of Ile du Gorée where unpleasant incidents have been reported where African-Americans emotionally affected by the site interacted aggressively with Europeans. On Rapa Nui (Easter Island) which is part of Chile there is an emergent political movement to reclaim the island's Polynesian heritage from its present Chilean control (Shackley, 1998e). Native people throughout the world are becoming increasingly vocal about who has the responsibility for managing their sacred cultural heritage (Carmichael *et al.*, 1994). Such locations often connect with what the Western world calls natural features (mountain, rivers, caves) but for many native people the notion of a sacred site carries with it a set of rules and regulations regarding visitor behaviour, and implies a set of beliefs to do with the non-empirical world.

A rather different view of site management issues is obtained if we plot visitor numbers against the emotive or spiritual quality of the site (Fig. 10.2). Sites which

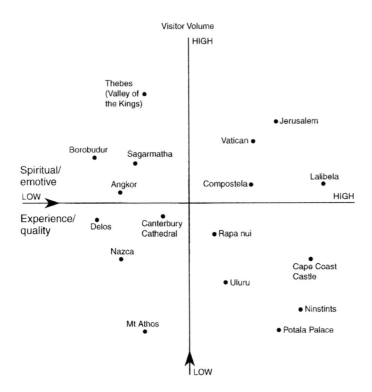

Figure 10.2 Classifying sacred sites – visitor volume vs spiritual and emotive quality

Figure 10.3 Sterility at the Borobudur temple in Indonesia, now located in an artificial parkland setting

provide the highest quality of visitor experience are emotive (Goreé, Ninstints), generating a powerful 'spirit of place' even if (perhaps especially if) visitors numbers are low. But the nature of the emotional or spiritual impact received by the visitor clearly varies with his or her motivation and cultural background. Tibetan Buddhists are more affected by the Potala than ethnic Chinese, since it is important to their own sense of national and religious identity. The rock-cut churches of Lalibela in Ethiopia (Carlisle, 1998) are of outstanding religious significance to the thousands of Coptic pilgrims who throng them each year, but to the European visitor may appear dark and tawdry. The nature of the experience obtained at Angkor Wat is affected by the persistent terrorist threat surrounding the site, and in any case can be described as more architectural than spiritual. The same is true for the Borobudur temple, where any spiritual experience is militated against by crowds of persistent hawkers, and by the site's location surrounded by artificially planted manicured green lawns. Archaeological sites like Delos, although constructed as sacred sites, have very little emotional appeal for the majority of visitors, since they are not 'working' spiritual sites. Places of high emotional impact also have problems with safety – a classic example is the famous 'Jerusalem effect' which regularly hospitalizes several dozen people a year overcome by emotion and hysteria when visiting the city.

The nature of the management challenges faced by sacred sites is not just related to difficulties with cross-cultural interpretation, but also depends on the physical structure of the sites. Some are isolated, others form part of a complex of buildings, some constitute integral components of large urban centres. The historic World Heritage-listed centre of Cracow, for example, includes 300 historic town houses, 58 churches, 600 historic buildings and 30 museums. Sacred sites are not only powerful cultural symbols but they need to present the visitor with an evocative experience by creating a visitor environment within which the original spirit of place is retained, while still creating adequate facilities and providing sufficient information. This is notoriously difficult to do, unless the site is extremely remote. The inaccessibility of the Native American Haida site of Ninstints in Canada contributes to both its lack of serious management problems and the high quality of visitor experience. At the other extreme the Valley of the Kings at Thebes (Egypt) sees 3000 visitors per day and has appalling management problems compounded by difficult conservation requirements and dire traffic congestion.

The easiest sites to manage are those where stability is high even if visitor numbers are high (such as the Vatican or Canterbury Cathedral) since this stability and control permits the development and implementation of effective visitor-management systems. Borobudur has become Indonesia's major tourist attraction, but is difficult to approach as a place of pilgrimage. Many Asian Buddhist visitors who come in spirit of reverence resent the fact that the temple is not freely open for worship, and indeed Borobudur is an island of Buddhism in a country that is now 90 per cent Muslim. This situation is analogous to that of the Christian monastery of St Katherine in Sinai. The management of sacred sites may need to be extremely sensitive, and difficult decisions must somehow be made. Auschwitz, for example, one of the largest Nazi extermination camps during the Holocaust, exemplifies the need to care for different ethnic and religious sensibilities. The site is not exclusively a memorial to Jewish dead (although these are in the majority) but is also recognized by Christians as a shrine to St Maximilian Kolbe, a Polish priest-martyr. The camp was restored by the Polish government after the Second World War but under Communism its guides were notorious for their anti-Semitic attitude, and displays in the museum still concentrate on Polish Christians. The building of a convent next door to the site by Carmelite nuns angered many Jews who felt it was another attempt to make Auschwitz into a Christian Polish shrine, and the sisters were relocated in 1993 (Adelsberger, 1996). Auschwitz now has the atmosphere of a museum, complete with interpretation for visitors including a documentary film and signboard in five languages. But the site also retains its sacredness as visitors, responding emotionally to grief and horror, perform ritual actions such as praying, lighting candles and laying flowers. Historians, Jewish survivors and the Polish government are currently debating whether the site should be managed as a museum to educate the public, or as a religious memorial. If it is to be a museum then some people feel that this should include rebuilding to enhance the visitor experience, including offering visitors the opportunity to experience the horror of entering the notorious 'shower rooms' and then seeing the crematorium. Others find this idea offensive, arguing that it would turn visitors into voyeurs and cheapen 'holy' ground.

Visitors to sacred sites often complain that the sheer pressure of numbers prevents them experiencing the numinous, and some site-management strategies have been developed to address this issue. At Westminster Abbey in London, which receives 2.5 million visitors/year (up to 17,000/day at peak times), much anxiety had been felt about stress to both buildings and visitors and a new policy, 'Recovering the Calm', was instituted in 1998. In an increasingly secular world visitors to a church do not necessarily know accepted codes of behaviour and upset worshippers by loud chat and milling around. Westminster Abbey had become a convenient waiting room or meeting point in central London, and the new plan involved a raised admission charge as a deterrent. Visitors were encouraged to be quiet and follow a well-marked route. Results seem to indicate that worshippers have returned in increased numbers, and criticism of the admission charge has been addressed by creating a quiet area in the nave for prayer, accessed by a special door. The plan required capital investment and staff training for a new 'ministry of welcome', and not all sites have either the funds or a management system to operate such procedures. Nor do all sacred sites need silence to preserve a sense of the numinous. On the island of Mont-Saint-Michel in France, for example, the vast monastic structure is an intrinsic part of a noisy commercialized urban area full of souvenir-sellers, probably much as it always was. Here the abbey was secularized after the French revolution but monastic life was resumed in 1966 for the 1000th anniversary of its foundation, with the community providing an interesting and unusual temporal management reversal. Many of the problems encountered in coping with visitors to the world's sacred heritage are also worsened by difficulties with ownership and the need to balance the requirements of visitor and visited. At Lalibela in Ethiopia, for example, the site is owned by the Ethiopian Orthodox Church but without properly-determined boundaries. Tourism provides vital revenues to support (among others) 560 priests and deacons, paying for salaries, festivals and the upkeep of churches (Carlisle, 1998), but the price being paid for unlimited and uncontrolled access is severe erosion of this fragile and non-renewable resource.

individual to withdraw from the complexity of public roles into private realms for self-gratification, whether in fantasy role-playing, netsurfing or practices designed to recover the inner self. In many ways this use of the Net is a type of tourism, which instead of exploring the external world creates a world for the individual. Individuals develop techniques to recreate a calm, centred internal world for themselves at a time when the external world is full of increasingly frantic activity. That world may include elements of traditional sacred rituals such as herbal oils, candles or incense as well as meditation or other practices designed to enable the person to identify the essential him or her in a world where this may be no longer clear. Externalizing these ideas accounts for the resurgence of interest in pilgrimage as a sacred journey of purification, at the end of which the real individual emerges.

The case study of Stonehenge discussed in Chapter 8 illustrated the phenomenon of social spatialization. The site is overburdened with meaning, and despite its ancient origins all the meanings given to the site today are modern, including the Druids whose society was founded at the beginning of the eighteenth century, although they present a claim to an unbroken line back to earlier times. Stonehenge is not just contested heritage where old and new interpretations of the significance of the stones fight it out; it also demonstrates the use of an ancient site to legitimize different sets of practices and individual lifestyles. The concepts of both heritage and festival are related to fundamentally opposing conceptions of time (Heatherington, 1992). Heritage implies continuity and a link with the past, but festival is about opposition to temporal authority. The archaeologist sees Stonehenge as a ritual site to be picked over and catalogued, mapping a dead time. The heritage tourist is also exploring a dead space, but nostalgia and the attempt to possess something different from the present leads to a re-temporalization of heritage space. The site becomes a space to be preserved rather than used, to be gazed upon but not changed, touched or used (Urry, 1990). Thus, when attempts are made to radicalize the use of that space, a dissonance arises. Exactly the same phenomenon is seen when attempts are made to modify sacred sites by the addition, subtraction or alteration of their features, perhaps to allow for some more contemporary use or the changing nature of their worshipping community. Because the space has become something to be gazed at, a space to be preserved intact much like a painting, the idea of altering the frame or adding a few more strokes of paint is generally fiercely opposed. At Stonehenge the visitors are worshipping the aura of the present, which they see as a living ambience created by the stones. It is interesting that such beliefs are held by an essentially nomadic element of society who exist disjunctively to everyone else but whose lives have some internal structure imposed by seasonality and festivals (Maffesoli, 1989).

Cultural tourism is sometimes regarded as a means by which the tourist achieves a level of personal transformation as a result of his or her visit to a symbolically significant destination. It is easy to see how this concept can be valid in the context of, for example, a pilgrimage to the Holy Land or a visit to a particular sacred shrine. However, it is less easy to see when the site becomes increasingly secular (although it is possible to identify considerable overlaps between the categories) such as a museum or visitor centre. Some would view museums as the settings for rites of passage which make us more worthy members of our own culture, although this seems excessively idealistic. The experience of visiting a sacred site, even when one is not actively involved in its 'ownership', undeniably inculcates a sense of history and tradition, a grounding in a particular belief system which the casual visitor can reject or convert into worship.

Contemporary humanity has a fear of chaos, produced as a result of modernization when both society and human relationships may be temporary. One result is to invent new rituals and new sacred sites, which may involve consumption and shopping (Shields, 1992). Another is to reinvent rituals and reuse ancient sacred sites, sometimes in new ways. Delaney (1992) commented on the History Hall of the Canadian Museum of Culture and the role it plays in developing good Canadian citizens by the purchase of Canadian knowledge and identity. The Hall is seen as ritual space, a place set aside or specially created by knowledge-possessing members of society in which a ritual (in this case the induction of new recruits) will take place. The new members must enter the special place, pass through certain rites, gain knowledge and pass out at the other side to gain full membership of the group. Ritual space needs to create a sense of otherness with its surroundings. It need not, and should not, be conflated with sacred space in the sense of belonging to some organized religion. Indeed, there could be good arguments for the identification of certain publicly utilized areas as ritual space which might include both mall and pub. Ritual space, *sensu strictu*, should divorce the participant from his or her surroundings so that the space becomes complete on its own, achieving a sense of timelessness or perhaps timefullness in which all sense of time is collapsed into a particular time frame. It is this sense of timefullness, that visitors to sacred space remark on but are unable to describe, which creates a powerful 'spirit of place' that affects visitors, and is affected by them. Foucault (1986) developed the term *heterotopia* for such ritual spaces, commenting that 'There also exist, and this is probably true for all cultures and all civilizations, real and effective spaces which are outlined in the very institution of society, but which constitute a sort of counter-arrangement of effectively realized utopia, in which all the real arrangements, all the other arrangements that can be found within society are at one and the same time represented, challenged and overturned: a sort of place that lies outside all places and yet is actually localizable.' (Foucault 1986: 15). To penetrate a heterotopia needs special permission and takes place after performing a certain number of gestures. One can see the similiarities here between the idea of sacred site as heterotopia and the overlap between sacred and secular sites, sacred and secular heritage and some aspects of contemporary cultural practices. Access to such sites is controlled by gatekeepers, but the rules for access are generally well known. However, when these rules are changed (perhaps by the introduction of a pay perimeter) or when the nature of access to the site is altered, both observer and site user become concerned. The sacred heterotopia exists out of time; attempts to lock it within a temporal framework and manage it as a business are doomed to failure. The process of initiation within the space involves the visitor submitting his or her senses and spirit to the perceived surroundings and actions of the space, in order to create a link with greater forces at work there. The ways of doing this are controlled by gatekeepers, who manage and conserve the rituals surrounding the site. When their activities extend into the contemporary business-related world, roles get confused and the visitor is unable to place a spiritual and temporal perimeter around the site, and becomes confused since the site no longer represents a space apart from the everyday world, but merely an extension of it. In a sense, the visitor both consumes the site and is consumed by it. The plays of Bertolt Brecht illustrate this point. Brecht considered that the psychic distance between viewer and play needed to be maintained in the theatre. Without appropriate distance between viewer and play the viewer would not be able to interpret what he or she was seeing, or to learn from the experience. Extending this argument into other performance fields should mean that the spectator at a sacred performance (such as dance rituals), from which he or she is separated by vast cultural distance, should be able to gain a clearer idea of what the performance is all about that someone enmeshed in the religious tradition represented by the dance. But of course this is not the case, as the watcher is unable to interpret the dance at more than a superficial sensory level without some form of interpretation or script. This does not mean that the impact of the performance is lessened, rather that it is different depending on familiarity with the concepts being portrayed. The same is true in the consumption of built heritage, whose impact on believer and non-believer alike may be just as great, though totally different.

Sacred space is complete and self-referencing, a system composed solely through signification of itself (Baudrillard, 1988) which creates nostalgia through 'a proliferation of myths of origin and signs of reality' creating 'a resurrection of the figurative where the object and substance have disappeared' (*ibid*.: 170). This is analogous to Foucault's final characteristic of heterotopia, 'creating a space of illusion that reveals how all real space is more illusory' (Foucault, 1986:17). The space offers compensation to those whose identity and history cannot be found or experienced in the realm of everyday life (Delaney, 1992).

VIRTUAL TOURISM?

It is a curious paradox that the contemporary resurgence of interest in a quest for the numinous, manifested in visiting sacred places, may eventually result in their closure. The writer has previously described this phenomenon as the 'Galapagos Effect', in the context of wildlife-based tourism, with its basic principle defined as 'the more fragile and endangered the site or species the more likely people are to wish to view it before it disappears, and the more likely visitor numbers are to grow rapidly'. It is interesting to speculate what form this phenomenon will take in sacred sites, many of which are already challenged to manage excessive visitor numbers. The most likely portfolio of solutions is management-based, as discussed in Chapter 5 above, but one alternative is that site will be visited virtually (on the net) rather than actually (on the ground).

God (however defined) is now big on the Internet. Religious sites are multiplying every day with some becoming extremely lucrative. Such sites are attracting venture capitalists and raising questions about the ethics of raising money from religion. An example is beliefnet.com which offers an online spiritual community for prayer but also carries advertisements. This religious market has been estimated at $40 billion/year. Online religious businesses include spiritual and religious tours to the Holy Land, Rome and Tibet. The tours can be actual (with the website used as a means of gaining information and booking) but they can also be virtual (with the website itself constituting the tour). Still other websites act as advertising for individual sites, churches, sects, cults and synagogues. Other sites such as Ibelieve.com, faith.com and mypotential.com have been besieged by venture capital investors (Steiner, 2000). New developments include funeral-cast.com which (for a fee) will camcast a burial live over the net so that people can take part in the ceremony even when not present. Almost all religious organizations and Christian churches have a web presence (with the exception of the Amish and the Shakers, whose sites are hosted by non-group-members). Some new Virtual Churches have been developed on-line to be non-denominational. Many established churches use their websites as both explanation and noticeboard, but some also exercise on-line ministry such as counselling and Bible courses. The net is unsurpassed as a networked medium between human beings, but only between those beings (or their representatives) with the education, training and IT equipment to take full advantage of it. At present, one of the major religious uses of the web is the transference of information between people with similar interests or members of religious organizations. The development of the cyberspace pilgrim site of the Order of St Benedict (http://www.cbsju.edu/osb) is a case in point.

Virtual religion is not only well established but has some interesting temporal and spatial realities. After a disagreement with the Vatican in 1995, the Roman Catholic Bishop Jacques Gaillot was dismissed from his See at Evreux in France, and consigned to the diocese of Partenia, actually a strip of uninhabited desert in Algeria. Gaillot responded by moving to Paris and developing a mission among the homeless, while at the same time establishing (with Papal permission) a Virtual Diocese in cyberspace. It is noteworthy that the Holy See's press release said that the Pope had urged Gaillot to 'commit himself more and more to the service of ecclesial fellowship' (Zaleski, 1997: 3). The virtual diocese of Partenia (http://www.partenia.org) is a fully empowered Catholic diocese which reaches thousands, potentially millions, of people via internet access. In what way is this kind of access to virtual religion and the development of virtual religious communities in cyberspace likely to reshape the spiritual life of our species and affect its propensity to visit sacred sites? One effect must be to broaden access to religion, but another is to potentially erode ecclesiastical hierarchies and change the way that we worship, not just within the Christian tradition. The web is organized laterally, not vertically, and websites bend the contours of our realities both physically, spiritually and psychologically. Websites also have infinite linkages, meaning that it is impossible to establish the boundaries of the religious communities that they represent, in any meaningful way. But websites also deal only with two-dimensional realities: no worshippers at Cyberchurch can (yet) smell the incense, although the combination of website with virtual reality makes this a likely future development. Since the online world is a world of mind alone various serious theological questions evolve: does this separation of mind from body have any effect on the nature of the human spirit? Do the artificial life-forms that populate the net have artificial souls? What effect does the web have on consciousness and on attention as a basic tool of spiritual reality?

Many writers on cyberspace talk about the net in the sort of evolutionary terms that Teilhard de Chardin wrote about, as a step to global consciousness. Teilhard identified consciousness with love, which connected, synthesized and held the entire universe together from individual quantum event upwards. Other writers have even suggested that the web is a holy tool, intended by God to help humanity. In practice, communities on the web do not seem especially divergent and few would admit to feeling the presence of God in cyberspace. One problem seems to be the limitations of the net as a communications medium. The subtle life-force energies (*prana*) which nourish the individual human being behind the words which s/he utters are missing, giving virtual communication a curiously sterile feel. The space left by this absent *prana* is filled by self-projection. Working with computers seems incapable of replicating true spiritual development which incorporates the truth of suffering engendered by having a body. Virtual communities do exist, but cyberspace does not ensure community, as the connectivity which it fosters is too often a one-way broadcast flow of information. Where there is interactivity on line, as in a chat room, community, in its broadest sense, can begin to exist. But most successful virtual communities are actually reinforcing and developing the boundaries and networks of 'real' communities established in the real world. Yet by enabling experiments such as Partenia, cyberspace can create new forms of faith communities that exist on a global level and are based on deep personal interactions. These need not necessarily be divorced from the needs of the larger societies in which they are embedded. It seems undeniable that the net communities do indeed represent spiritual tourism sites in some form, attracting pilgrims and worshippers who have made a journey, providing information, access, explanation and community. Sacred sites can now be virtually visited for a number of reasons, some cultural, some spiritual, with their web presence sometimes constituting a preliminary to, and sometimes a replacement for, the actual visit.

A POSTMODERN ESCHATOLOGY

Of course, it is not possible to repress the past without denying the future: postmodernity is itself a symptom of the need to suppress bad memories of Auschwitz, Hiroshima, and the other genocides on which modernity was built (MacCannell, 1992). Thus, the central drive of postmodernity is to stop history in its tracks, and the central drive of postmodern tourism is to discover places that seem to exist outside of history: unspoiled nature and 'savagery'. Fukuyama commented

> At the end of history the struggle for recognition, the willingness to risk one's life for a purely abstract goal, the worldwide ideological struggle that called forth daring, courage, imagination, idealism, will be replaced by economic calculation, the endless solving of technical problems, environmental concerns, and the satisfaction of sophisticated consumer demands. In the post-historical period, there will be neither art nor philosophy, just the perpetual caretaking of the museum of human history. I can feel in myself, and see in others around me, a powerful nostalgia for a time when history existed (Fukuyama 1993: 18).

And it is that nostalgia, of course, that created a heritage industry which continues to expand and diversify. That nostalgia for greatness, for spectacle, for spiritual nourishment also stimulates the endless demand for pilgrimage, whether sacred or secular, where the visitor can be physically located at a point where significant events happened, removed temporarily from the concerns of the workaday world and its rampant consumerism. Perhaps it is that phenomenon that makes the association of merchandising with sacred sites so repugnant to many. Within the Christian tradition, the distinction between sacred and secular is encapsulated in the story of Christ's cleaning of the temple when He symbolically removed commerce from a sacred site using a whip of cords.

The quest for the numinous seems inextricably connected with a distancing of the visitor from the world, accomplished in the context of a sacred site by the crossing of a perimeter into sacred ground. Fukuyama's vision of a postmodern world where no great art is made will intensify the human need to visit sites where the art of earlier eras is preserved, especially sites whose art and architecture are a testament to the glory of something both eternal and invisible. Sacred sites will become the locations where humanity, mired in a bog of secularity, can still admire the view of the numinous. They will become beacons testifying to quite different value systems. It has been interesting to note, in recent years, the increasing popularity of houses of religion as places of retreat and even as training grounds for battle-weary businessmen. This phenomenon is matched by an emergent literature of business texts drawing on the sacred as a means of interpreting the values of the modern world, and changing them (e.g. Handy, 1996). Only by removing themselves from the world, albeit temporarily, can individuals change their personal focus from an obsession with outward things to a quieter and more reflective consideration of inward things, things of the spirit, things neglected in daily life, for which there is no time. This book has looked at the abandonment of millions to religious ecstasy in the great feasts and dances of Asian festivals, and methods for regulating crowds numbering hundreds of thousands in St Peter's Square. Such people are temporarily removed from the concerns of daily life, immersed in a crowd of fellow-believers, a temporary member of a large group of people welded together in community of purpose.

Current fashions in movies tend to favour both reappraisals of unpleasant events in a more favourable light (e.g. *The Thin Red Line, Saving Private Ryan, Schindler's List*) as well as fantasy films (Disney), science fiction and horror. These different genres actually have something in common, since they transport the watcher beyond the confines of his or her mundane life and enable him or her to speculate on the existence of something more. The means by which this is accomplished is immaterial, but varies with the tastes and motivations of the individual. Attendance at a *Star Trek* convention is, for some, no less a pilgrimage than walking the road to Compostela, and has many of the same motivations (Porter, 1999). At the former, tourists include individuals who role-play, and identify with mythical characters, changing themselves from who they are today into persons or beings that they would like to be. The motivations of visitors to sacred sites that form part of our global heritage are not so very different. All are seeking an experience to change them, but not all are seeking that experience for the same reasons. The managers of sacred sites have to cater for this need while avoiding bringing the attendee down to earth. The experience should be essentially spiritual, uncontaminated by technical and commercial realities. Sacred sites should offer the attendee a window on infinity. As Albert Einstein once famously said, 'The fairest thing that we can experience is the mysterious'. It is the task of sacred sites to manage the mysterious and reach for the sublime while coping with the prosaic. Whatever the shape of the postmodern world, increasing numbers of people are going to be looking at sacred sites for some means of defining a more acceptable reality.

Bibliography

Adelsberger, L. (1996) *Auschwitz: A Doctor's Story*. Boston, Mass.: Northeastern University Press.

Ahmed, Z. (1992) 'Islamic pilgrimage (Hajj) to Ka'aba in Makkah (Saudi Arabia)'. *Journal of Tourism Studies* 3(1), 35–43.

Airey, D. A. (1998) 'Cracow (Poland)', in M. Shackley (ed.) *Visitor Management; Case Studies from World Heritage Sites*. Oxford: Butterworth-Heinemann, pp. 46–66.

Airey, D. A. and Shackley, M. (1998) 'Tourism development in Uzbekistan'. *Tourism Management*, 18(4), 199–208.

Allcock, J. B. (1988) 'Tourism as a sacred journey'. *Society and Leisure*, **11**, 33–38.

Allcock, J. B. (1994) 'Sociology of Tourism', in S. F. Witt and L. Moutinho *Tourism Marketing and Management Handbook*, 2nd edn. New York: Prentice-Hall.

Amoako-Atta, B. (1995) 'Sacred Groves in Ghana', in B. von Droste, H. Plachtor and M. Rossler (eds) *Cultural Landscapes of Universal Value: – Components of a Global Strategy*. Gustav Fischer Verlag /Unesco Stuttgart, pp. 80–96.

Austin, N. K. (1997) *The Management of Historical Sites of Emotional Significance to the Visitor: the case of the Cape Coast Castle*. Unpublished PhD thesis, Scottish Hotel School, University of Strathclyde.

Baddeley, O. and Brunner, E. (1996) *The Monastery of Saint Catherine*. London: The Saint Catherine Foundation.

Bahn, P. and Flenley, J. (1992) *Easter Island, Earth Island*. London: Thames and Hudson.

Barbeau, C. M. (1963) *Totem Poles* (2 volumes). Ottawa: The Queen's Printer.

Baron, R. and Byrne, D. (1987) *Social psychology: Understanding Human Interaction*, 5th edn. Boston: Allyn and Bacon.

Baudrillard, J. (1988) 'Simulacra and simulations', in Poster, F. (ed.) *Jean Baudrillard: Selected Writings*. Stanford: Stanford University Press, pp. 56–83.

Bauer, Y. (1996) 'The impact of the Holocaust'. *Annals of American Academy of Political and Social Science*, **548**, 14–22.

Bayor, R. H. (1993) 'Historical encounters: intergroup relations on a "Nation of Nations"'. *Annals of American Academy of Politics and Social Science*, **530**, 14–27.

Belk, R. W., Wallendorf, M. and Sheery, J. (1989) 'The sacred and the profane in consumer behaviour: theodicy on the Odyssey'. *Journal of Consumer Research*, **16**, 1–38.

Bender, B. (1999) *Stonehenge: making space*. Oxford: Berg.

Berger, J. (1992) 'Expectations theory and group processes'. *Social Psychology Quarterly*, **55**(1), 3–11.

Berger, J. and Norman, R. (1995) 'Evaluations and formations of expectations'. *American Journal of Sociology*, **101**(3), 721–46.

Bethell, D. (1972) 'The making of a twelfth-century relic collection', in G. J. Cumming and D. Baker (eds) *Popular Belief and Practice*. Cambridge: Cambridge University Press.

Bishop, P. (1989) *The Myth of Shangri-La*. Berkeley: University of California Press.

Bista, J. S. and Heide, S. (1997) 'An account of cultural heritage and nature conservation in Mustang, Nepal'. *International Journal of Heritage Studies*, **3**(3), 168–73.

Bizzaro, F. and Nijkamp, P. (1996) *Integrated Conservation of Cultural Built Heritage*. Series Research Memoranda 12. Amsterdam: Vrijuniversiteit.

Boniface, P. (1995) *Managing Quality Cultural Tourism*. London: Routledge.

Boniface P. and Fowler, P. (1993) *Heritage and Tourism in the Global Village*. London: Routledge.

Boorstin, D. J. (1964) *The Image: a guide to pseudo-events in America*. New York: Harper and Row.

Borg, J. van der, Costa, P. and Gotti, G. (1996) 'Tourism in European Heritage Cities'. *Annals of Tourism Research*, **23**, 306-21.

Bowman, M. (1998) 'Belief, legend and perceptions of the sacred in contemporary Bath'. *Folklore*, **109**, 25–31.

Brockman, N. C. (1997) *Encyclopedia of Sacred Places*. Santa Barbara: ABC-Clio Inc.

Brown, D. and Loades, A. (eds) (1995) *The Sense of the Sacramental*. London: SPCK.

Bruner, E. M. (1996) 'Tourism in Ghana; the representation of slavery and the return of the black disaspora'. *American Anthropologist*, **98**(2), 290–304.

Bywater, M. (1994) 'Religious travel in Europe'. *Economist Intelligence Unit Travel and Tourism Analyst*, **2**, 39–52.

Burns, J. (1995) 'Holy Island balks at religious tide'. *Sunday Times*, 17 December, p. 95/1.7.

Carlisle, S. (1998) 'Lalibela (Ethiopia): a religious town in rock', in M. Shackley *Visitor Management: Case Studies from World Heritage Sites*. Oxford: Butterworth-Heinemann, pp. 139–60.

Carmichael, D., Hubert, J. and Reeves, B. (1994) *Sacred Sites, Sacred Places*. London: Routledge.

Caspary, H. (1995) 'The cultural landscape of Sagarmatha National Park in Nepal', in B. von Droste, H. Plachter and M. Rossler (eds) *Cultural Landscapes of Universal Value – Components of a Global Strategy*. Gustav Fischer Verlag/Unesco Stuttgart, pp. 154–62.

CCB (1992) *Holy Land Pilgrimage: A Guide for Visitors*. London: Council of Churches for Britain and Ireland.

Ceballos-Lascurain, H. (1996) *Tourism, Ecotourism and Protected Areas*. Gland: IUCN.

Chadran, M. D. S. and Hughes, J. D. (1997) 'The sacred groves of South India: ecology, traditional communities and religious change'. *Social Compass*, **44**(3), 413–27.

Chippindale, C. (1986) 'Stoned Henge: events and issues at the Summer solstice'. *World Archaeology*, **18**(1), 38–58.

Cleere, H. (1995) 'The evaluation of cultural landscapes: the role of ICOMOS', in B. von Droste, H. Plachter, M. Rossler (eds) *Cultural Landscapes of Universal Value: Components of a Global Strategy*. Stuttgart: Gustav Fischer Verlag/Unesco, pp. 50–60.

Clifford, J. (1994) 'Diasporas'. *Cultural Anthropology*, **9**(3), 302–38.

Clough, J. (1994) 'Dzongs of Praise' *Guardian*. 9.4.94, pp. 40–1.

Cobb, J. (1998) *Cybergrace: the Search for God in the Digital World*. New York: Crown House Publishing.

Cockerell, N. (1996) 'Egypt'. *EIU International Tourism Reports*, **2**, 5–20.

Cohen, E. (1992) 'Pilgrimage Centers: concentric and excentric'. *Annals of Tourism Research*, **19**, 33–50.

Colpe, C. (1978) 'The sacred and the profane', in M. Eliade (ed.) *Encyclopedia of Religion* vol. 12. New York: Collier-Macmillan, pp. 511–26.

Cooper, C., Gilbert, D., Fletcher, J. and Wanhill, S. (1998) *Tourism: Principles and Practice*. London: Longman.

Csikszentmihalyi, M. (1975) *Beyond boredom and anxiety*. San Francisco: Jossey-Bass.

Dalrymple, W. (1998) *The Age of Kali*. London: HarperCollins.

Davies, D. (1994a) 'Christianity', in J. Holm and I. Bowker (eds) *Sacred Place*. London: Cassell, pp. 33–62.

Davies, D. (1994b) 'Raising the issues', in J. Holm and I. Bowker (eds) *Sacred Place*. London: Cassell, pp. 1–8.

Delaney, J. (1992) 'Ritual space in the Canadian Museum of Civilization: Consuming Canadian identity, in R. Shields (eds) *Lifestyle Shopping; the subject of consumption*. London: Routledge, pp. 136–49.

de Oliver, D. (1996) 'Historical Preservation and Identity: the Alamo and the production of a consumer landscape'. *Antipode*, **28**(1), 1–23.

Dorfles, G. (1969) 'Religious trappings', in G. Dorfles (ed.) *Kitsch: the World of Bad Taste*. New York: Universe Books, pp. 141–2.

Durkheim, E. (1911) *Elementary Forms of the Religious Life* (trs. J. W. Swain). London: Allen & Unwin.

Eade, J. (1992) 'Pilgrimage and tourism at Lourdes, France'. *Annals of Tourism Research*, **19**, 18–32.

Eco, U. (1990) 'Fakes and Forgeries', in Eco, U. (ed.) *The Limits of Interpretation*. Bloomington: Indiana University Press, pp. 172–204.

Edensor, T. (1998) *Tourists at the Taj: Performance and Meaning at a Symbolic Site*. London: Routledge.

Eliade, M. (1981) *The Sacred and the Profane: The Nature of Religion*. New York: Harcourt Brace and World.

Falwell, J. (1980) *Listen America!* New York: Doubleday.

Feifer, M. (1986) *Tourism in History: From Imperial Rome to the Present*. London: Stein and Day.

Feilden, B. M. and Jokilehto, J. (1993) *Management Guidelines for World Cultural Heritage Sites*. Rome: ICCROM, UNESCO and ICOMOS.

Fladmark, F. M. (ed.) (1994) *Cultural Tourism*. London: Donhead.

Foley, M. and Lennon, J. (1996) 'Heart of Darkness'. *International Journal of Heritage Studies*, 2(4).

Foucault, M. (1986) 'Other spaces; the principles of heterotopia'. *Lotus International*, **48/49**, 9–17.

Frazier, J. (1935) *The Golden Bough: The Magic Art and the Evolution of Kings*, 3rd edn, 12 vols. New York: Macmillan.

Frost, P. and Bartle, J. (1995) *Machu Picchu Historical Sanctuary*. Lima: Nuevas Imágenes.

Fukuyama, F. (1993) *The End of History and the Last Man*. London: Penguin.

Geertz, C. (ed.) (1998) 'Blurred genres: the refiguration of social thought', in *Local Knowledge*. New York: Basic Books, pp. 19–35.

Getz, D. (1991) *Festivals, Special Events and Tourism*. New York: Van Nostrand Reinhold.

Gilbert, D. and Joshi, L. (1992) 'Quality management and the tourism and hospitality industry', in C. Cooper and A. Lockwood (eds) *Progress in Tourism Recreation and Hospitality Management*, vol. 4. London: Bellhaven, pp. 149–68.

Glasson, J., Godfrey, K. and Goodey, B. (1995) *Towards Visitor Impact Management*. Aldershot: Avebury.

Gleeson, J. (1994) 'Gospel Simplicity'. *Antique Collector*, **65**(4), 84–9.

Gnoth, J. (1997) 'Tourism motivation and expectation motivation'. *Annals of Tourism Research*, **24**(2), 283–304.

Goffman, E. (1959) *The Presentation of Self in Everyday Life*. New York: Doubleday.

Golding, F. (1989) 'Stonehenge: past and future', in H. Cleere (ed.) *Archaeological Heritage Management in the Modern World*. London: Unwin Hyman, pp. 256–64.

Graburn, N. H. (1989) 'Tourism: the sacred journey', in V. Smith (ed.) *Hosts and Guests: the Anthropology of Tourism*, 2nd edn. Philadelphia: University of Philadelphia Press, pp. 21–36.

Graefe, A. R., Vaske, J. J. and Kuss, F. R. (1984) 'Social carrying capacity: an integration and synthesis of twenty years' research'. *Leisure Sciences*, **6**, 31–45.

Graham, B. and Murray, M. (1997) 'The spiritual and the profane: the pilgrimage to Santiago de Compostela'. *Ecumene*, **4**, 389–409.

Gunn, C. (1988) *Vacationscape, Designing Tourist Regions*. New York: Van Nostrand Reinhold.

Haber, W. (1995) 'Concept, origin and meaning of "landscape"', in B. von Droste, H. Plachter, and M. Rossler (eds) *Cultural Landscapes of Universal Value: Components of a Global Strategy*. Stuttgart: Gustav Fischer Verlag/Unesco, pp. 38–42.

Hall, C. M. and Weiler, B. (1992) *Special Interest Tourism*. London: Belhaven Press.

Hart, C. (1992) 'The Jesuit Missions to the Guaranis', in *Masterworks of Man and Nature: Preserving our World Heritage*. Paris: Unesco, p. 26.

Handy, C. (1996) *The Age of Unreason*. London: Arrow Books.

Hartmann, R. (1989) 'Dachau Revisited: Tourism to the memorial site and museum of the former concentration camp'. *Tourism Recreation Research*, **14**(1), 41–7.

Hawass, Z. (1998) 'Site management: the response to tourism'. *Museum International (Unesco Paris)*, **50**(4), 31–7.

Heatherington. K. (1992) 'Stonehenge and its festivals: spaces of consumption', in R.Shields (ed.) *Lifestyle Shopping: The Subject of Consumption*. London: Routledge, pp. 83–99.

Herbert, D., Prentice, R. C. and Thomas, C. J. (eds) (1989) *Heritage Sites: Strategies for Marketing and Development*. Aldershot: Avebury.

Hewison, R. (1987) *The Heritage Industry: Britain in a Climate of Decline.* London: Methuen.

Heyerdahl, T. (1952) *American Indians in the Pacific: The Theory behind the Kon-Tiki Expedition.* London: Allen and Unwin.

Hobbs, J. (1996) *Mount Sinai.* Cairo: American University in Cairo Press.

Holm, J. and Bowker, J. (eds) (1994) *Sacred Place.* London: Cassell.

Huet, M. (1978) *The Dance, Art and Ritual of Africa.* London: Collins.

Hughes, J. D. and Swan, J. (1986) 'How much of the earth is sacred space?' *Environmental Review*, **10**(4), 247–59.

Inskeep, E. (1991) *Tourism Planning: an Integrated Planning and Development Approach.* New York: Van Nostrand Reinhold.

Jackson, R. H. and Henrie, R. (1983) 'Perceptions of sacred space'. *Journal of Cultural Geography*, **3**, 94–107.

Jenkins, S. (2000) *England's Thousand Best Churches.* London: Penguin.

Jenner, P. and Smith, C. (1992) *The Tourism Industry and the Environment.* Economist Intelligence Unit Special Report 2453.

Kaiser, T. (1990) 'Dealing for dollars: the antiquities market'. *Journal of Field Archaeology*, **17**, 205–10.

Kanter, R. (1977) *Men and Women of the Corporation.* New York: Basic.

Kaur, J. (1985) *Himalayan Pilgrimage and the New Tourism.* Delhi: Himalayan Books.

Kiley, S. (1995) *Sunday Times*, 13 July, p. 40.

Klieger, P. C. (1992) 'Shangri-La and the Politicization of Tourism in Tibet'. *Annals of Tourism Research*, **19**, 122–5.

Kluckhohn, C. (1949) *Mirror for Man: The Relation of Anthropology to Modern Life.* New York: McGraw Hill.

Kotler, P. (1994) *Principles of Marketing*, 6th edn. New Jersey: Prentice Hall.

Kramer, M. (1988) 'Tragedy in Mecca'. *Orbis*, **32**, 231–47.

Langman, L. (1992) 'Neon Cages: shopping for subjectivity', in R. Shields (ed.) *Lifestyle Shopping: The Subject of Consumption.* London: Routledge, pp. 40–83.

Layton, R. and Titchen, S. (1995) 'Uluru: an outstanding Aboriginal cultural landscape', in B. von Drost, H. Plachter and M. Rossler (eds) *Cultural Landscapes of Universal Value.* Stuttgart: Gustav Fischer Verlag Jena/Unesco, pp. 174–82.

Le Clère, M. (1990) *Guide des Cimetières de Paris.* Paris: Hachette.

Lena, M. (1993) 'The Mission of Taizé'. *The Month*, **26**(2), 46–52.

Lew, A. (1987) 'A framework of tourist attraction research'. *Annals of Tourism Research*, **14**(4), 553–75.

MacCannell, D. (1973) 'Staged authenticity: arrangements of social space in tourist settings'. *American Journal of Sociology*, **79**, 589–603.

MacCannell, D. (1992) *Empty Meeting Grounds: The Tourist Papers.* London: Routledge.

MacDonald, G. F. (1983) *Haida World Heritage Site.* Vancouver: University of British Columbia Press.

McGirk, J. (2000) 'Beer ad shoot wrecks Inca Treasure'. *Independent* 13 September, p. 13.

McNichol, T. (1987) 'False Profits'. *New Republic*, **196**, 11–12.

Maffesoli, M. (1989) 'The sociology of everyday life (epistemological elements)'. *Current Sociology*, **37**(1), 1–16.

Mayo, J. (1988) 'War Memorials as political memory'. *Geographical Review*, **21**, 62–75.

Messenger, P. (1989) *The Ethics of Collecting Cultural Property. Whose Culture? Whose Property?* Albuquerque: University of New Mexico Press.

Middleton, V. (1994) *Marketing in Travel and Tourism*, 2nd edn. Oxford: Butterworth-Heinemann.

Moldoveanu, M. (1998) 'The world of the Cistercians'. *Museum International*, **500**(3), 33–8.

Morrow, L. (1990) 'Trashing Mount Sinai'. *Time*, **135**(12), 2.

Murray, M. and Graham, B. (1997) 'Exploring the dialectics of route-based tourism: the Camino de Santiago'. *Tourism Management*, **18**(8), 513–24.

Nolan, M. L. and Nolan, S. (1992) 'Religious sites as tourism attractions in Europe'. *Annals of Tourism Research*, **19**, 68–78.

Nowak, M. (1984) *Tibetan refugees*. New Brunswick, NJ: Rutgers University Press.

Oechslin, W. (1984) 'Nature and its reduction to architecture'. *Daidalos*, **15**, 44–53.

O'Guinn, T. C. and Belk, R. W. (1989) 'Heaven on Earth: consumption at Heritage Village USA'. *Journal of Consumer Research*, 16 September, 227–38.

Opler, M. (1935) 'The concept of supernatural power among the Chiricahua and Mescalero Apaches'. *American Anthropologist*, **37**, 65–70.

Otto, J. and Ritchie, B. (1996) 'The service experience in tourism'. *Tourism Management*, **17**(3), 165–74.

Page, S. (1995) *Urban Tourism*. London: Routledge.

Park, C. (1994) *Sacred Worlds: an Introduction to Geography and Religion*. London: Longmans.

Pawek, C. (1969) 'Christian kitsch', in G. Dorfles (ed.) *Kitsch: The World of Bad Taste*. New York: Universe Books, pp. 143–50.

Pfafenberger, B. (1993) 'Serious pilgrims and frivolous tourists: the chimera of tourism in the pilgrimages to Sri Lanka'. *Annals of Tourism Research*, **10**, 57–74.

Philp, J. and Mercer, D. (1999) 'Commodification of Buddhism in contemporary Burma'. *Annals of Tourism Research*, **26**(1), 21–54.

Pieper, J. and van Uden, M. (1994) 'Lourdes: a place of religious transformation?' *International Journal for the Psychology of Religion*, **42**(2), 91–104.

Pilbrow, R. (1979) *Stage Lighting*. New York: Drama Book Specialists.

Pocock, D. (1996) 'Place evocation: the Galilee Chapel in Durham Cathedral'. *Transactions of the Institute of British Geographers*, New Series **21**, 379–86.

Porter, J. (1999) To Boldly Go: *Star Trek* Convention Attendance as Pilgrimage', in J. Porter, and D. McLaren (eds) *Star Trek and Sacred Ground*. New York: State University of New York Press, pp. 245–71.

Price, N. (1994) 'Tourism and the Bighorn Medicine Wheel: how multiple use does not work for sacred land sites', in D. Carmichael (ed.) *Sacred Sites, Sacred Places*. London: Routledge, pp. 259–64.

Reeves, P. (2000) 'Papal visit makes holy site a "Mount of Bulldozers"'. *Independent*, 15 March, p. 14.

Richards, G. (1996) *Cultural Tourism in Europe*. Wallingford: CAB.

Rinschede, G. (1992) 'Forms of religious tourism'. *Annals of Tourism Research*, **19**, 51–67.

Rivers, J. (1998) 'Thebes (Luxor, Egypt)', in M. Shackley (ed.) *Visitor Management: Case Studies from World Heritage Sites*. Oxford: Butterworth-Heinemann, pp. 161–82.

Roof, W. (1983) 'America's voluntary establishment: mainline religion in transition', in M. Douglas and S. Tipton (eds) *Religion and America*. Boston: Beacon, pp. 173–86.

Ryan, C. (1991) *Recreational Tourism; a social science perspective*. London: Routledge.

—— (1995) *Researching Tourist Satisfaction: Issues, Concepts and Problems*. London: Routledge.

Shackley, M. (1993) 'The land of Lo: the first eight months of tourism'. *Tourism Management*, **15**(1), 17–26.

—— (1994a) 'Monastic Rituals and extinct animals; the significance of a meh-teh mask at Ngon-qu Janghub Ling Monthang Choedhe Gompa, Nepal/Tibet'. *Anthrozoos*, **8**(2), 82–4.

—— (1994b) 'When is the past?: authenticity and the commoditization of heritage'. *Tourism Management*, **15**(5), 172–3.

—— (1995) 'Lo revisited: the next 18 months'. *Tourism Management*, **16**(2), 150–1.

—— (1996a) 'Too Much Room at the Inn?' *Annals of Tourism Research*, **23**(2) 449–63.

—— (1996b) *Wildlife Tourism*. London: International Thomson Business Press.

—— (1996c) 'Visitor management and the monastic festivals of the Himalayas', in M. Robinson, N. Evans, and P. Callaghan *Culture as a Tourist Product*. Newcastle: University of Northumbria, pp. 409–23.

—— (1997) 'Tourism and the Management of cultural resources in the Pays Dogon, Mali'. *International Journal of Heritage Studies*, **3**(2), 17–27.

—— (1998a) *Visitor Management: Case Studies from World Heritage Sites*. Oxford: Butterworth Heinemann.

—— (1998b) 'Visitor Management', in A. Leask and I. Yeoman (eds) *Heritage Visitor Attractions: An Operations Management Perspective*. London: Cassell, pp. 69–83.

—— (1998d) 'Visitors to the world's oldest cities: Aleppo and Damascus, Syria', in D. Tyler, M. Robertson and Y. Guerrier (eds) *Managing Tourism in Cities*. London: John Wiley, pp. 109–23.

—— (1998e) 'The cultural landscape of Rapa Nui (Easter Island, Chile)', in M. Shackley (ed.) *Visitor Management: Case Studies from World Heritage Sites*. Oxford: Butterworth Heinemann, pp. 66–82.

—— (1998f) 'Ninstints (Canada)', in M. Shackley (1998a), pp. 182–94.

—— (1998g) 'A golden calf in sacred space?: the future of St Katherine's Monastery, Mount Sinai (Egypt)'. *International Journal of Heritage Studies*, **4**(3/4), 123–34.

Shields, R. (1992) *Lifestyle Shopping: The Subject of Consumption*. London: Routledge.

Shoval, N. (1999) 'The challenge of urban tourism management in a historic city and a pilgrimage centre: Nazareth as a case study', in J. van der Borg and A. P. Russo (eds) *Tourism Management in Heritage Cities*. Technical report 28. Venice: Unesco.

Simpson, B. (1993) 'Tourism and tradition: from healing to heritage'. *Annals of Tourism Research*, **20**, 164–81.

Singh, T. V. and Kaur, J. (1986) 'The paradox of mountain tourism: case references from the Himalaya'. *UNEP Industry and Environment*, **9**(1), 21–6.

Sizer, S. (1999) 'The ethical challenges of managing pilgrimages to the Holy Land'. *International Journal of Contemporary Hospitality Management*, **11**(2/3), 6–12.

Solomon, M. (1996) *Consumer Behavior: Buying, Having and Being*. New Jersey: Prentice Hall.

Stabler, M. (1996) 'Are heritage conservation and tourism compatible? An economic evaluation of their role in urban regeneration', in M. Robinson (ed.) *Tourism and*

Culture. Newcastle, Centre for Travel and Tourism, University of Northumbria, pp. 417–46.

Steiner, R. (2000) 'Three clicks to heaven'. *Independent*, 3 September, 3:16.

Sumption, J. (1975) *Pilgrimage: An Image of Medieval Religion*. Totowa, New Jersey: Rowman & Littlefield.

Swarbrooke, J. (1995) *The Development and Management of Visitor Attractions*. Oxford: Butterworth-Heinemann.

Sweet, J. (1989) 'Burlesquing "the other" in pueblo performance'. *Annals of Tourism Research*, **16**, 62–5.

Te Heuheu, T. (1995) 'A sacred gift: Tongariro National Park, New Zealand', in B. von Drost, H. Placher and M. Rossler (eds) *Cultural Landscapes of Universal Value*. Stuttgart: Gustav Fischer Verlag/Unesco, pp. 170–4.

Thorncroft, R. (1997) 'Travel: God and cosmic vibes'. *Financial Times*, 31 May, 18.

Thubten, J. N. and Turnbull, C. (1983) *Tibet: Its History, Religion and People*. New York: Penguin.

Tuan, Y. (1978) 'Sacred space: exploration of an idea', in K. Butzer (ed.) *Dimensions of Human Geography*. Chicago: University of Chicago Dept. of Geography Research Paper 186, pp. 84–90.

Tuffour, K., Oduro, W., Ghartey, K., Beeko, C., Juam-Musah, A. and Bamfo, R. (1992) *Study of Traditional Conservation of Biodiversity in Ghana*. Accra: Forestry Commission Technical Series.

Turner, V. and Turner, E. (1978) *Image and Pilgrimage in Christian Culture: Anthropological Perspectives*. Oxford: Blackwell.

UNESCO (1995) 'Operational Guidelines for the Implementation of the World Heritage Convention' (WHC/2/revised February 1995). Paris: Unesco World Heritage Centre.

Urry, J. (1990) *The Tourist Gaze*. London: Sage.

Uzell, D. (1989) 'The hot interpretation of war and conflict', in D. Uzell (ed.) *Heritage Interpretation*, vol. 1. London: Belhaven Press, pp. 33–47.

van Tilburg, J. (1994) *Easter Island: Archaeology, Ecology and Culture*. London: British Museum Press.

Vuconic, B. (1996) *Tourism and Religion*. Oxford: Pergamon Press.

Wall, G. (1983) 'Tourism cycles and capacity'. *Annals of Tourism Research*, **10**, 268–70.

Walle, A. (1993) 'Tourism and traditional people: forging equitable strategies'. *Journal of Travel Research*, winter 1993, 14–19.

Walsh-Heron, J. and Stevens, T. (1990) *The Management of Visitor Attractions and Events*. New Jersey: Prentice Hall.

Weiler, J. (1998) 'Dollars and sense: the economics of conserving built heritage'. *Heritage*, **1**, 17–20.

Wells, M. and Sharma, U. (1998) 'Socio-economic and political aspects of biodiversity conservation in Nepal'. *International Journal of Economics*, **25**(3/4), 226–43.

Westover, J. and Collins, G. (1987) 'Perceived crowding in recreation settings'. *Leisure Sciences*, **9**, 113–27.

Wilson, C. (1997) *The Atlas of Holy Places and Sacred Sites*. New York: Reed Publishing.

Wright, J. (1966) *Human Nature in Geography*. New York: Harper and Row.

Wright, J. and Yi Fu Tuan (1976) 'Geopiety: a theme in man's attachment to nature and to place', in D. Lowenthal and M. Bowden (eds) *Geographies of the Mind*. New York: Oxford University Press, pp. 11–29.

Wullschlager, J. (1998) 'Flanders Field Museum'. *Financial Times* 9 August, 17.

Zaleski, J. (1997) *The Soul of Cyberspace: How New Technology is Changing our Spiritual Lives*. New York: HarperCollins.

Zarkia, C. (1996) 'Philoxenia receiving tourists – but not guests – on a Greek Island', in J. Boissevain (ed.) *Coping with Tourists: European Reactions to Mass Tourism*. Oxford: Berg E. Hahn Books, pp. 143–73.

Ziffer, K. (1989) *Ecotourism: the Uneasy Alliance*. Washington: Ernst and Young.

von Droste, B., Plachter, H. and Rossler, M. (1995) *Cultural Landscapes of Universal Value*. Stuttgart: Gustav Fischer Verlag.

Zepp, I. (1986) *The New Religious Image of Urban America: The Shopping Mall as Ceremonial Center*. Westminster, Md.: Christian Classics.

Index